Princeton Theological Monograph Series

Dikran Y. Hadidian

General Editor

45

Where Is My Home?

A Theology of Hope as the Outcome of Despair:
A Survivor of Nazism, Communism and Exile
Remembers the Forces that Shaped His Faith

WHERE IS MY HOME?

A THEOLOGY OF HOPE
AS THE OUTCOME OF DESPAIR: A SURVIVOR OF
NAZISM, COMMUNISM AND EXILE
REMEMBERS THE
FORCES THAT SHAPED HIS FAITH

Zdeněk F. Bednář

*To Joanie and Paul, with Rich memories
for our common ministry and much love*

PICKWICK PUBLICATIONS
ALLISON PARK, PENNSYLVANIA

March 12, 99

Published by

Pickwick Publications
4137 Timberlane Drive
Allison Park, PA 15101-2932

Printed on Acid Free Paper in the United States of America

Library of Congress Cataloging-in-Publication Data

Bednář, Zdeněk F.
    Where is my home? : a theology of hope as the outcome of despair /
Zdeněk F. Bednář.
      p. 340 + xii cm.
    "A survivor of Nazism, communism, and exile remembers the forces
that shaped his faith."
    ISBN 1-55635-036-8
    1. Bednář, Zdeněk F. 2. Narrative theology. 3 Christian
biography--Czech Republic. 4. Christian biography--United States.
I. Title.
BR1725.B415A3 1998
270.8'2'092--dc21
    [B]   98-38872
                                                 CIP

CONTENTS

PUBLISHER'S NOTE

It gives me great pleasure to publish the spiritual memoirs of Zdeněk F. Bednář, written in the form of narrative theology, and therefore rightly included in the *Princeton Theological Monograph Series*. Bednář writes from the perspective of this century about his life and growing faith. *Where Is My Home?* is a document of the twentieth century, its refinement and inhumanity, it is a family saga, a portrayal of growing up in the terror of religious bigotry, then through the economic depression, seven years of Nazism, the horror of communism and finally the perplexities of becoming an exile, The book, written in flowing prose is punctuated not only by Bednář's wit and humor, but also is richly permeated with the observations of the writer trained in theology as well as in political philosophy, church history, and social ethics.

On a personal level I must register here a remarkable irony. The author and I came to the USA the same year, 1946, to study at the Hartford Seminary Foundation. Denny, as everyone called him, came from Prague, formerly Czechoslovakia. I came from Beirut, Lebanon. He was the youngest son of Dr. and Mrs. František Bednář. His father was the dean of the faculty of theology as well as a professor of Law at Charles University. His mother was a learned, cultured woman *nonpareil*.

At Hartford also both of us met our future spouses. Little did we know that we were the lucky ones of the last decade of that extraordinary institution. In the sixties the Foundation entered a period of decline culminating in the sale of the campus and the tragic disbursement of its truly famous Case Memorial Library for "thirty pieces of silver."

Dr. Bednář and I met as colleagues, and after fifty

years since our graduation we had a chance to renew our friendship while working on the publication of this significant work.

The book is not just a look backward, it provides a mirror in which we may see ourselves today. Denny was extremely lucky, and richly blessed by hardships which refine some and destroy others. Though he passed through many ordeals, he has never stopped celebrating life, seeing glory and promise in the least of people. His dearest hopes were realized when Václav Havel appeared on the scene, giving his tortured land liberty, and also the dictum of "living in the truth."

As I read these pages I have often recalled the words in 1 Peter (1:6 and 7). "In this you rejoice, though now for a little while you may suffer various trials, so that the genuineness of your faith, more precious than gold, which though perishable is tested by fire, may rebound to praise and glory and honor at the revelation of Jesus Christ."

Dikran Y. Hadidian
November, 1998

INTRODUCTION

FROM THE ROOM CALLED
"REMEMBER"

The distinguished novelist Frederick Buechner stirs our imagination as he writes about a room named "Remember."[1] It is a room in which we lose our anonymity, we know who we are, and to whom we belong. Being lost, once again, we can orient ourselves. Indeed, we are more and more reminded that we are what we remember, that we are rememberers. Tragically, when we forget who we are, we forget that God has been involved in our lives, in our history, and easily we start living in the illusion that we are self-made masters of our destinies. In the Bible the leaders of Israel have a special mission to remind their people of God's mighty deeds in the past, saying to them "Oh, my people, remember." In Exodus, the indefinable God, who prefers to be known as "I am who I am"[2] introduces himself to Moses precisely when this refugee begins to consider his exile and the horrid oppression of Israel in Egypt as permanent. He says to him: "Moses, Moses ... I am the God of your Father, the God of Abraham, the God of Isaac and the God of Jacob ... I have seen the great affliction of my people in Egypt, I have heard their crying ... and I have come down to deliver them out of the hand of the Egyptians."[3] As a leader on whom God counts, Moses first of all has to remind the oppressed people of their past, and to affirm that this God of their past was also the God of the future.

Recently when I was asked to give my faith journey at one of the now distinguished Forums of Bangor Theological Seminary held at Hanover, NH, on the poster it was billed as "Theology of Hope as the Outcome of Despair: A Survivor of Nazism, Commu-

ix

nism and Exile Remembers the Forces that Shaped his Faith." Of course, I have realized that my faith and my theology have been shaped by the view from the room called "Remember" but as I worked on that lecture and finally delivered it on April 2, 1997, it was a manifold revelation to me that some remembering was still painful for me, that my passionate yearning for a different kind of society was still as fresh as the morning dew. Secondly, I realized that my life, covering almost three quarters of this troubled century lived under three political systems on two sides of the Atlantic, has been so rich and full that one could not possibly squeeze it into a lecture without some strict editing of the mighty acts of God in my life. Thirdly, and most astonishing was the reception of my exhausting lecture by a very varied audience and the many requests to have it in print. Lastly, it is a revelation to me that I would not mind being recycled and having a chance to live it all over again, for the God given love and joy outshines everything.

The contemporary emphasis on narrative theology and on sharing our personal journeys of faith is a definite departure from the forms of the thirties and forties in which any personal testimony was considered a sign of poor taste, and it is enriching, for as we listen to the faith journeys of others, we are reminded of similar experiences, and we feel a wonderful sense of commonality.

It seems like yesterday when preachers found a favorite illustration in a bright boy, who, fascinated by the dramas of history asked his father "What did you do during the revolution?"

"I survived!" was the answer.

The people in the congregations chuckled and then the preachers proceeded to dissect the father as the prototype of a pseudo-Christian. Today I would not be as severe.

In this century we have often won great struggles for human liberties, and at the same time we have lost something of our souls. Among the political leaders of today, no one seems to speak as eloquently about this paradox of winning great struggles in behalf of human liberties and not having the spiritual and moral motivation to enjoy them and maintain them, as president Václav Havel.

In our feverish activism, we have often forgotten who we are, we have not chosen "the good portion."[4] The horrid tyrannies of this century did not leave us unmarked. As Havel often says, we have maintained gallant struggles for the triumph of the truth but we have not yet learned to live in truth. This century has been not only liberating, but also a cruel dehumanizing century. During the last sixty years the map of the world has changed so much that our parents would not be able to orient themselves. Many political scientists speak of this century as of another one hundred year war, which started in Sarajevo in 1914. World War II was a direct continuation of World War I. This war has continued in the decades of the Cold War, in numerous wars such as in Korea or Vietnam, in enormous and exhausting struggles against colonialism, and on and on. To survive this century with a bit of dignity, with faith alive, and love and hope dominating one's heart, to be a part of the holy remnant is an achievement, and a testimony to God's special grace. We are survivors, we remember the forces that have shaped us, the chisel of the eternal sculptor who achieved the ultimate in the cross on the hill of Golgotha, and who still, ever so tirelessly, is chiseling, until the world will be as He perceived it and intended it to be.

PART I

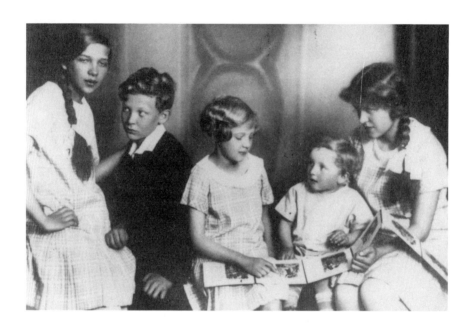

The Bednář children in 1926.
From left to right:
Nadia, Blahous, Bohunka, Zdeněk and Vera

THE LITTLE ONE

In hundreds of caricatures Linus has especially endeared himself to me. In a reflective mood, he ponders the awesomeness and the perplexity of the world and says: "The minute I was born, and stepped out on the huge stage of history I knew this role was not meant for me." With that I fully identify! Of course biblical theology constantly talks about the necessity of going into the unknown, about "creative insecurity," about obediently going where we do not want to go. With a deep humility I must confess that very often I have been an unwilling pilgrim on the pilgrimage of life and faith. Of course, very often I shudder as I observe many well meaning contemporary parents portraying life to their children as an escalator: all you need to do is to earn good grades, so that you may get to some outstanding university, and then you go up, and up and up until after two or three graduations you land in a lofty job in the corporate world and know eternal bliss. What a big lie that is! My greatest fortune has been that my parents gave me the understanding that Christianity is not an option, but also that it is not an insurance policy. By their fortitude and their living, they radiated the deep conviction that God has a purpose for my life, and that he will have the last say about our efforts and the outcome of history.

When my mother awaited my birth, the birth of a fifth child, she was not exactly thrilled. There was a difference of twelve years between my oldest sister and myself! I was born in the parsonage of the historic and prestigious St. Kliment church of which my father was the minister. No child had been born in that parsonage for decades, and there was a great rejoicing at my birth, but also some anxiety when it became known that I did not open my eyes. When I did not open my eyes for almost two days, the family doctor braced himself to tell Mother that she had given birth to a blind boy. I do not doubt that Father tried to comfort Mother and to give the tragedy some theological meaning! Just at that moment I opened my eyes, and ever since that moment I have seen more than is believable! Regardless of the diagnosis of my "blindness" I really believe that I was afraid of the twentieth century.

The wise men and women from east and west, north and south came to see me, and Mother carefully recorded their presents. One of the truly wise men of this century also came to look at me when I was still very little. It was Albert Schweitzer. When I asked my oldest sister about the occasion, she smiled and said "During that visit Dr. Schweitzer did not show much reverence for life, particularly for you! Your brother, and we, your sisters, who were taking care of you, were pretty mad at the famous visitor!" She explained that Dr. Schweitzer, who was a good friend of my parents, was practicing for his concert at St. Kliment church. After the concert, as always he planned to come for supper, but this time, just before leaving for his performance at Smetana Hall, he asked Mother if he could bring a few friends after the concert. Mother was delighted.

She always prepared enough food for a few more, but Schweitzer came back hungry and in the company of about thirty of his admirers! Mother was frantic, wondering what to do. I was screaming, wanting to be nursed. She woke my sisters to take care of me, then she sent our helper in a taxi to the nearest restaurant with a laundry basket to bring any food that was available. It was close to eleven at night. Hurriedly she rearranged the table for a buffet supper. From a distance she could hear me screaming. At last the food arrived. Luckily, this was a "slow night" at the restaurant and there was plenty of everything. Mother felt that it was a great triumph when she beckoned the guests to the dining room table laden with food. Nobody was even surprised, Schweitzer being the main attraction. Then Mother rushed to the nursery, she embraced and kissed my sisters and brother assuring them that they were the best children in the world. Then she nursed me and happily sang for me a lullaby.

This was very typical for our family. Mother would have done anything possible for anyone of us, but also she did not hesitate for a minute to wake us after ten thirty at night, and summon us to help. The thought that we would be tired and sleepy in school the next day, never crossed her mind. Her priority in that moment was to make Albert Schweitzer happy, relaxed, refreshed for his immense work in Africa. She understood how important it was for Schweitzer to have contact with people of influence if he was to raise enough money to translate his dream into reality: a hospital in Lambarene! I presume today Mother would be reported by neighbors for abusing her children, and we would be the first ones to defend her, because she gave us a true sense of family and of responsibility for one another. On her part, I do not doubt that she would say: If Albert Schweitzer, that great genius, can work to exhaustion to atone for the sin of Western civilization, the least we can do is to sacrifice something for his well being: the children are not excluded.

Mother's compelling love was always able to create a community. Only now do I realize that we were truly a family as long as she was in our midst.

*   *   *   *   *

No memory from my early childhood is as strong as the sense of love, security and joy of belonging to a large family. There was a definite order to each day. After breakfast, Father's prayers before we went to school, all meals were shared around the long table in the dining room, there was always plenty of laughter, my brother and sisters mimicking their teachers, and talking about their experiences. After supper or later in the evening Father again led us in prayer before we disappeared in our rooms. Late in the evening Mother never failed to go from room to room and check on us. If we were sad or upset or worried she would sit down on the edge of the bed and talk with us until we were calm again.

Of course, in the morning after my brother and my sisters hurried away to school, I was thrown into an adult world, and at times it seemed to me that the adult world had forgotten that I was only a child, and I had to defend myself by saying, "I'm still little." Many people obviously remembered this and have called me "the little one."

The parsonage, with its constant procession of people coming in and out, was a wonderful place. Just about everybody stopped by to see me, some brought little gifts to me, others stayed

for a while and played with me. On Sunday morning, when Mother
took me to church, I knew a great many people, waved to them and
they waved back to me. The old custodian, Vancura, who lived
with his wife downstairs in the parsonage, was unquestionably my
favorite. Being fat, shaped like a ball, he moved about rather slowly, always speaking in the plural, saying "here we come." Vancura
had a splendid mustache and an endearing smile. He was always
scolding my brother and sisters for their sliding on the brass railing
of the staircase, and yet it was Vancura who introduced me to this
thrill. Ever so carefully he seated me on the railing about a yard
from him and I happily slid into his arms, wanting more and more
of this fun. "Enough!" Vancura said, "we must do some work!"
Every so often, with the permission of Mother, he took my hand
and we waddled across the street to Kliment Church and I helped
Vancura "to dust," while he was vacuuming. Once in a while professor Urbanec, our distinguished organist, was practicing and I
was filled with awe. After sitting quietly in a pew for a long time I
could not resist the urge to go to the source of the majestic sounds,
and climbed the steep stone steps to the balcony. For the first time
I saw a man playing with his feet as well as with his fingers. I was
scared. I can still see the silhouette of the organist. He moved his
head to the keyboard, his long graying hair covering his forehead,
then he swayed to the tempo of the music, then his eyes closed, he
leaned backward, his long hair hanging from his head. Professor
Urbanec seemed to understand my sensations. He smiled gently
and invited me to touch the pedals. I could not. He showed me the
pipes and the workings of the royal instrument. I sat down again,
ready to listen. That day I fell in love with Bach's "Toccata and
Fugue in D Minor." The three staccato sounds, and then the enormous swelling of sounds echoing through the high vaulted sanctuary, the torso of the organist twisting, his head moving backward,
his eyes closed, his lips suggesting singing. It was so beautiful that
I wanted to cry, and I ran to Vancura.

Another fascination was the high, high pulpit. As far as I
was concerned it always needed dusting, the carving of the railing,
the pulpit itself. Vancura put his forefinger across his lips, which
meant "you must not tell a soul" and he let me crawl up to the pulpit. I could not see over the railing, but I was fascinated by the

sound board. Looking up from the pulpit it was like looking up into an upside down ice cream cone with lights along its edges. Before going home from our church excursion we went to the sacristy and Vancura gave me a great many boxes from wedding rings, some wooden, others were covered with velvet, brocades and other fine fabric or even leather. They were my cherished possession and I could play with these boxes in the most imaginative ways.

I was still quite little when Mother took me for the first time to the National Theatre for the performance of Smetana's opera, "The Bartered Bride," which left an unforgettable impression on me. I was dazzled by the immensity of the chandelier and all the glitter contrasting with the splendid maroon velvet upholstery of the seats. Intentionally we came early so that Mother could explain to me the set up of the orchestra while the musicians were tuning up. She helped me to identify the instruments, many of which I had never seen before. As the big chandelier slowly dimmed the opera house, the conductor lifted his baton and the orchestra started playing the exuberant, exquisite overture. I was in ecstasy even before the great opening chorus. It was like a wonderful dream. Mother told me the story of the opera, but the diction of the singers was almost perfect, and I had no difficulty in following the plot. Most of the choruses and arias are easily singable, and I fell in love with the role of Kecal. All the way home Mother and I were singing his gutsy "I know a girl, she has plenty of money, money she has!" From that performance on, I lived in the fantasy world of the opera, visualizing myself as a conductor, or as a singer. I could hardly wait to be taken to the opera again, and Mother did not disappoint me. We saw quite a few performances together and the love of grand opera has never left me. I remember the fascination with Dvorak's beautiful fairy tale *Rusalka* in which the same Vilem Zitek, who sang the role of Kecal in *The Bartered Bride* sang the role of the waterman. A performance of Gounod's *Faust* is also in my memory. Of course, *Faust* was totally over my head but the last scene with the orchestra and the organ made a most memorable impression on me. Margaret, so beautiful and tender, went to heaven, and the doomed Faust simply could not go with her, he just had to watch her going away from him to the realm of glory which he was not able to enter. It seemed to me cruel, but already then I sensed that there was something immensely right in that scene. Of course I asked about it and Mother confirmed that evil people indeed cannot really enter the realm of goodness and beauty.

Not all excursions with Mother were as pleasant as going to an opera. Mother had a beloved mentor and minister, Jan Karafiat, who in his retirement lived only a few blocks from us. He never married, and did not take his retirement kindly. In fact, most of the time he was so difficult that his housekeeper Marianka, who had been taking care of him for years was ready to quit. Karafiat had a great affection for both my mother and father. He remembered Mother as a young girl. He admired her parents, and knew her brothers. We went to visit Karafiat every week. The visit had a double purpose. First of all, Mother had to listen to all the complaints of Marianka and negotiate the terms of truce, and then she had to listen to Karafiat, pacify him, urge him to make some concession to Marianka, and at last they came to a subject or two of serious discussion. Jan Karafiat was not only an outstanding minister who had a great following but above all he was known as the author of the celebrated book for children, *The Fireflies*. This book, appearing in edition after edition, illustrated by some of the finest Czech artists was the "good night" book of Czech children, regardless of their religious upbringing until the arrival of the Communist tyranny which declared that book superstitious and unfit for the training of a socialist mind. *The Fireflies* must be counted among Czech classics.

This is a book written in exquisite prose, embellished with such "Czechness" of expression that it is untranslatable but it sings with music, so that it is a delight to read aloud. The children memorize its passages without knowing it, and to this day, the prayer used by the fireflies, is often prayed at the dinner tables of the Czech protestants. Here is a story of a family of fireflies, and particularly of the youngest, Broucek. It is an exemplary loving, forgiving family. In the company of his Father and at times on his own, Broucek is discovering the world: the friendly dark in which the fireflies go out to perform their God given duty, to bring light; the realm of nature, the unpredictable such as Broucek's confrontation with the June bugs, and finally the realm of human beings. Karafiat is an absolute master in portraying the intricacies of nature, all ordained by God. The time comes for Broucek to take his lantern and join his father and uncles in going out at night bringing light. Broucek is terribly frightened, but is assured of God's unfailing love. On his first night out, the breathless Broucek and his father rest for a while on the window sill of a large church, while the evening service is going on. There is no end to Broucek's questions, and his father seems to use this opportunity to explain the whole Calvinistic theology. "The Fireflies" has been translated into dozens of languages, and although the beauty of the book seems lost in translations, it is also understandable that without its Czech poetry, the book is pedantic and with its chief emphasis on obedience to God's design for life and the world as the basis for happiness and peace, it is offensive in an increasingly secularized culture.

The Fireflies certainly belonged to my dearest possessions when I was a child but little did I know then, that in less than thirty years our affection for this book would be used as one of the many proofs that we were enemies of the people. Long before his death, Jan Karafiat appointed my father as the executor of his literary work. Father felt very honored and took that assignment as a sacred trust. Late in the forties, just in the middle of the exhaustive struggle against the communist's ruthless rise to power, Father was appalled, yes infuriated, when he had discovered that the Russians, without asking for permission, published their "translation" of The Fireflies. The book was beyond recognition, the text was totally adjusted to the teaching of Marx-Leninism, and any mention of God was deleted. The Russian translation of Karafiat's work to this day illustrates what takes place when such theology as Calvinism is "liberated." In the best case it means a return to Feurbach, who changed the biblical assertion that the sovereign God is love, into Love is God! Father did not hesitate a minute to write an editorial about the Russian translation of "The Fireflies" for leading newspapers. He documented the falsification of the text. The article appeared on the front page of the papers and was widely quoted, since it appeared just at a critical time when the communists desperately tried to prove that Christianity and the communists could coexist. The communists and their fellow travelers never forgot that article.

Mother explained to me long before our first visit at Jan Karafiat's that he was very lonely and therefore at times "difficult," nevertheless, I expected him to be like one of the characters in "The Fireflies" and I was looking forward to meeting this man for whom my parents had such admiration. As we came, Marianka welcomed us at the door, and then spilled out all her problems at once. Mother assured her that she would consider all the problems very seriously. Jan Karafiat already awaited us in the living room. He greeted us warmly but formally, addressing me as "young man." The large sunny room was furnished with a Victorian round table, a long narrow sofa, a few matching easy chairs. Karafiat seemed to fit the decorum, and was dressed in a dark suit. His shirt was starched and immaculate. Mother sat down in what appeared to be "her" chair, Karafiat next to her at the round table. They immediately jumped into a lively conversation, meanwhile I seated myself on the long sofa and studied the room. I wore dark, short velvet pants and short white socks, I cannot forget it, because the sofa was upholstered with horse hair, and I felt as if I were seated on an ant hill. As I scratched myself, Karafiat, speaking in his high pitched voice, reprimanded me, "Young man, control yourself!" Mother gave me a pleading look. For me the visits at Karafiat's were always the same torture of sitting on the same sofa. On the way home Mother always praised me, and often we stopped in a pastry shop. Indeed, Mother was petrified that Karafiat would judge her according to my misbehavior, and therefore before every visit at Karafiat's I was promised something special. It was a perfect bribe. When I remember those visits now, I just cannot comprehend how such a tender book as "The Fireflies" could ever come from the pen of a man who appeared so terribly distant to children.

On the other hand, I recall with absolute adoration the gentle smiling face of Rabindranath Tagore. When this great Indian poet came to Prague, my father was translating his lecture. I do not know whether he was coming to our house for tea or just making an unexpected call. Regardless of the situation, and the genuine efforts of my parents to control my boundless curiosity, again I broke the cardinal rule of not running to the front hall when the doorbell rang. I have no idea what was the reason for the fascination, per-

haps I wanted to be the first one to announce the arrival of someone outstanding, or perhaps in the boredom of my childhood I had
been expecting someone to arrive to break the monotony of my
days, or simply that I found sheer joy in getting to the door much
faster than our slow moving housekeeper, but the minute the bell
rang I flew like lightning to the door. So it was when the great poet
came. Yes, I met Rabindranath Tagore before anyone else came to
the door, and I was scared to death, for here was a tall man,
dressed in a rich purplish gown, his flowing beard almost to his
waist, saying something like, "Oh you beautiful child, come, I
want to embrace you." Against my strictly protestant upbringing I
was ready to fall on my knees and to repeat at least three "Hail
Mary's." Later on, I was told that indeed Tagore liked me, but I
knew that before I was told, although I could not understand him. I
presume, however, that if I were given the choice between the Nobel prize poet Tagore, and the comparatively obscure Karafiat, I
would still cast my vote for Karafiat. I would forgive him his pedantic mannerism, and his prickly sofa, because he was a special
friend of my parents but above all, because he gave us "The Fireflies," a book which was formative for me, and which with some
pain I had to learn to outgrow. Nevertheless, I cultivate thyme,
which the fireflies love, in my garden, and on some August night
the children of our children summon us to the porch, saying, "The
fireflies are out!" We watch them and they silently speak to us
about the obedience which we lack, and which Karafiat described
so well.

Zdeněk with his Mother, Marie Novotna Bednář

THE HEIR OF THE REFORMATION

Just before I was to enter the first grade my father was appointed as a professor of Law but also of Practical Theology and Social Ethics at the University. The appointment meant saying goodbye to our St. Kliment family and moving out of the parsonage to a house of our own. I was not too happy when I was told about the move but then as long as we were all moving together, and Vancura and the rest of my friends would be coming to visit, it was all right.

Mother was definitely an urban woman, and although father would have preferred a family house with a garden, he submitted to Mother's wishes. Mother's rationale was this: we spend almost three months a year at the Bednář family homestead in Moravia where we maintain a huge orchard and garden. Mother had no illusions about what it meant to maintain even a small garden. The two decided on an apartment house. They found just the right apartment house which was in poor condition but which had tremendous possibilities. It was located in a section of Prague which was becoming fashionable as the people were increasingly moving from the center of the city, changing the despised periphery into respectable suburbia. The house was a part of buildings which were only on one side of the street, and, therefore, the house offered an awesome view of the hilly outskirts of the city. Besides, the house was in walking distance of my school and of the tram station for others. It was in the very vicinity of Prague's largest park with immense gardens, pavilions, play grounds for children, large ponds with ducks and swans, wonderful pathways to ride scooters or bicycles, and hills for sledding in winter. It was ever so typical for my parents: they found a centrally located place with a view in a deteriorating apartment house, and then they called an architect and asked him to add two more floors to accommodate us.

Since Mother wanted to have the view from most of the rooms, the main entrance on the top floor had an enormous hall, the whole width of the house, just right for me to ride a scooter! The rooms were all new, almost mysterious, but to me the house was cold, it had no memories, no Vancura, strangers lived all around, but there were quite a few children in the neighborhood and I was just ready to enter the first grade.

*   *   *   *   *

The Czech Reformation was, so to speak, in my blood, for I come from a family of the survivors of the Hussite revolution, of the church which was outlawed, and brutally persecuted over three hundred years. Already in the first grade I began to understand the horror of religious bigotry and hatred, yet I had every reason to be proud. More than one hundred years before Luther, the followers of John Hus, who on false charges was condemned to death and was burned at the stake in 1414, achieved a complete reformation of the church and society. The dogma of the Middle Ages was smashed. First of all, the Bible was given to the people, the altar railing separating the privileged clergy from the lay people was removed, and the common people were given the chalice. The documents of the trial of John Hus at the Ecumenical Council in Constance show the sheer horror of the leaders of the mediaeval church at the thought of the Holy Scriptures and the chalice in the hands of common people! Cardinal D'Aily literally trembled as he shared with the Holy Fathers the horrible news that the Hussites also encouraged even the peasants, and even the *women*, to read the Gospel! There is no doubt that the representatives of the decaying Christendom had reason to be worried, and to be prepared to fight to protect their own vested interest, for at that time, Bohemia was resounding with such revolutionary thoughts as the idea of the sovereign people under the sovereign Lordship of Jesus Christ. *Sola Scriptura*! Not the Pope, nor the church's prelates but the Holy Scriptures were the authority for every Christian, "*Religionis Causa, Libertatis Ergo*,"—for the cause of religion, therefore, for the cause of human liberty. We cannot have one without the other.

Here began the long, exhaustive search for justice and for a responsible society. The condemnation of John Hus to death was to end heresy, but instead it resulted in long wars in which quite incredibly the immense power of the crusaders could not prevail. The rebellious Hussites became "the warriors of God" who fought in blood not for their standing in the world but yearning to liberate the truth of God. To the horror of Rome, for a short time the reformation flourished in the Czech lands, that is until Rome succeeded in encouraging a split, an inner struggle, and eventually a war between the conservatives and the radicals of the Hussite movement. Rome used its enormous power: the rebellious people were placed under the interdict which meant not only starvation, but also the paralysis of the then already famous Charles University, and above all, the horror of not receiving the rites of the church. No baptism without which there was no salvation, no confession, no last sacrament for the dying. It was not difficult to humiliate the Czechs, to bring them down to their knees. Rome, with its brilliant scholars, understood that freedom was bound to lead to fracturing, to different interpretations, but the Hussites of different parties did not fall on their knees, there was bloodshed between them in the battle at Lipany, and then the crusaders came and finished the bloody job. As I write this, I look left and right as if I were spreading some horrid heresy, yet exactly on this day the Holy Father, Pope John, is in Prague. Before celebrating an ecumenical mass at St. Vitus cathedral he embraced the representatives of the reformed churches, and in his homily stated that John Hus was to be rehabilitated or better said, counted as one of the great reformers of the church. There were such enormous crowds that I was glad that I was not in my native city and that I could witness this historic scene in the comfort of our living room, watching the television coverage. What would the rehabilitation of John Hus mean in terms of the dogma of the Roman Church, the dogma of Papal Infallibility?

After the tragic defeat at Lipany, the adherents of the reformation were given six months, either to emigrate, or to return to the fold of obedient Roman Catholics. My forebears, as many others, decided to stay and perpetuate their faith secretly. They took an enormous risk, and to this day the walls of our homestead and the surrounding Moravian hills speak of their suffering.

Fortunately I was born into the world of freedom and democracy, when the surviving protestants could go out of their hiding places and worship in their sanctuaries. But most certainly, political freedom and democracy do not necessarily mean acceptance. From the first day in the first grade on, I was the only protestant in the class. The teachers treated me as the son of a heretic, the children laughed at me. On top of it all, my mother insisted on giving me a ham sandwich for lunch on Fridays, and I was certainly assured of my ultimate destiny. I begged my mother not to give me any meat on Fridays and she said, "Why, my boy? We all have to learn to defend our faith. When they laugh at you, when they question you, just say that Jesus never taught anything about fasting on Fridays." In those days there were quite a few priests teaching in public school, and all properly behaved children crossed themselves whenever they met a priest. He was a representative of Jesus. I was told at home never to do that, just to say, "Good morning, Father." I tried to do that, and therefore I spent most of my school days being punished for disrespectful behavior. I can still hear the screaming teacher, pushing me into the corner of a classroom saying, "You insolent cub!" There was no use complaining to my parents, the teachers seemed to have absolute power to make my life miserable. I was treated as a heretic and was graded as such. At times I really wondered why this believing in Jesus Christ had to be so difficult. Today my catholic friends are shocked when I humbly confess to them that until I came to the USA, the cross meant nothing to me but persecution.

The good thing about this period of my childhood was that I learned to define my faith at a very early age. Of course, I was encouraged by the knowledge that my brother and sisters were involved in the same struggles and conflicts, several times being forced to change schools. Nobody can imagine how profoundly our parents were aching for us, their children. Day by day they were encouraging us, tirelessly telling us that it was not true that we were hopeless, stupid good-for-nothing heretics but that we were wonderful, beautiful, that God had some special destinies for us. Above all, they loved us most, by sharing with us the family history, the stories of the old homestead and of the village Vir where we spent every summer. It was a beloved locality where we used the word "our": it was our home, our orchard, our village and our people, a village in which the family has been settled for centuries, where we belonged and were understood. Nowhere else did Father remember so much and remember aloud as at the homestead: here under the flooring of the dining room, our forebears hid the Bible and the chalice, in this room the persecuted brothers and sisters of the Hussite tradition often met late in the evening to study the Scriptures. Once in a while a German pastor would arrive incognito in the village. He was selling linens, and was taking orders for future deliveries, and at night he preached at the homestead, baptized children, and administered the Lord's Supper. The group grew in numbers, many young people became a part of that persecuted church. In the whole village there was not a room big enough to accommodate the group and elaborate plans had to be made for worshipping outdoors.

In the thirties my father wrote a chronicle-like book, *Spark in Darkness*, a collection of narratives based on local documents describing the gallantry of these men and women. An ideal place for worship services was found deep in the woods, on a plateau, next to the ruins of the ancient castle of Zubstejn. The leaders, however, were extremely cautious and proceeded in their plans on the premises of the New Testament that in dealing with principalities and powers they had to be as gentle as doves and as sharp as scorpions. Long before the first outdoor worship many came out of the woods as if paralyzed by fear, spreading dreadful stories throughout the villages about being pursued by demons. Never again would they enter these haunted woods! Their whispering propaganda worked so well that the local priest was concerned and invited some inquisitors to investigate the case. To calm his parishioners he announced his plans, and the day on which the inquisitors would come. They were to be remembered in the prayers of all. It was not any minor affair. A commission of inquisitors arrived, and after a short mass, they gathered at the parsonage. While they were enjoying plenty of food and wine, the "plotters" hid themselves high in the trees, and when the slightly tipsy inquisitors entered the woods, there was howling of hyaenas, and supernatural sounds. The inquisitors ran out of the woods trembling, invoking Virgin Mary and proclaiming these Moravian woods definitely haunted.

All people of the Holy Catholic church were warned not to enter these premises, and thus the secret reformed Christians worshipped in those woods in reasonable safety for a long time, until they were betrayed. Because of the treason many endured incredible suffering in the dungeon in the nearby castle of Pernstejn. These were formative stories of my childhood but as Father told them they always had their own happy ends: The Lord God has the last say. He never gives up on his people who try to do his will. His truth is marching on and he will ultimately triumph. Somehow my Father could not leave it with that assertion, and in one form or another he reminded us that we have a costly, noble heritage, and urged us to ask, "Is this safe in our hands?"

I had hardly overcome some of my fears in school and won the favor of a few teachers when the period of great suffering had spread throughout Europe due to the economic depression. Suddenly there were bread lines, people were coming to the door begging for a bowl of soup. At home the atmosphere was tense. I was wishing for a bicycle for Christmas and was told that there would be no bicycle, that we would be lucky to have a tree. I had no idea what was happening and was troubled. Mother was told in no uncertain terms to economize, but there were the same number of people to feed, and the usual number of guests. There is no use portraying my father in terms of the last decade of this century, he was a child at the end of the nineteenth century, a patriarch and as such, he was destined to be the manager of financial affairs and not to share any of his worries. Yes, we lived in a splendid apartment on the top floors of a six story house. Father invested all Mother's money in real estate. We had another apartment house, and of course, the luxury of the homestead with its never ending upkeep. The taxes were horrendous. I remember one particular scene. I was playing with a new set of blocks, building a very intricate castle. The design and the instructions were complicated, and father enjoyed helping me. A visitor was announced but Father motioned to me that it was all right for me to stay. It was the *concierge* of our two apartment houses, Mr. Weigl, whose job was also to collect the rent. Mr. Weigl scrubbed the stairs of the house but when he came with the payment of rents he was dressed as a junior banker and carried a slim brief case under his arm. Usually he was all smiles—undoubtedly Father gave him a generous tip. I continued building my castle but my ears were certainly open to the conversation. "The news is not good today," sighed Mr. Weigl. "Well, Mrs. Konecna could not pay more than half of the rent this month. She said that she will pay as soon as she can. Tonik, as you know, is out of work. Honest to God three kids! What can he do? That old Holikova, she is something else! I know that she never goes anywhere but the minute she hears my steps she pretends that she isn't at home . . ." One bad news followed another. Later on I heard father telling Weigl, "As long as we can scrape enough money to pay the taxes it is all right. Goodness, we cannot put the people out in the streets! We must help them as much as we can."

Weigl politely nodded, and was ready to leave. Father gave him the tip saying, "Sorry, it's not more." "Professor, you shouldn't do it. I am much obliged," repeated Weigl, and was out of the door. I can still see his outstretched hand while he repeated the rehearsed line, "You shouldn't do it."

"That spineless Cretan," father said as soon as Weigl left. For a long time he sat at his desk staring at the column of unpaid rents, and brooding over problems for which he had no solution. Very often now I feel that father deprived himself of a great deal of love by not sharing with us his financial anguish. We would all have supported him, but he acted as probably all fathers of that era acted, he was grouchy, tense, and we, the children, had no idea what was actually happening.

Both my parents really suffered seeing the great misfortune of so many all around us, and although the budget at home was tight, they always seemed to have enough money to help everyone—the students at the University, the people on our street, friends from the church, the people from the village of the homestead. They realized, however, that feeding the starving was not a solution, and they had lengthy debates about it, sitting at the dining room table long after each meal. Mother seemed to come prepared with a list of names. Obviously they planned an action; they were going to their affluent or influential friends and asking them for jobs for the people they knew. Father had some doubts but Mother was determined. Many times Mother came home from her extensive teas and visits triumphant. Father could not believe his ears and smiled approvingly.

One particular scene from that period was deeply chiseled in my memory. As always in summer, we were at the homestead, but father was away somewhere abroad giving lectures. A distant relative of strong views, but also of great abilities, was visiting us for a few days. It must have been late in August because the apple and pear trees were literally covered with fruit, their branches bending to the point of breaking. The brilliant relative was indeed very helpful. Immediately he took us to the woods to cut branches to use for the support of the fruit trees. It seemed we spent hours going from tree to tree putting a support under every laden branch.

Mother went behind us with a bushel basket, picking up the apples that had fallen, promising to make some strudel. Everyone was exclaiming over the incredibly rich harvest. It was a hot August day, and all of us children could hardly wait to jump into the cool waters of the river Svratka. Our jobs were done, and we announced our wishes to Mother. She knew that the road to our swimming place in the river was under construction and she said, "Can't you wait until four? I don't know, but somehow it does not seem to me right that the Bednář children would go swimming while those poor workers are slaving there earning ten cents an hour." Our relative remarked that the wood which we stacked by the gates before his arrival was an absolute disgrace, and that he would be glad to show us how the wood ought to be stacked. Well, he did show us how, and without a word we all obeyed his orders. The result was an object of art. As soon as we finished stacking the wood we ran home to change and then hurried to the river. Mother laughed, seeing our happiness, and did not spoil it by giving us any instructions. What a special joy it was to swim in Svratka and then simply stand under its waterfall!

It was one of those incredible August evenings. We ate late, and then as we stepped outdoors the orchard seemed covered with fireflies, Mother always looked at the sky and pointed at Jupiter and Aldebaran, quoting a line from Shakespeare. It was a friendly, happy evening which we wanted to last longer, but our tired bodies commanded sleep.

Late during that night I heard a great commotion in the orchard. My window was wide open and I could hear the strong voice of our guest. The lights were on in the hall. Hurriedly I got up, and dressed in my blue pajamas. I ran downstairs and to the veranda and then through the dark garden to the orchard following the voices. Mother was on the way to "the scene" and I caught up with her. She held my hand firmly. We walked a short distance. In the moonlit orchard I saw two wagons at the gate. One full of the wood which we had so carefully stacked that afternoon, the other full of apples. Our visiting relative yelled and turning to Mother, said, "Look what they did, scoundrels! Tell them to stack the wood exactly as it was, and leave the apples here!" Mother was stout and short, but in a moment of that kind she always grew in stature. Without a word she looked around trying to identify the faces of the thieves as if she wanted to say, "Do I know you neighbors?" There was a pause of an awful silence. The moon illuminating the strangers, the silhouettes of their wagons, the fireflies in the thirsty grass. "Well," said Mother, clearing her voice, "if people have to steal apples to have something to eat, and the wood to keep the kitchen stove going, there is something terribly wrong in this world. Let them go!" She turned around, took me by the hand and we walked toward the house. Of course, our visiting relative, who overextended himself in protecting our property and assumed the role of a man in the absence of our father, was humiliated. Furiously he yelled at my mother, "You Prague elitist! You have no sense. You will bring this homestead to ruins!" I noticed that Mother cried, but she squeezed my hand as she led me to my room, ignoring our guest, refusing to enter into any discussion with him. Little did we know that night that one day those dark silhouettes in our orchard would prove to be good neighbors to us in the night of our need.

The view from the homestead at Vir. In the front corner is the "youngest" part of the orchard. On the left of the road is a wooded outline of the villa occupied by Oberst Ohler. The "Big" building is a school house, the birthplace of Zdeněk's Father, the domain of his grandfather, school principal.

THE PINK SATIN BLANKETS AND
THE FIRST CLASS BUMS

In the early thirties a ham sandwich was not a problem even on Fridays! Every day most students ate bread spread with mustard for lunch, and those of us who ate bread spread with margarine felt a bit guilty and out of place. Poverty and the tremendous needs of people all around us were daily the subject of conversations at our dinner table. Mother and Father suddenly decided that I should invite two boys from unemployed families to share meals with us. Since very often, when some decisions or ideas were debated, my parents spoke French, English or German, which I did not understand, I do not know the exact rationale for the decision. I am sure, my parents first of all wanted to be helpful, but they also wanted me to have a better concept of poverty, to deepen my sense of social responsibility. In retrospect I chuckle that quite obviously it never occurred to my parents that this involvement might give me also a less desirable education. The boys were not screened, the choice was mine. Simply one day I came home in the company of two permanent dinner guests, saying, "Mother, this is Eman, and this is Vrana." Mother welcomed them warmly, and asked them to join me in the ritual of scrubbing hands before dinner. Mother certainly did not intend to teach the boys the dinner etiquette, but the scrubbing of hands in plenty of soap was an imperative. There was something grotesque about the first dinner with the boys. Eman was the giant of the class, and Vrana was the peanut, but both looked as if they stepped out of the pages of "Oliver Twist." They were dressed in rags, Eman's head was covered with a mane of curly, unruly hair, falling down to his shoulders. Vrana was petit, his hair was straight black and also long. Those boys were proud, they desired to be first class bums. I can still see that long, white damask covered dining room table, Father at one end,

Mother at the other. As always, Father said "let us pray." I held my breath, and with semi-closed eyes observed the scene. Typically, Vrana piously closed his eyes and held his clasped hands right under his chin. Eman, most uneasily looked at the ceiling as if he were saying to himself, "Lord, how much does one have to endure for a lousy meal!" The boys ate with great gusto. The sound effects were a bit too much for Father and later I overheard him saying to Mother, "Why on earth did you have to serve soup!" Actually, although no word was ever said, the boys shortly were totally acclimated, they ate the soup quietly, and thought it was fun to help Mother to be seated. Why did I choose these two? I was always fascinated by Vrana, the clown of the class, and Vrana, as a good politician, would not make a major step without Eman. Everyone was afraid of Eman. Vrana, the smallest solicited his friendship, which he reciprocated by the fruits of his natural resourcefulness. Vrana and I became good friends. He was fun to be with. Never complaining, he carried poverty with great dignity. He was a born clown, who was totally free of envy—a little devil who knew how to humiliate those who had power over him. In school he was politeness incarnate, always bowing to our teacher, Miss Zednikova, always saying, "May I help you?," and at the same time plotting a miserable day for the teacher, and a wonderful entertainment for the class. Vrana was musical. When he was tested in our class in music appreciation, the teacher marvelled and said, "Vrana, you have an almost perfect ear!" "Thank you, Miss Zednikova, I am glad that there is something perfect about me." Then when the same teacher tried to teach us national folk songs, accompanying us on the piano, Vrana was in his element. There was one song "Good night beloved, good night, good night . . ." which Miss Zednikova considered one of the greatest treasures of the Slovak national folk songs; all in a minor key, and the text sentimental enough to make every third grade boy giggle. Not Vrana. He took the role seriously, stationing himself in the second row. When the teacher gave us the pitch and walked by us, she would explain, "Very nice, Vrana." The minute she was a few steps away, Vrana sang with a tremendous gusto, loud and intentionally so flat that we were convulsing in laughter. As soon as the teacher returned Vrana was on perfect pitch, saying "What a shame, they are not getting it."

Then there was the case of Vrana's violent sneezing which usually occurred when the teacher wanted to make some crucial point, "Stop that obnoxious sneezing Vrana!" "I can't help it, Miss Zednikova, I am allergetic!"

"The word is allergic."

"Yes, allergic, I am terribly allergic, and I am always sneezing after a dinner of squirrel stew. Have you ever eaten squirrel stew? It's delicious. My mother says that the rich do not know what whey are missing. It's much better than dog food. Do you know why? It's because the rich people do not feed the dogs right, the dogs now have very little meat, except the police dogs, but they are hard to get. Have you ever eaten dog meat goulash. It's delicious!"

"Enough!" shrieked Miss Zednikova, getting green in her face, "no more of squirrels and dog meat goulash. And stop sneezing, or I shall send you to the principal."

"Oh, Miss Zednikova, I'm so sorry that I am upsetting your stomach, I shall never mention the squirrels again, except I had to explain that I am allergetic, I mean allergic, to squirrel meat."

Vrana was a marvelous observer of life around him and could mimic every teacher, the men and women of his neighborhood. Strangely enough he detested beggars, always reminding me, "My father says they have no class." In Vrana's company I discovered unknown streets and sections of Prague, museums and galleries which charged no admissions, and to appreciate such free spectacles as big weddings and funerals. The splendor of the horse drawn, glass enclosed hearse with fluttering flowers on it's roof, the bands playing Chopin's funeral march over and over again, the uniformed men carrying huge bouquets and wreaths. We always joined the procession of mourners walking to the cemetery, yearning to know how the spectacle would end. We learned the Latin liturgical phrases very quickly. At weddings we were more interested in the limousines than in the bridesmaids. Another show to which Vrana introduced me was watching Cardinal Kaspar riding from his palace in a golden coach drawn by two pair of white horses to St. Vitus cathedral, less than a quarter mile away. "Have you noticed his red satin slippers?" Vrana always seemed to notice every minute detail. Our every excursion was followed by acute yearning for some pastries. If I had some money in my pocket it was not enough to buy cream rolls but Vrana always had a solution. He would go to the kitchen of a gourmet restaurant and ask the pastry chef for the remnants of pastry. Shortly, he was back with two bags full, crumbs of chocolate cakes, broken pieces of delicacies; I can still see us sitting on the steps of some church, or on a park bench enjoying every morsel, and Vrana ever so adult-like saying, "Life is beautiful." As far as I remember, whenever I did not have any money, which was quite often, Vrana still somehow mysteriously disappeared and in a few minutes came up with refreshments. I enjoyed watching Vrana's sheer joy of eating. I learned early that it was wise not to ask any questions. Vrana often mentioned that kids of my set would never understand the intricate art of becoming a good bum. Nevertheless we were friends, and I considered it a great compliment, or at least an admission that I was acceptable, when he invited me as the only guest to celebrate his birthday feast of horsemeat steaks. I promised to bring a cake.

The family lived on the sixth floor of a big tenement house, and the apartment consisted of one big, narrow room. The walls were painted yellow, and although there was only one window, the room appeared bright. A window box outside the window served as a refrigerator. On each side of the window was a single bed with a high, and elaborate headboard. Vrana immediately explained that the beds of his parents appeared very high because the mattresses of the children were stacked under these beds during the day. "You should see it at night!" he exclaimed, "We are camping every night. We do not use blankets, we cover ourselves with coats. It's fun, the only trouble is that when we start giggling we cannot stop, and dad gets very mad." Vrana was the youngest and had four sisters. All of them were helping Vrana's mother. A small kitchen gas stove was on the left and right next to it was a folding table which was festively set. On the other side of the room was a large lavabo sink, an armoir and a pot belly stove with an easy chair in front of it. The room was filled with excitement and laughter. After the supper and the big birthday cake, Vrana was given a few dice, and a big board for table games made by his father. All of us joined in a lively game of Halma. Later on Vrana complained that everybody was getting cold and his father put some wood in the stove, reminding us that it was a special treat. The birthday party made a deep impression on me, and that night, as I went to bed in a warm room, with plenty of blankets, I thought of Vrana and his family sleeping on mattresses on the floor, each covered by a coat. It troubled me, because I knew, that we had more blankets than we needed. That thought haunted me until one day, when the house was quiet, I went and opened the wide doors of the so called guest linen closet. There were stacks of sheets, pillow cases, blankets and on the top shelf satin covered comforters. There were at least five pink ones, I could not remember ever seeing them. Before I knew it I stuffed four comforters into two big bags and I rushed to Vrana's apartment. My good deed was greatly appreciated and remained a secret for several months until the house was in turmoil in preparation for the arrival of some important guests. To my horror, I overheard Mother telling the housekeeper to use the pink satin comforters in one of the guest bedrooms. When a frantic search for the pink comforters began, I had no choice but to confess my deed. I remember quite distinctly that I gave my confession a sort of sermonic preamble about our neighbors in need and compassion. To my surprise my gentle Mother was absolutely furious, speaking as loudly as I never had heard her before, so loudly that everyone could hear her saying: "So our little son enjoys playing a cavalier! How magnificent of you to give big gifts that cost you nothing!! Listen, my magnanimous man, I want those blankets back right now, and I mean now! If you want to give blankets to Vrana's family that's fine, you shall withdraw all your savings, and we shall buy blankets but now go, and don't come home without those pink blankets!" Of course Mother knew, that by that time, the blankets would be so filthy that they would be of no use, but she insisted. I can still feel the horrid humiliation, the oozy feeling in my stomach as I had to tell Vrana's mother and ask her to give me the blankets back. "Holy Virgin, Mother of God! You swiped them?" she exclaimed, "Are your not ashamed? And here I thought that you were a decent kid, and from such a good family! Well, I am going to return the blankets to your mother myself. I want to talk to her about cleaning them." That evening when Vrana came to our house for dinner, he sensed the tension, the unusual quietness and the lack of laughter. Immediately he asked, "Did someone die?"

"No, Vrana, but the pink blankets which Zdeněk gave you are mine. He took them."

Vrana burst into uncontrollable laughter saying "Mrs. Bednář, Zdeněk is not any thief, he cannot even lie."

"Vrana, we do not take anything from our houses and give it away without asking. What does not mean anything to you, may mean a great deal to someone else, and we may not use as gifts things which are not ours."

"But . . . we knew the blankets were from you and not from him."

"Precisely, Zdeněk pretended that we were gracious, which we are not."

"But you are . . ."

"Enough of it. Now let us eat!"

The blanket affair and Mother's enormous obedience to principle had a profound influence on me. I could not look into Mother's eyes, I could not ask her to forgive me until I emptied all my piggy banks, and closed my savings account. No matter how I counted my resources, I did not have enough for the blankets. At last, Mother, who was advising me, smiled, we embraced and she promised to help me out. Happily we went out to shop for some blankets. Vrana was more than happy when I came to their apartment with the new blankets "You see, I told you, Mom, I told you!" he repeated, as they admired the blankets. I felt good all over.

Later on, Vrana offered to walk with me toward my home, and he gave me a little friendly sermonette, "You know, your mother is something else! I would never dare to lie to her, but I'm surprised at you. How could you ever be so stupid as to steal from your mother! You never, steal from those you know, but never, I mean n e v e r, from those you love!" After a long pause, he said, "You are very fortunate that you come from your family . . . but my father says that people like your mother and father probably will have a lot of trouble, because they are too decent; and you? Good God! I don't know, but you would never make even a third rate bum."

TREASON: AN INVITATION TO CORRUPT PEACE

The years of economic depression were hardly behind us, and there were already signs of new horrid danger in the rising power of fascism and Nazism. It was the era of great stars, and Hollywood poured out dozens of remarkable movies. They were a must for us to see and most of them led us into a wonderful world of unreality, but even going to the cinema provided a disturbing element, for in the classical era of film, before the main feature one was treated to a cartoon and to a newsreel. Here it was in black and white: The bloody civil war in Spain; Mussolini marching against the innocent in Abyssinia with tanks; Hitler shrieking at the Nazi Party Rally in Nürnberg, spelling out his plans for establishing a one thousand year German Reich, and announcing that his patience with all enemies of the German people was running out. His followers appeared drunk with power, tens of thousands were cheering Hitler with endless *Sieg Heil! Sieg Heil!* I was a teenager at that time, studying at a popular gymnasium, enjoying my new friends, and ahead of me were dances, romances, and the first big ball at the Lucerna Palace. A tuxedo was on my Christmas wish list. I wanted to have a good time and was just hoping that Hitler and his movement would pass away as a bad nightmare. Unfortunately perhaps the majority of adults in the Western democracies entertained this teenage wishful thinking.

As that time I was also preparing for membership in the church by attending confirmation classes led by our pastor, Dr. Josef Krenek, for whom I had a tremendous admiration and respect. Dr. Krenek was a graduate of Union Theological Seminary in New York and was a pastor of several churches in the USA before assuming his pastorate in the Kliment church in Prague. He was a tremendously gifted preacher. In a very real sense he was our Fosdick. Sunday after Sunday the church was filled to the rafters, and the big balcony seemed to be the gathering place of students. Every so often after church we went to a nearby cafe to discuss the sermon. Much of his magic was not only in his oratorical skill but primarily in his superior knowledge of world literature and history, and of the culture of which we were a part. Every Sunday we were reminded of some book we were to read or of some play which was worthwhile. He was familiar with every good movie as well as with contemporary music and art, and reacted to them from the point of view of the Gospel. At times he hit the nail on the head so forcefully that we were mad at him. He was equally fascinating as a teacher of the confirmation class. He certainly did not treat us as boys and girls, for him we were the decisive future generation. At times, I thought that he was rather heavy in wanting us to understand "the rod of God's anger," to be ready to bear the consequences of the sins of our fathers and mothers. Each point was elaborated by the history of Israel, and examples from contemporary life. It took me the whole week of fun to be ready for another dose!

Although I enjoyed my social life, there were realities one could not ignore and which were evil companions of my happy days. The location of my native Czech land is not exactly enviable. There is no use in moralizing and giving us Switzerland as an example of a sound neutrality. How often during my long stays in Switzerland I envied its location and hundreds of years of peaceful prosperity! Bohemia is not surrounded by impregnable Alps, and friendly neighbors. It is largely surrounded by Germany and then Russia in the background, on the other side. Paul Scherer used to say that there was quite a difference between seeing a roaring lion in the Bronx Zoo and seeing the same roaring lion freely walking on Fifth Avenue! That is what our many friends in the thirties simply could not understand. When Hitler triumphantly conquered Austria without any opposition from the civilized world, not only was he mere kilometers away but also he was actually present in the Czechoslovak Republic in his paid agents whose job was to create incidents in which the Germans would appear as innocently persecuted people. Secondly, the Nazi agents had the assignment to cultivate the friendship of the fiercely anti-Jewish Monsignor Josef Tiso, as a future separation Slovak leader. At the same time, our friends abroad perceived Hitler as a contained and somewhat grotesque evil.

The members of the German minority in Czechoslovakia had their own schools, their own universities, their own theaters and opera and were fully represented by their elected representatives in the Czechoslovak Parliament. All of a sudden under the leadership of Konrad Henlein, our Germans became our enemies. Over night they decorated their homes with the flags of the German Reich and started to greet one another with outstretched arms shouting, "*Sieg Heil!*" A great many of them paraded in uniforms, with the swastika on their arm bands. Day by day they staged some demonstration, calling for a plebiscite, expressing their deep desire to belong to Great Germany. The provocations were incredible and yet our government, trying to prove our good will to the outside world, ordered the police not to respond to violence with force, and the radio continually warned the Czech public to do the utmost to ignore the Nazi provocateurs. The Germans in those days were so obnoxious that as I remember, many of us preferred to walk rather than face some provocation in trams, or buses.

Even before the ill fated Crystal Nacht, the Jews who could afford it, began escaping to the West via Czechoslovakia, Thomas Mann, Einstein, and Stefan Zweig among them. The Jews in the Czech Republic were petrified, many still hoping against hope. The richest and the best informed, such as the coal magnate Petchek, started to sell their possessions at ridiculously low prices. In our neighborhood, the huge Petchek Palace surrounded by a stately park was suddenly on the market. My mother hated that palace and always referred to it as "the monument to banality." The palace was sold to the USA to serve as its embassy. The papers reported that the spokesman of the embassy had stated that the USA could not refuse the purchase for the given price. To this day the residence of the American Ambassador in Prague is one of the plushiest in the world.

My sister, Nadia, who at that time studied in Germany, and lived with the family of a German pastor, an old friend of my father, suddenly appeared home. At the parsonage she witnessed a party in honor of the birthday of Adolf Hitler at which he was already toasted for his conquest of Europe. The fate of the Czechoslovak Republic was for her hosts already a *fait accompli*.

Somebody obviously gave instructions to Weigl to clean and to reorganize the cavernous cellars under our apartment house so that there would be space enough for everybody to use it as an air raid shelter. One day, before dinner, suddenly Father opened a huge box containing gas masks for each one of us. I was upset, disgusted, thinking that my parents were alarmists. As a victim of my own upbringing I repeated for myself and for everybody who was listening: We have a friendship treaty and military alliance with France which possesses the unbeatable Maginot Line, we cherish the friendship and military treaty with Great Britain known not only for its enormous power but also for its sense of fair play. We, ourselves, have an extraordinary army, and our own Maginot Line built according to the French plans. The Soviets also stand in readiness to help. What on earth is there to worry about?

Our parents certainly did not want to ruin the joys of youth for us but they felt duty bound to share with us, their children, their immense anxiety. Father elaborated: Hitler is loudly talking about attacking Czechoslovakia. We think he is bluffing. Of course, we could never fight Hitler alone, but he is not ready for a world war. Everything now depends on the attitude of the Western world, if France and England lose their nerve, and show hesitation, we are all lost.

I was thinking about Father's resume, it was not a preacher's assumption. Indeed Father was never isolated by church leaders or by university colleagues. I marveled at the diversity of the circle of his friends. His closest, dearest friend was the chief of our Foreign ministry, Consul Jiri Sedmik, through whom Father met a great many men involved in foreign affairs. Other friends who frequented our house included industrialists, bankers, philosophers, politicians, educators, physicians, artists and poets. On the wall of his study there was always a large photograph of President Benes, with the inscription "To Dr. František Bednář, with appreciation and in sincere friendship, Edward Benes." Father was very attached to Dr. Benes, and although he never talked about it, he visited at the Castle often and remained extraordinarily faithful to President Benes all his life. I did not doubt that Father's interpretation of the international situation was not the result of just his own analytical reasoning. Everything depended on persuading the British and the French that the Czechoslovak crisis was not a crisis of an isolated nation but a crisis of the Western democracies.

Father, who was educated in England, and held degrees from Edinburgh and St. Andrews had a great many influential friends in Great Britain. Our Foreign Ministry and Father's English friends arranged speaking engagements for him at British Universities and even an address at the House of the Lords. Perhaps most important were his private visits with prominent leaders of the British religious, political and cultural life. Father was especially appreciative of the help and encouragement of the late Archbishop of Canterbury, Dr. Temple. Although these journeys were always exhausting, Father always seemed to return from England refreshed in optimism. Unfortunately, Mother never shared that optimism. Both my parents were incredible anglophiles, who shared rich memories of their student years in England, but in that critical period, their perception of the British thinking totally differed. Perhaps it was due to the fact that Father spent most of his student years in academic communities and churches, while Mother, as a student of music, moved more in the wealthy, aristocratic circles. Father genuinely believed in the power of British public opinion, he believed that some church leaders and journalists who understood the situation would be able to exercise the decisive influence. Mother, on the other hand, was convinced that the opinions of all the good people in England would be over-ruled by the British aristocracy "and my dear, you might just as well face it, they will not move a finger until they will feel the sword of Hitler on their own necks." Father could not tolerate such thought, he was furious, he felt stabbed, as if Mother talked critically about the dearest members of his family, as if she were destroying something very dear to his heart. Mother understood, everybody knew her thinking, but she no longer spoke about it and continued supporting Father at his every step. Undoubtedly she was also worried about Father who was terribly overworked. At that time he was the dean, he taught his courses in three fields, and always held some colloquia for special students at our home, and just when he yearned for some unity there was a considerable theological warfare. Well, Karl Barth and his followers smoked pipes and drank Slivovitz while the followers of Emil Brunner stood at a judgmental distance. Karl Barth himself cracked a joke that his dearest hope was not to be a Barthian, but the reality was not a joke. He and Brunner did not speak to each other. And then there were those impossible liberals! Just to figure out some congenial seating arrangement at a faculty dinner was an act of diplomacy. Mother was patient, but to the surprise of Father she refused to stage separate dinners for the protagonists of conflicting theological and philosophical views. Of course, Father was not neutral in this conflict of thought, and pounded his typewriter, writing one article after another. He was an editor of a monthly journal, his books were coming out, the galleys had to be proof read, and there was always the preparation of new lectures. Although Father possessed a very good memory, for the first time he did not trust himself, and I can hear him walking back and forth in his room, studying the Latin text he was to deliver in presenting honorary degrees. He seemed to enjoy us growing children, more than ever, and to his joy there was always laughter at the dinner table. Otherwise he often escaped to the homestead, to be in his orchard and above all in his bee house. Yes the bee house was enlarged, and Father had a couch installed in it! That was one place in the world where nobody would bother him.

It was obvious that we were heading toward a horrid crisis. When I recall those critical months it seems to me quite incredible that the churches in the world seemed to be quite paralyzed by self interest, and were totally unable to make any unified statement against Hitler. The Pope coined the phrase "our hearts are with the afflicted" and did nothing. Karl Barth issued a brilliant statement against Naziism, but ecumenism as yet was not in the vocabulary of the Christians of the twentieth century.

It is now known to us that suddenly Hitler started negotiating with the British Foreign Secretary, Lord Halifax, assuring him that he does not see any reason why the German and British people could not live together in peace. We did not know anything about Hitler's secret efforts to persuade France and Great Britain to talk about us without us, but we felt a definite pressure from our allies to do the utmost to show good will toward the Nazi minority in the Czechoslovak Republic. The Czechoslovak Foreign Office answered "what more can we do to show our good will?" Under the pressure of France and Great Britain we were trying to accommodate the Sudeten Nazis, and the Nazis in our land in general, so much so that there was a public outcry. To our absolute astonishment the British government of Neville Chamberlain simply told us that it was sending Lord Walter Runciman on a mission to study the Czechoslovak-German situation. We felt morally beaten. Our allies, the British, were sending a mission to us which we never invited, but for which we were to pay. Lord Runciman arrived with a considerable entourage and settled in a comfortable castle of a German nobleman. Lord Runciman wasted no time. After his official visit at Prague Castle with President Benes, he immediately made a friendly call on the leader of the Nazi party, Konrad Henlein. There is no doubt that Lord Runciman at first was convinced that the conflict between the Nazis and the Czechoslovak Republic could be resolved through diplomatic negotiations. Many knowledgeable diplomats were interpreting Runciman's mission as an effort of the British to buy time. Although the French government was secretly involved in joint efforts with Great Britain to negotiate with Hitler, publicly the French foreign minister, Bonnet, expressed astonishment and lied, saying that Runciman's mission was purely a British affair. At home the atmosphere was unbearable. When we saw in the papers President Benes graciously dealing with Runciman, and then pictures of Runciman playing golf with the Nazi nobility, or attending the German Opera house, our stomachs were turning and both parents, at last in unison remarked "well at last we know who represents the real aristocracy!"

Most fortunately Ruciman's mission coincided with my confirmation which called for a major family celebration. There were over thirty of us confirmands and Dr. Krenek seemed proud of us. I felt goose pimples all over my body as we entered the Kliment church, and professor Urbanec played Bach's *Toccata and Fugue in D Minor* ever so masterfully. Did he play it because he remembered me as a little child listening to him while sitting on the floor of the balcony, watching him full of awe and wonder? Of course, many remembered me as the parsonage child and showered me with love and gifts. I remember also the exquisite table Mother set for our family feast, but most strongly I remember a conversation, or rather confrontation, with Dr. Krenek shortly before the service. We were all lined up, ready to process from the parish hall. Dr. Krenek greeted all of us individually and when it came to me he asked me to step aside. We stood by the window and he looked into my eyes and said, "Very difficult times are coming for our churches. Zdeněk is this not a good day to make the decision to become a minister?" I was stricken with panic; from childhood on I had suffered with horrid stage fright. I could think of other excuses none of which I could verbalize. I just stuttered, "No, I know I could never do that." Dr. Krenek looked at me and said rather sharply, "Zdeněk, I really did not ask you what you can and cannot do. I asked you whether or not you would consider the enormous privilege of being a minister. Who are you to decide what God can and cannot do through you?" I remember that I was impressed by his incredible toughness to a student, but my answer was firm. I was thinking about my brilliant brother, my sisters and their promising careers. In the bourgeois climate of my youth I certainly wanted to be somebody, and not a minister in some hick town of Moravia! Little did I know of Luther who says so beautifully that when we feel like somebodies even God cannot make anything out of us, that we have to feel like nothing and then God can really shape us for his purposes. I knew that I was hurting Dr. Krenek whom I loved and admired. I even felt that I was resisting the Holy, but I stood firm saying, "I am sorry, very sorry, I have no idea what I want to be, all I know is that . . . ."

"I hear you," Dr. Krenek replied, touched my shoulder and walked away.

Well, I hardly said my "No" to God before I was on my knees saying "God, God, God," having absolutely nothing else to say.

We were finished. The Western democracies represented by Premiers Chamberlain and Daladiers made a pact with Hitler in Munich, at a conference about a sovereign nation without even inviting its representative. At two in the morning, the French and British ambassadors arrived at the Prague Castle demanding an immediate audience with President Benes. They behaved against any diplomatic protocol because they were not coming to bring the president any information but rather an ultimatum. President Benes knew both of these diplomats well from their years as envoys in Prague. In his memoirs which are so meticulously documented for the benefit of researchers, Dr. Benes writes that as he hurriedly dressed to receive the ambassadors, despite all his immense exhaustion he was surprised by his calm. The ambassadors read the instructions of their governments: An agreement was reached between Great Britain, France and the German Reich. The German army will cross the Czechoslovak boundaries at such and such a time. The refusal to accept the conditions agreed on at Munich would mean a military conflict between the German Reich and the Czechoslovak Republic in which France and Great Britain would not feel bound by any previously signed treaties. Benes writes that as the ambassadors were reading this message of treason they were choking in tears, and he felt a very profound pity for them. He assured the diplomats that he would answer after the consultation with the government according to the constitution of the State. Before the members of the government gathered with the president for emergency session, the president also received a notice from the Polish president that the Polish armies were joining the Führer in crossing the Czechoslovak boundaries in claiming their "historic" land. Marshal Horthy of Hungary likewise joined Hitler at that hour, and his armies marched to take their "historic" slice of Czechoslovakia. We were abandoned. Of course, the Soviet Union alone remained faithful, and its ambassador verbalized its readiness to assist us in case of aggression. Realistically that assurance did not mean anything because the Soviet Union, at that time, did not have access to the Czechoslovak territory. Nevertheless, the Soviet posture at that time of despair meant a great deal.

The British prime minister, Chamberlain, arrived in London from Munich, saying, "Peace in our time," and he was greeted as a hero of peace by thousands. Later on, speaking to huge crowds, ever so humbly he said he just tried to save the British people from bloodshed "for a little country about which we know nothing." The crowds were singing, the bells were ringing, and already at that time the Soviets through the Communists in Czechoslovakia started their incredible propaganda.

The news of Munich was spreading slowly. The radio summarized the ultimatum submitted to the President, and it's conditions. The refugees from our Sudeten land were pouring in with incredible stories, kicked out of their houses, factories and workshops by the Nazis. They were coming, carrying just bundles of clothing. Everyone, in desperate tension, awaited the decision whether to accept the dictates of the Western powers or to fight Adolf Hitler and his armies. The majority of the government and certainly the majority of the Czechoslovak people, not fully realizing the total hopelessness of our situation, wanted to refuse the Munich dictate and to risk war with Hitler. The nation was glued to the radio awaiting the decision which was to be announced by the President.

At home, Father was desolate, Mother was a stone. Nobody was talking, there was just the familiar voice of the radio reporter, his news punctuated by our exclamations of unbelief and hurt. I ran to Vrana's apartment. As everybody else Vrana's Father was sitting by the radio, his head in the palms of his hands, crying. Hearing the latest news of Benes' capitulation, he took an axe and in utmost despair smashed the radio into pieces. Only then did he notice me and shouted, "Get out of here. Those who have loved the traitors are the traitors, understand? Where is the beloved England of your Father? Only the Soviets stayed faithfully with us! I don't want to see you here ever again. You belong to the skunks!"

Tens of thousands of people poured out into the streets to demonstrate and to march on the Castle. Some watching these crowds and their passionate anger were worried about the possible revolution for it was obvious that the police were doing absolutely nothing to stop the crowds. Frantically, that night we left Prague for our beloved homestead in Moravia, but even there, where we always felt that we were among our own, we felt a chilly reception, some venting their anger and saying, "Here go the lovers of England! You have loved the traitors, you lied to us, saying that this would never happen!" It was Mother who somehow managed to say, "Are you not ashamed to kick a man who tried to do so much, who believed in decency and was betrayed by those whom he had trusted?" At last we were alone, the house was chilly, and significantly our housekeeper and her husband who always had been present upon our arrival were nowhere. As we carried the wood and started the fire in the antique tiled stove we could feel their eyes, their hostile pleasure: The lovers of England, of democracy, can fix the fire for themselves! We ate sandwiches and huddled around the radio. The late broadcast ended with quotes from the statement issued by our ambassador to London, Jan Masaryk. I cannot remember whom he was addressing but he said that the Czechoslovak nation was asked to make an unreasonable sacrifice for the peace of the world. Nobody has any moral right to dictate such a sacrifice. The Czechoslovak nation, the nation of St. Wenceslaus, John Hus, Commenius and Masaryk takes the cross laid upon its shoulders by the mighty of the world with incredible courage. If indeed the Czechoslovak sacrifice will guarantee peace in the world, the Czechs and Slovaks will lift up their hearts, but if as we believe, this sacrifice is just another step of Adolf Hitler in the conquest of the world, if the immense suffering imposed on Czechoslovakia is for nothing, may the Lord have mercy on the souls of those who prepared Munich! With that thought we were all leaving for our individual rooms, wanting to be alone to fight the sorrow of being betrayed, and above all to level with the fact that the very decency of our culture was defunct. Hitler was Hitler, no one expected any decency from him, but we believed that the leaders of France and Great Britain would act according to the Christian faith they professed. Indeed our anger at them was balanced by a profound feeling of a need to pray for their souls.

A political scientist realizes that at Munich much of this century was decided. Of course, enlightened British politicians such as Winston Churchill or Anthony Eden were profoundly ashamed of their government but they also knew that Munich actually encouraged Hitler in his future moves of conquest. At the same time in the Soviet Union, Stalin had no illusion about Hitler, but the cowardice of the Western powers surprised him, and encouraged him to seize the new opportunities for the advancement of Soviet power. In Prague not only the streets but also the universities were buzzing with the same melody: Only the Soviets can be ultimately trusted. While this propaganda pushed by the communists was making considerable progress, the people in the West lived in a total delusion and with a few exceptions actually believed that Hitler would keep the promises made at Munich. President Benes, of course, had to resign, but before he fled to the West he sent a message to his friends, among them to my Father, stating that the Second World War was inevitable. Hitler has far reaching plans not only for the liquidation of the Jews but also for reducing all Slavic nations to the role of laborers and providers for his Reich. He concluded his message with an appeal to start right away to save as many leading personalities as possible from elimination for the sake of the future of the nation. It was only natural that immediately in the post Munich days, when we were back in Prague, Father called us together to meet in the dining room, half whispering he was telling us about the wishes of President Benes. Father was worried about the safety of the distinguished and much loved Czech theologian Josef L. Hromadka, an outspoken critic of Franco, and of the fascists in general. He shared with us that Hromadka wanted to get out and that we ought to help him to leave as soon as possible. After a pause, Father reminded us that our helping Hromadka would be possibly very dangerous for us later on. We really did not know what Father talked about, but we all agreed that Hromadka deserved any help possible. Of course, at that time, Father did not mention that certain money deals were involved so that Hromadka and his family would have the necessary cash after their arrival in Switzerland. In the notes which Father sent to me shortly before his death, he elaborated on some details of Hromadka's escape. According to the notes, Hromadka made public his intention to deliver his "Long scheduled" lectures in Switzerland, and he was asking the Dean to negotiate with the ministry of education to grant him a month of absence with pay. When Hromadka came to my Father with his request, he also told him that his extremely wealthy and influential father-in-law, Dr. Lukl, miraculously secured not only the passports for him and the whole family, but also the permission of the offices of the German Reich. Naturally Father did not want to know any details, but such miracles in those days did not happen without a considerable sum of money. The exit then was not Hromadka's problem, his problem was that he was not allowed to take out any, or hardly any, money. He turned first to my uncle, professor Adolf Novotny, a faculty colleague, a pedagog for whom Dr. Hromadka, according to my Father showed very little respect. Dr. Novotny who was also the Secretary of the World Sunday School Association was rather surprised when Dr. Hromadka came to make a friendly visit. He made the purpose of his visit shortly clear: "I am leaving for Switzerland and then to the USA. I desperately need some funds to enable me and my family to travel to the USA, and to have some money before we get established. It is my understanding that the World Sunday School Association has money abroad. Would you be able to secure some funds which would be available for me at the time of my arrival in Geneva?" Dr. Novotny assured Hromadka that indeed the World Association had some funds but that the transaction which Hromadka requested would have to be approved by the president of the World Association, who was my father. In reading the note of my father it surprises me that Hromadka went to Dr. Novotny first. He certainly knew who the president of the Association was, and also he could not be as naïve as to think that Dr. Novotny could arrange the transfer of funds by himself. In the thirties the World Sunday School Association was a prestigious organization of which John D. Rockefeller was the good godfather. Indeed, Rockefeller believed that a sound Christian education was essential for the survival of Western civilization, and because Rockefeller was one of the leading spirits of this movement, he attracted to it a great many prominent, affluent personalities of the world. I am mentioning this because in the Nazi vocabulary people like Rockefeller were termed as most dangerous plutocrats, the tools of the evil powers of the Jews and Masons! At that time it was only wise on the part of my uncle and of my father to downplay their work in the Association. In his note Father writes, "Novotny and I spent many hours discussing Hromadka's request. Novotny rightly reminded me that if the transaction ever leaked to the Nazis that we both would be guilty of high treason. I was aware of it, decisive was the fact that Hromadka was in danger, and that he stood for a just cause, that he could accomplish a great deal abroad. We agreed to notify Dr. Kelly in Glasgow secretly and instruct him to give Dr. Hromadka ten thousand dollars. Hromadka was deeply grateful, and when he was leaving he told me that he would never forget my help and friendship. Of course, when Hromadka left, both Novotny and I lived through days of utmost anxiety, and were prepared for everything." I am mentioning these details of Hromadka's escape only because Hromadka later on played a very important role in my father's life, and Father's note seems to me important. As we debated Hromadka's escape around the family table, I think we would have voted to take the risks, even if we had known the financial details, because we thought a great deal of Hromadka. Father had another item on the agenda, and Mother was increasingly more tearful. He announced that someone from the embassy of the USA came to tell him about the concern of many friends about Father's safety. He was offered a professorship at some American university (I really cannot remember which one). Father said that he could not make a decision of such magnitude without the agreement of the whole family. He was choking as he announced that the condition of the escape was that only Mother and Zdeněk would go along. My heart was fluttering in anguish. Everybody seemed upset. Father called for discussion and then for a vote, "All in favor of the proposed plan for escape say yes." The dining room resounded with the loudest, "No," and I was the happiest guy in the world. We shall face Nazism together! It was one of the great moments of my life. We were happily embracing one another. My brother said, "There must be some champagne in the cellar," and before we knew it, we were toasting to each other, affirming our love and determination. It was a true love fest, I think the last one of the family.

The notes of my Father include also these lines, "Soon we heard that Hromadka arrived in Geneva and received the promised funds. Dr. Lukl came to tell me about it, and was extremely happy. I was somewhat shocked when Dr. Lukl suddenly asked me if I could arrange it so that the allotted rationing of coal of Dr. Hromadka would be delivered to Lukl's cellar! I was greatly troubled but at home there was good news awaiting me. Someone had delivered a large envelope. I opened it quickly, and read the message: Dr. Bednář, we do not want you to be anxious. I personally removed from the files of the police, of the Ministry of the Interior and also from the former Ministry of Foreign Affairs all documents of your activities before the Gestapo will get to them. I am so glad that I could do this. I repeat, there is nothing reported in the files under your name. I was deeply moved by the note. Someone risked his life for us. How do we deserve a day of safety bought at the cost of such an enormous risk?"

THE SWASTIKA AND MY TUXEDO

The post-Munich period was like a Wagnerian overture leading to *Götterdämmerung*. Already in the opening scene of the first act, Adolf Hitler stood in the open window of the Prague castle shouting, "Czechoslovakia has ceased to exist!" The crowds responded with a deafening *Sieg Heil! Sieg Heil!* Everything was perfectly staged. The uniformed Germans played the major role in the spectacle but also thousands of extras were secured from Czech schools and factories. They were to represent the great joy of the Czechoslovak people for being incorporated into the Great Deutschland. Our school was assigned a place very near the first courtyard of the castle. We were taught how to shout, how to smile, how to greet Hitler with outstretched arms. It was a first class extravaganza made for export. Film makers were everywhere ready to produce a documentary on the superior German military might, and on a bloodless conquest. Our group was hardly established in our assigned space when I spotted Vrana in another group about ten yards from us. We had not seen each other since that awful scene in his apartment when his father literally pushed me out of their door. Soon we were in each other's arms, glad to see each other, saying, "What are you doing here?"

"What?"

"What?"

The bands played fortissimo and planes were flying extremely low, their enormous noise symbolizing power. Any conversation was impossible. As always Vrana assumed leadership, and ever so discretely and politely, inch by inch, we were pushing ourselves through the crowds until we found ourselves in the oasis of total quietness at the back of the cavernous nave of St. Vitus Cathedral, in the heart of the castle. We sat down and whispered to each other. We had so much to talk about! Not a soul was around, but as the time of Hitler's arrival was approaching, Vrana glanced at his watch and whispered, "I don't think it's too swift to stay here. Surely the Gestapo will come to check the cathedral! Let's get out of here!" Then both of us noticed that the heavy door to the bell tower was ajar, and before we knew it, we raced up the three hundred sixty seven steps to view the arrival of Hitler from the heights. Although it was a windy, misty, cold day, the view from the top of the bell tower was so incredible that we stood there speechless. All around us we could see the shadowy outlines of the familiar, majestic buildings telling us their stories, but what was truly breathtaking was the view of the reality of that day. It was like a scene from *Gulliver's Travels*. From the perspective of the bell tower of St. Vitus cathedral the arriving Hitler appeared like a midget riding in a matchbox Mercedes Benz. The goose stepping SS troops looked like pitiful black creatures one could step on. Vrana cleared his throat and with a genuine gusto spat down only to be surprised by the quick, shocking result of his manly effort to spit on the conquerors; his saliva was all over his jacket! I was splitting with laughter as Vrana was exclaiming, "Holy virgin! So it's true! It's true! You can't spit against the wind!" We ran down the winding steps of the bell tower laughing, and discretely re-entered the crowds.

At home it was like an inferno. My father tried to destroy his correspondence—anything in his study which could endanger somebody else. The "visit" by the Gestapo was more than probable. The compromising material seemed to pour out of dad's study in bushel baskets, and landed at the stoves in different rooms. All of us took turns in this effort to destroy the evidence. I knew that this was important, although instinctively I believed that the Gestapo had more important criminals on their agenda that night than us; but I was also disgusted, mad. This was the week of the big ball. In my room, a handsome, double breasted tuxedo, stuffed with tissue paper, was hanging in the closet.

After that sleepless night, I looked out of my window, and watched the squirrels climbing the trees, and the sparrows chirping on the window sills. They were enviably free. That day I was afraid even to cross the street. The German intellect, the innate sense for technology, order, punctuality and the usual obedience to superiors in the service of Adolf Hitler had incredible, astonishing results. Almost over night the streets of Prague were renamed. The schools were closed only for a few days, and were reopened as German schools. The classrooms were decorated with portraits of Hitler, the old textbooks were burned and replaced with new German text books. The official language was German, the students who could not manage in German were dropped and disappeared. In a few days everybody mastered greeting the teachers and professors with outstretched arms, saying "Heil Hitler." The goal of the education was a total germanization. German officers supervised the schools, and since they inspected the classrooms almost daily they initiated a system of fear. The professors were afraid of failing in teaching the propaganda and being shipped to concentration camps, the students were afraid of the teachers and of being shipped as hard laborers far away not to be seen, and in every classroom there were a few new students, whose obvious job was to report on both the students and the instructors. There was a new daily paper, "Der Neue Tag." The brutal persecution of the Jews began much sooner than expected. All Jews were forced to wear a yellow arm band with the star of David and a sign, "A Jew" and the stores and public buildings started to carry big signs "Jews not Permitted"—*Juden Verboten* or a more positive sounding sign "For Aryans Only." Some of my friends did not even know that they were Jews, and all of a sudden they had to wear a yellow arm band, and we had to meet under the cover of night.

At the railroad stations the preparations for the transport of the Jews began. The criminality was planned publicly without any shame and for all the world to see. It is simply not true that the Germans or for that matter the British or the Americans or the French did not know what was happening.

According to the papers some shameless Czechs began hoarding food, while in reality we could see German officers confiscating food and supplies at depots and mills and sending them to Germany. Ever so politely, for the sake of Czech people very strict rationing of food was instituted, a rationing on which no one could survive. The black market was born. Everyone had to deal on the black market in order to survive, and those who were caught were shot or sent to concentration camps. Life of enormous risk-taking began, and to a point, I had to unlearn what I had learned. To lie, to steal was not wrong, it was the only way to survive. To lie, to steal, to pretend was not against God, it was against the Nazis and therefore for God. For the first time I realized that only in fairy tales was evil presented as hideous, here every brutality had the facade of propriety. Most incredibly the Germans succeeded in a short time even in a task about which the Czechoslovaks had debated for the decade: The traffic turned from left to right, the cars, the buses, trucks and trains, bicycles, everything on wheels started moving on the right side. Many people were truly astonished and wondered why educated evil was progressing with such phenomenal speed, while goodness seemed to move only by inches.

I was a bewildered, angered, frightened, disgusted teenager. Yes, I was disgusted, I could not comprehend what was happening, and I was afraid even to verbalize my anger. Before 1938 in our family conversations, we used to distinguish between the Nazis and the Germans or between "good Germans" and "bad Germans." How many German ministers from Sudeten Land Mother used to entertain! After the occupation of the Czechoslovak Republic the distinction was gone, the good Germans simply blended with the majority, our German friends, to the best of my memory, no longer existed. In the West most people really believed that Hitler's demand of incorporating Czechoslovakia into Germany was his last demand, but among the German people, as many of Hitler's followers document, the bloodless conquest of Czechoslovakia was nothing short of a miracle. Hitler was bluffing about his military might. His entry into Prague was the proof that he was indeed the God-sent messianic leader of Germany. Albert Speer writes about it in his memoirs saying that the conquest of Czechoslovakia before the eyes of a frightened world now completely convinced the Germans of their leader's invincibility. Further more, Speer recalls Hitler's impression of the extraordinary, massive fortifications at the Czech borders. The test bombardment showed that the German weapons would not prevail against them. Hitler was ecstatic about the military loot from the former Czechoslovakia, and about the fortifications which were suddenly his, exclaiming, "We have all these without loss of blood. What a marvelous *starting* position we have now. We are over the mountains and already in the valleys of

Bohemia."[5]

Whenever possible, in the evening, we huddled around the radio to listen to the BBC news while someone stood guard by the door, everyday hoping for some sign of weakness in the German Reich. There was not any. Of course, even as a teenager I believed that ultimately Hitler would be beaten, but at the same time I was aware that a mad man and his mad followers, determined to conquer the world, had total power over our lives. I could not comprehend my mother who was actually saving some canned apricots and pears and some food products for the tough times! I wanted to eat those apricots now, arguing, "How do we know that there will be any future?" My heart was rebelling, I desperately wanted to seize every day, every opportunity to have some fun, to live fully, and undoubtedly I had caused some great anxiety to my parents. Unfortunately the opportunities for fun were extremely limited, the old cafes were full of noisy Nazis, and one could not visit in them, but there were the old picturesque streets of Prague, the chance to take long, long walks through such royal parks as Stromovka. We went to galleries and museums, yearning to react to something, yearning to talk to each other and have deep discussions. Above all, we loved to gather in somebody's room, listen to phonograph records, to take a few steps of the fox trot . . . our friendships became extremely dear. Suddenly we shared what we had never shared before, our anxieties, hopes and fears for ourselves and also for our loved ones. There were arrests in the families of my friends and we encouraged and upheld one another. We marveled at ourselves. We did not need to spend a penny, and every so often we had such a good time that we did not want it to end. The young people loved to come to our house because it was a big establishment but especially because my mother had a very, very special appeal to young people. At times my room was packed. We called it "Zdeněk's Salon." Perhaps it was only natural that already we, the youngsters, were very much concerned about the civilization of which we were a part. How could Hitlerism come into being in the nation of Beethoven, Goethe, Heine, Luther, Einstein, and the host of giants of the Western civilization? The more we debated the question the more we sensed that there was something rotten in Denmark. At the same time we were fascinated by reading forbidden literature, actually we are indebted to the Germans for helping us to become literate. We read the same forbidden books and then we discussed them. At times we read certain passages together. How memorable was our discussion of Andre Gide's, *Pastoral Symphony* or of, *Little Man What Now?* by German writer Hans Fallada. At times the room was so noisy and shaking with laughter that Mother came to tone it down before the whole neighborhood would suspect us of some plot; yet I could see that nothing could make Mother happier than hearing us laughing. Indeed, there was the healing power of laughter, and any group was a gathering of new political jokes which then went from person to person. Humor of Svejk's tradition permeated and upheld the nation. It always began with the question "Do you know what?"

"What?"

And a joke followed.

"Do you know what?"

"What?"

"Goebels just announced that he was uniting the Ministry for Arts with the Ministry for Food Production."

"What? Why?"

"Well, he explained that it only made good sense because the production of food is one of the greatest arts in the German Reich."

Some of the jokes were undoubtedly based on reality which was adjusted for popular consumption. Who could ever forget the story of the statue of Mendelssohn, a joke which even became a title of a book fifty years later. I can tell it just as I heard it for the first time in my "salon" by a friend, a master narrator.

"Did you hear about Mendelssohn?"

"What about him?"

"Well a friend of mine was passing by Rudolfinum last night, and noticed a number of SS men walking on the roof of the concert hall and with a flashlight examining every statue. Quite a few people stopped and watched, it must have been quite a sight. My friend has a number of friends among the members of the symphony and what happened is this. SS Gruppen Führer Karl H. Frank went to a concert, and as he was driven through Prague he was obviously pleased with the speedy Germanization of the city.

As he stepped out of his car and walked the splendid steps to the symphony hall, he looked up at the illuminated statues, and he almost had heart failure. "Unbelievable!" he shouted, "there is Mendelssohn on the roof. That Jew will be removed before the end of tonight's concert!" An officer in his party promised to carry out the order, saluted and left to organize the mission. Shortly under his command eight or ten SS men marched to Rudofinum and immediately ran to the roof. The officer stood there expecting that "the case of Mendelssohn" would be finished in a minute, but to his surprise he noticed that his men were all over the place, looking at each statue with flashlights, attracting the attention of the public in the street. "What's the matter, idiots, smash him at once! This is a scandal!" he yelled and to his fury the puzzled SS men came to him saying "The statues are not marked. How do we know which one is Mendelssohn?"

"Can't you recognize a Jew when you see one?" he shouted. "You have five minutes! Land alive, don't you recognize the statue of a man with the biggest nose?"

"Jawohl!"

"Natürlich!" were their responses and shortly, sledge hammers in their hands they surrounded a statue of a composer with the biggest nose. The officer came forward and seeing the statue he froze in terror and then shouted "Stop! For Christ's sake stop! Stop! Do you realize that this is a statue of Richard Wagner, the god of our dear Führer. "You almost smashed the great prophet of Germany. Cretans, gerade aus! I shall look for Mendessohn myself!"

My room was resounding with laughter, there was no maliciousness in this humor. We laughed and felt good because here the super race was rebuffed. Each one of us could hardly wait to tell the story at home or to someone else.

Although we were dutifully taking the new daily, and listening to the propaganda on the radio, the real news then was communicated person to person. When we gathered at the dinner table Father's first question was, "So, what's new?" At other times someone announced, "Just wait 'til I tell you what I heard today!"

Every night after dinner, Father led us in prayer, and then we embraced one another. Mother often could not control her tears.

We all knew that this was too good to be true, that it would not last much longer. As the youngest I was petrified, I looked at the worried face of Mother and wanted to cry, "I have never had enough of you!" My brother and my three sisters were so dear to me that I could not imagine life without them. Night after night I dreaded the thought of being left alone somewhere in the world.

Of course, the case of Dr. Hromadka's eacape to the USA via Switzerland became known to the Gestapo shortly, and Father, as the dean of the faculty, had to endure hours of interrogation by the Gestapo. Also a high officer was assigned to the theological faculty and Father was accountable to him. Although these days were marked by enormous tension and anxiety, our grace period lasted longer than ever expected. One day after long hours of interrogation and threats, dad came home feeling sick. He was so exhausted that he seemed limping and went straight to the sofa in the living room, the only room which was heated. He seemed to be groaning as we covered him with a blanket. He had a slight fever, his face was bright red, and he breathed heavily.

"Would you like some Slivovitz?", asked Mother, offering a strong plum brandy which the Czechs of that era used as a remedy for any illness under the sun. When Father shook his head, Mother summoned our family doctor who came almost at once. After examining Father, he looked concerned and in a whispering voice told us that Father's blood pressure was extremely high and that he had probably suffered a minor stroke, and that other strokes might follow. He asked us to give Dad as much quiet rest as possible, and promised to be back in the evening.

Mother acted as the captain of the ship and followed all the doctors orders most diligently. As far as I remember we were to whisper only, and walk through the long hall in slippers. Yes, she even arranged to have the front door bell disconnected. The doctor came back in the evening, as he had promised, and was examining my father when there seemed a loud commotion, and then knocking on the large front door, which was a part of a frosted glass wall. "Geheime Stadt Polizei!" someone shouted. Our little dachshund, Rigo, went berserk and it took all my strength to hold him in my arms. Behind the frosted glass of the door and the front walls of the hall the Gestapo officers appeared like mountains. Mother pulled herself together and went to open the door. Her "hoch Deutsch" was so perfect that the chief officer assumed that she was a cultured German and addressed her as "Gnädige Frau" and inquired about Herr Professor Bednář. Mother explained. Of course she was immediately asked where she learned to speak German so well. The man was impressed and for a moment appeared respectful. Mother explained the situation to him and added that he and his men had to take full responsibility for the possible deterioration of my father's condition, "Our responsibility is for the safety of the German Reich," he snapped and motioned to his men to follow him. The sound of boots echoed through the long hall suggesting a small army. The hall had a checkered ceramic tile floor, and every step sounded like three. Only the chief officer went to my father's bedside: The rest of them spread throughout the house. Holding Rigo in my arms I feverishly prayed, "Dear God, you love him, please let him die, let him die, so that they cannot touch him!"

My father was a thoroughly honest man, he had many faults, but he was always honest, he could not lie, and would not know how to lie. His theatrical abilities were absolutely nil. He would not ever be able to fake illness, and yet this was the first assumption of the Gestapo. He was cross examined while the doctor kept his eye on him. Father's German was also flawless, after all he was a graduate of German Universities, but there was a certain hesitation in his speech, and once in a while, we were told he slouched. He looked awful. The Gestapo man came to a quick conclusion that the old Bednář was kaput or would be kaput if not in a few days then in a few months. No use to waste dear German money and space in a concentration camp for him. The verdict was: "You will leave Prague for your homestead as soon as possible, and you will report at my office in Prague regularly according to my instructions. Heil Hitler!"

As soon as the men left, we all gathered around Father's bed, not daring to say a word, but smiling. At last we were sure that the men were really gone. The doctor broke the silence, "I really need a glass of Slivovitz!"

For several days Father just slept but he was making an obvious and marvelous recovery. Usually Father did all the planning for every trip or a long stay at the homestead, this time Mother took over and to the surprise of all, when Father felt up to the long trip, and his doctor approved of it, everything was ready. Actually without Father's knowing anything about it, Mother sent to the homestead a big shipment of winter clothing, and some kitchen equipment ahead of time, and they left for the homestead with only one suitcase, as if they were going for a weekend. Everything happened so quickly and my youth was definitely over, as if it were a luxury only for those who could afford it.

There was no place under the sun which Father loved more than the homestead and his native village of Vir. Mother fully shared that love. While the world was rapidly changing around us, Vir remained the same, the landmarks were the school house, the old maple tree, the post office and one inn at each end of the village. To the disgust of the lazy geese a few cars and trucks passed by, but at night one could not hear anything but the soothing humming of the river Svratka. My parents accepted the fact that the homestead was getting older along with them, and there were always some repairs, but they resisted any change in the familiar landscape. When the old, old pear tree under which my great grand father proposed to his wife began to lean, expert tree men were summoned to save that tree. It was naïve, but somehow we all had expected that the village of the homestead was exempted from the happenings in the world. It had always served us as an oasis of peace, and we thought that it was destined to stay that way. As my parents were arriving at the homestead, it was a terrible shock for them to see a flag with a swastika flying from above the entrance to a villa neighboring our orchard. It was upsetting enough to hear that the former occupants of the villa, our seasoned neighbors, Josef and Rita Rotter, the owners of the local factory for woolens, were among the first Jews to be dragged away to their slow death, but it was terrifying to hear that the Rotter's villa, with its manicured garden in which every rose bush was treated as a child, was now the seat of Herr Oberst Ohler and his wife Magda. I am not exactly sure about the name Ohler. It is very ironic because he was the only SS man who was not just an evil man in a black uniform, this man was an evil man with a name, a man I can remember also in slacks and sweater, but I am not exactly sure of his name. Perhaps it is because on the few occasions when I met him I always addressed him as Herr Oberst or according to his rank. The village of Vir was his domain, he was in charge of expanding the former Rotter's factory, which under his management was running on three shifts and was producing heavy military uniforms. Above all, he was in charge of order in the village and was to dispel any rumors of foreign enemies hiding in the deep woods around Vir. When he was making his daily inspection of the factory he always wore the uniform of an SS officer and his entourage was a show of power. First several soldiers on motorcycles, then a jeep with soldiers holding pistols in their hands, then the limousine, and again a jeep and the noisy motorcycles. Noise seemed to me a very important part for the Nazis in demonstrating their power. Ohler was usually accompanied by his wife Magda who seemed to command more authority of terror than her illustrious husband. It was Magda who arranged the security procedures, who ordered the installation of immensely powerful floodlights in the eaves of the villa so that at night, the garden and the surrounding fields were lit like a supermarket parking lot. Several vicious Dobermans roamed the garden, and whenever the Ohlers stepped outside the garden, two dogs accompanied them. Considering that the Ohlers lived in a tiny, obscure village, their house was a fortress, and the security measures seemed grotesque. Frau Ohler supposedly was possessed by fears but many believed that she was astute and that her understanding of reality was better than her husband's.

The homestead was never left empty, and the beds upstairs were always ready just in case Father would unexpectedly decide to come for a few days. Also in the winter time we often came for skiing. Our former housekeeper, Ruzena lived at the homestead with her family. Her husband was a shoemaker who maintained a fine workshop at the homestead and employed several apprentices. The sound of hammers and the whistling of the apprentices belonged to the melodies of the homestead. Ruzena had worked for my parents since she was fourteen, and her parents, and her grandparents had worked at the homestead before her. Whenever there was some special occasion, such as a wedding, Ruzena came to Prague to help us out. She was a loving, highly intelligent and capable woman, proud of her work, proud of the fact that a great many guests complimented her on the outstanding way she served at the table. Ruzena was totally dedicated to Mother, and cherished her open affection and praises. She was the only one who moved with the Bednář's from place to place and was the second mother to the five of us children. It was only natural that when she had planned to be married, my parents offered the young couple to make their home at the homestead. Although Ruzena loved the homestead, undoubtedly this was to be only a provisional arrangement, but Ruzena and her family stayed for decades, and her own daughter was married from the homestead. Endowed with enormous curiosity and ability to collect news, Ruzena was the living information service. When my parents arrived at the homestead, Ruzena welcomed them with open arms and detailed information on all the developments in the village. The very next day, my parents tried to get established and to make the spacious rooms more cozy for year round living. As always Ruzena and the apprentices were helping in such an endeavor. This operation was interrupted by the arrival of Herr Oberst Ohler. Ruzena and the apprentices disappeared, and Mother was the first to welcome the new neighbor. He was dressed in his SS uniform and this was an official visit. He was a slender man of short stature. His head was shaved, and appeared polished. He had expressive blue eyes, his hands were always gesticulating. One thing which distinguished him from others was that he never yelled. He was cultivated, soft spoken. As Mother led him to the living room to introduce him to my father, Ohler too was taken by surprise when he heard my parents fluent "Hoch Deutsch," and yet before he assessed them and their surrounding, he also found out that Father studied at his home town of Halle! He was also fascinated by my mother's command of German literature and music, his great love. Mother served tea. The conversation was about Goethe. He was surprised by Mother's preference for Schiller because he was less titanic in his poetry. Herr Oberst remarked that he would like to continue the conversation about the word "titanic" in the future, and I guess, Mother was sorry that she had ever used that term. The new conversation was about the German theology of Schleiermacher and then about Halle, street by street. The visit was long, the conversation was lively, although very exhausting, especially for Father. It became obvious that Ohler knew about the orders of the Gestapo in Prague, and that one of his duties was also to guard the Bednárs and to report on them and their activities to Prague. It was also obvious to my parents that Ohler, who majored at Halle in philosophy and literature, was bored stiff in Vir. As he was leaving the homestead he asked my father, "Professor do you play chess?" When Father nodded with a smile, Ohler said, "See you then at three tomorrow. Auf Wiedersehen!"

Ever since that day Ohler came to the homestead to play chess almost every afternoon often bringing some coffee and other unheard of treasures. During my parent's exile at the homestead at least twice I was stricken with deep, uncontrollable yearning to be with them and to my joy I got sick, and was ill enough to be excused for three or four days. Both illnesses were faked. To this day I do not know whether my faking a serious allergic reaction was so perfect that I fooled the old school doctor, or that the doctor was kind, and read my mind. The horrid brown blotches under my eyes were a shoe polish which I rubbed so hard that the skin of my face was raw and even some blood was showing. I was a sight of misery unable to control the horrid itching. The doctor gave me not only some ointments to apply to my face but also some pills, and excused me for four days. Leaving the doctor's office I congratulated myself but now I wish to thank that doctor for not reporting me and for overlooking my amateurish job. He gave me an incredibly beautiful visit with my parents. I took the night train and in the morning an old neighbor from Vir was awaiting me at the Bystrice station with his carriage. It was late in spring, the violets and also the yellow primroses were blooming by the road side. At home there seemed no end to hugging and kissing, and Rigo followed me at every step. I just could not tell my parents that I was faking my illness, and although I felt fine I was applying the prescribed ointment to my face which actually gave my ailment some authenticity. My parents did not ask any questions, but pampered me, and I loved every minute of it. Mother prepared a feast for every meal and there was much we had to tell each other. Father was explaining to me the role of Oberst Ohler and just at that moment he arrived. I was so petrified by his sudden appearance that I almost greeted him with "Heil Hitler." He was terribly sorry about my illness and explained that the purpose of his visit was to invite me to play some tennis with him that afternoon. The Ohlers restored the old tennis court to perfection. Since I heard from my parents about the Russian and Czech partisans and some British paratroopers hiding in the woods of Vir, I was not at all surprised that Oberst Ohler asked me to play on the side of the tennis court which was bordering our wood land. It was a strange feeling to play several sets of tennis against the feared, hated representative of our cruel enemy, and to know that he was a target of the paratroopers hiding in the woods! Suppose they consider me a collaborator? Every time before I served I looked back. Although I had not played tennis for a long time I was in good form that afternoon, and I had Ohler running all over the place, yet remembering my duty to give Ohler at least a marginal sense of triumph. His playing was slow, predictable and studied. He won three sets six to four and was absolutely elated. He even added to his ego by telling my Father that I was absolutely colossal.

It is strange and ironic but the time my parents were confined to the homestead was perhaps their happiest time I could remember. For the first time in years they were in charge of their schedule. Father was busy "farming" bringing in the wood, walking through the orchard and checking on the trees, talking to his bees, and spending a great deal of time at his typewriter. To the delight of Rigo almost every day they went for a walk, and came home so tired that they were ready for a nap. Actually the almost daily visit of Ohler was a time consuming nuisance! Although my parents realized how fortunate they were, as the rumors about the partisans were spreading, both Mother and Father feared that while Ohler was performing his duty, he was also thinking of himself. He knew that Mother and Father were highly respected and loved by the people of the village. In case of a conflict with the partisans it was easy to imagine that he would take Mother and Father as hostages. In that type of warfare everything was possible. For the first time in years Mother cooked, and above all, she had time to read. The kitchen, with a huge tiled stove, was the warmest room in the house. Rigo was glued to his pillow near the kitchen stove. Although the kitchen lacked modern conveniences it was extremely homey, and mother could prepare spectacular meals in it. There was a large table with a scrubbed wood top the color of butter. On that table Mother could stretch the puff pastry for strudel to amazing proportions, and she also enjoyed using the three ovens in the antique wood stove.

By the large kitchen window looking out into the garden, there was a table at which my parents ate. At the table every morning they also sat and read aloud professor Zilka's book on the parables of Jesus, and they often wrote us about their Bible study. At the table my Mother also liked to read until late at night or to write letters. Father typed his letters upstairs and we heard from him frequently. Mother insisted on writing separately to each of us children. After reading these letters we felt the impulse to answer them right away, and it was a blessing that in corresponding with our parents we often expressed our feelings better than we would have verbalized them face to face. In writing letters to them it came naturally to say, "we love you, we are grateful to you, we pray for you." It was easy to put our feelings on paper. Of course Mother never stopped being our mother, and was constantly plotting some supply of food for us in Prague. Quite often someone appeared at our door in Prague delivering a package with butter and lard and eggs which were greeted as holy manna.

The old housekeeper Ruzena stopped by several times every day to visit with Mother. They covered a lot of territory as rememberers of the past but Ruzena also brought along the latest news and was a constant source of information on what she could get on the black market for Mother's use and her shipment to Prague. The greatest joy of my parents at that time was that they lived only five kilometers away from my older sister Nadia and her two children. She was married to a county doctor at the age of twenty one, and although she was happily married, she missed Prague terribly, and always envied us having Mother and Father near. Now it was the mutual turn of parents and daughter to enjoy each others company. Nadia's husband, Jiri Plch, possessed an enormous sense of humor, and was captivating in sharing his experiences as a country doctor. My parents always provided an appreciative audience. Once in a while Jiri and Father enjoyed a long game of cards, and it was a matter of course that Nadia and family stayed for dinner. Nadia and Mother also had good times together planning Christmas and mastering such arts as making soap, producing strong after dinner drink which called for the use of honey;

or taking apart old hand knitted sweaters, and knitting "new" scarves and gloves.

At first, the people of the village were afraid to come near my parents in the daylight except when they went to the shoemaker's shop, but soon my parents had visitors who were coming regularly and never empty handed. This bucolic intermezzo was often interrupted by the Gestapo summons for Father to appear at the office in Prague. He was always required to bring a report from his physician, and therefore to our great joy, every visit at the Gestapo also meant a several day family reunion. Already after the very first trip from the homestead to Prague's Gestapo Headquarters, it was obvious that Ohler and somebody else reported Father's every step. They knew for instance about every visitor and were especially concerned about two visits of the nearby minister. Otherwise Father's file was indeed removed before the Gestapo could get their hands on it, for the investigating officer knew nothing of Father's previous activities. He knew, however about the old time neighbors at the homestead. Immediately next to us, in a house which used to be a part of the homestead, lived Ambassador Jaroslav Cisar, and right next to him was the villa of Dr. Jaroslav Stransky. Both Dr. Cisar and Dr. Stransky and their families escaped to London, and Dr. Stransky was a member of the Czechoslovak government in exile. The Gestapo was aware of the connection between London, Moscow and the partisan groups. It was essential for them to eliminate those who were providing partisans with directions from abroad. They were suspicious of anybody. It was obvious that visits at the homestead had to be limited to the minimum. My parents also suspected that one of the apprentices at the shoe workshop was doing more than fixing shoes. Above all, it was clear that Ohler's information concerning Father's health did not agree with the reports of our friendly doctor. It was therefore advisable for Father to be more sickly, and not be well enough to play chess with Herr Oberst every day. Also Mother had to take walks solo but enjoying the company of Rigo, often getting lost as she was investigating unknown vistas of the woods and mountains. Father never liked her going on these excursions alone, but she loved it.

Ruzena told me that the last time Mother and Father were leaving the homestead for Prague, just before Christmas 1944, although it was to be only a few days stay Mother could not control her tears, and as the sleigh was taking them to the railroad station, Mother profusely thanked Ruzena for all her help, and then she waved to her with her handkerchief until the sleigh disappeared in the distance. According to Ruzena she also could not stop crying and seemed to know that she would never see Mother again.

Shortly after their departure the sleepy village of Vir and the surrounding towns were deeply shaken. Oberst Ohler and his wife Magda were shot by the paratroopers as they went on their daily winter walk with their dogs. For security reasons the Ohlers never took the same walk often. This time they walked a narrow road to the neighboring town in which my sister lived. Suddenly the Russian and Czech partisans jumped on them from both sides of the road. Ohler and his wife both had their pistols and although they were wounded, they fought to their last. The Gestapo, the German soldiers, the Czech police arrived almost immediately and found the Ohlers and their dogs dead. Then a long and fierce fight between the paratroopers and the Nazi forces took place. The Germans combed the woods until, at last, late in the evening, all was quiet, and the chief of the operation announced that the foreign agents were all liquidated. Until that day the stories of soldiers being dropped off and paratrooping from British and Soviet planes seemed unbelievable, suddenly everyone heard that there were armed enemies of the German Reich in the spreading mountainous territory of Vir.

The village became a fortress, soldiers, SS men, the Gestapo were everywhere. A German police car equipped with loudspeakers went ever so slowly through the village "Achtung! Achtung!" shouted a voice into the loudspeaker announcing the martial law. No one was to leave his or her home after eight in the evening. Then came the announcement that gave everyone shivers. Anyone giving any assistance to a foreign paratrooper will be shot along with all the members of the family. This car went round and round the village making the same announcement, and continued in this known technique of Nazi terror for hours: "If you give any assistance to foreign paratroopers and agents not only you, but also your wife, your children, your brothers, sisters, and your parents will be shot. All enemies of the German Reich will be eliminated without any mercy!" This announcement was echoing through the valley of the village, and in every house the people were hugging each other. The Gestapo knew that the murder of the Ohlers would have been impossible if the partisans, hiding in the woods did not have some assistance from the village folk. It was a night of terror. The Gestapo went from house to house. Many arrests were made. If Father and Mother had been at the homestead that night undoubtedly they would have been arrested, or taken as hostages. Perhaps it was fortunate that at that time we had no idea that my sister Nadia, a mother of two little children, was tight-lipped while she went through the greatest horror and anxiety of her life. That night when it was risky even to step outside, one of the partisans quietly entered her house looking for the doctor. When Jiri came out, the man said, "Doctor, we need your help, some of our men and officers were badly hurt."

"Let me take my bag."

"Jiri, what on earth will happen to us and to our children?" cried Nadia desolately.

"Mrs. Plch," said the man, "your husband is loved and respected, he has no choice, he is under the orders of the Liberation army!"

They blindfolded Jiri and took him to the place of disaster in a German police car which the paratrooper had somewhere confiscated.

Thirty years later Dr. Jiri Plch received a very gaudy decoration from the Soviet Union for heroism. It was revealed then that Jiri had operated on a Soviet general and saved his life, and the lives of several wounded partisans on that fateful night, following the murder of the Ohlers.

TOTALLY ENGAGED

Being the youngest in the family, I lasted in school, and in living at home, in seminormal circumstances, the longest. Our family began to break up. Shortly after my parents were sent to the homestead, my brother Blahous was sent to Hungary, and we did not hear from him. The fiancé of my sister Bohunka, successfully escaped to England, joined the Czechoslovak air force in exile and tragically was among the first ones reported as missing in action. Many of our friends heard that news on the Czech broadcast from England and brought the sad tiding to us. Just at that time my sister was sent to work in a factory. My oldest sister, Vera as a pharmacologist was needed where she was. I realized that my life could not go on in this fashion forever, the question was what was ahead of me, and at times the uncertainty of my tomorrows haunted me. I continued maintaining my "salon" although the circle of my friends was shrinking, and after one of our classmates was executed we were more and more careful in getting together. A new venture in my life was that I followed the announcement in the church, and joined a Bible study class led by the much loved and admired New Testament scholar, Dr. Zilka. Since my parents were studying his book on the parables we had even more to write about in our letters. For the first time I felt religiously liberated, as this biblical scholar without blinking an eyelash reminded us that the Bible contains much of fiction. For the first time I heard the distinction between the Jesus of history and the Christ of faith. I was the youngest in the class of mostly elderly ladies who could not understand a teenager asking many questions of a prominent scholar. They let me know that the absence of my parents was obviously showing in my behavior but Professor Zilka acted as if those questions were very important and took a great deal of time to answer them. I appreciated that and especially his closing prayers. He was never whining, his prayers sent us out with the great affirmation that nothing can ever separate us from the love of Christ.

At that time I also was fascinated by Dostoevsky's *Crime and Punishment* and absolutely fell in love with Sonia, and the concept of the hidden Christ.

Our daily bread, or the lack of it complicated our lives. We were broke. Buying things on the black market was beyond our resources. My parents were at Vir, and we all worried, especially because my sister Nadia was a diabetic and insulin which she had to have to survive was then available only on the black market. Just in those days I experienced a miracle, or at least I perceived it as such. A woman appeared at our door. She introduced herself as Mrs. T. and told me that she was led to discuss with me a very urgent matter. She appeared as a visionary, everything about her was exaggerated, she spoke with the pathos of a great tragedian. I led her to father's study, a sunny room lined with bookcases and she exclaimed, "Here I am, in the very room of a theologian and a very great man, a noble, great man!" After this monologue I was almost sorry that I ever let her in, but I did ask her to sit down. She took a deep, deep breath, she told me in a confidential, hissing voice that she was led to know that the dear professor and his family were in a great financial crisis. "As it happens, I have quite a bit of cash, and I would like nothing more than to help you out and buy this house. Please, tell your father. Of course, we would reach an understanding that you could continue living here as long as you wish. My husband and I, and our two lovely boys would take one of the apartments on the second floor. I need the answer from your lawyer in a week."

"Yes, indeed I shall try to explain this to my parents," I stuttered. "I am very grateful to you."

As I led her to the door she said, "I know my dear boy that these are difficult times for you. My son, the younger one, is only one year older than you are. You must be courageous, I know that some very great things are ahead of you."

As she left I was shaken. She was led. By whom, by what? She knew my name, she knew our financial situation, she acted as if she knew all about us.

As I shared the news with my sister, Vera, she categorically answered, "An agent." We called several lawyer friends, most of them Masons, and they all felt that there was something fishy, but agreed that we ought to proceed in a strictly business way. To the amazement of all, the house was sold and Mrs. T. agreed to all the conditions worked out by our lawyer. We could occupy the apartment as long as we wished, had the use of the garden, and she was granted permission to move to the second floor, and, of course, it was her privilege to make any changes in the house. She paid according to the agreement. Once again we had some cash in our hands. I felt like a hero but Father failed to say so. He did write that obviously we were dealing with a spiritualist, and that he was extremely glad that God had chosen her to help us out in our dire need. My father interpreted everything in theological terms. I had no idea what was meant by a spiritualist, but very obviously according to Father, the Lord God never depended only on his own. He does not mind using pagans to achieve his purposes. By the grace of God our help came through a spiritualist.

Mrs. T. and her family moved into the apartment house much earlier than expected and as soon as they moved in, the painters came and painted all windows bright red. When you looked at the six story apartment house, all you could see were the bright, lipstick like outlines of every window. It was so appalling that I rushed to Mrs. T. to ask her for an explanation, after all, I was the only one among my friends who lived in that crazy house with bright red windows! Mrs. T. very kindly explained to me that she was a spiritualist, and that at the séance the medium told her that the house would be protected from bombing if the window frames were painted red. I did not know what to think, but before leaving I asked "Mrs. T., when the Gestapo will come for your son, what will he do, what will you do?"

"We think a great deal about it, but we are not worried, we trust that in our meetings we shall be told what to do. I hope very much that our son, Tom, and you will become friends. It would be good for both of you."

That was a bit too much for me.

The only reasonable disadvantage of my staying at home in reasonable comfort so long was that meanwhile day by day, month by month, and year by year the Nazis had perfected their technique of eliminating their enemies, the unwanted, the inferior species, especially the Slavs. Yes, there was a change in thinking, and in policy. We do not know whether Hitler learned from Stalin or Stalin from Hitler, but we do know that as the war against the Soviet Union dragged on, and there was not any "blitzkrieg" as expected, it was Hitler, who according to the documents of the Nurenberg trials developed the brilliant scheme of using the men and women from the occupied territories as a slave labor force. He speculated that over two million people in his occupied territories were available. Forced labor, as perceived by Hitler, was designed not only to keep the German factories running, and roads and bridges, and railways in bombed areas repaired while the German men were fighting at the front, but also to eliminate undesirable people who were unfit for his future empire. Hitler shouted at his closest collaborators that thanks to his leadership a shortage in the labor force never needs to be a problem in Germany. Millions of laborers were available, all that was needed was a good organization, determination and discipline on the part of those whom he had entrusted with leadership in this task. If they are unable to succeed in this undertaking they must be considered lazy saboteurs, and as such deserved death. Hitler was literally hoping that after his victorious war only the fittest would be left to enjoy the new Germany. When this dream collapsed at the end of World War II, Hitler had no compassion even on the German survivors. He was not interested in helping them, because as he said to Speer, the best of the Germans were already dead anyway.

One day when I came home from school, as usual I was sorting the family mail, and there was a surprise for me. My eyes stared at a large, impressive envelope addressed to me. It was sent by registered mail. The envelope was bedecked with swastika insignias. Well, it was not an invitation to a reception by Goebels but here it was! I was congratulated for my perception in joining other students and in volunteering my life for the service of the German Reich. The total war declared by the Führer calls for a total engagement of the young generation. Finally the letter came to the point. I was to report for my assignment the very next day at six thirty in the morning at the stadium hall, formerly used for trade fairs. I was to bring only bare essentials, everything would be provided for me. I sat down at a table and read the letter over and over again just to be sure that I understood every word. Then I just stared into space totally overcome by the beastliness of the Nazi evil, and by its civility. This was too clever for the good people of the world to comprehend. Here I was being summoned to report for hard labor, and the word labor was never even mentioned. I was congratulated for volunteering in the total engagement! Of course, I was not the only one who received the same congratulations that day, and as I mentioned my news to some friends and neighbors I became a victim of the flourishing whispering propaganda, some of which was so exaggerated that I had to laugh. Almost everybody seemed to know about transports of laborers, and about a great many people who were shipped to Berlin and other large cities to remove the time bombs dropped by the allies. On the other hand I had friends who were like characters from the comedy absurd saying to me "What on earth do you worry about? You always have some possibilities. When you go there tomorrow they will ship you away or they will not ship you away, if they don't ship you away, everything is fine, and there is another 'either or.' Of course, you may be shot, but if you are shot, you cannot do anything about it. So what do you worry about?"

Hurriedly I wrote to Mother and Father and to a few friends, pathetic and slightly dishonest letters. I was writing them about being confident and full of trust in God. There was no other way of writing, because I was frightened, and the minute I began to open my heart, I was in a puddle of tears.

That night I feverishly prayed my begging prayers telling God that I was a young and innocent boy, and that I came from such a nice family, definitely not meant for Berlin. Then I prayed for a huge air raid or an earthquake, after all, for God everything was possible, and he was able to save my life! Not an airplane was heard that night, and God was obviously unimpressed by my prayers. I was very much afraid of oversleeping but after an almost sleepless night I actually saw the sunrise from the window of my bedroom. I loved my room filled with so many treasures reminding me of the happy days of my youth. I wanted so much to return to my room, and to find it untouched. The sky was brilliant, I had forgotten how beautiful the sunrise is. I guess the last time I saw a sunrise was on Easter morning, when we sang Hallelujah, and affirmed that the Easter sunrise was a cosmic event, an epilogue to the tragedy of Good Friday. As I was thinking about it, I felt ashamed of my begging prayers, I felt like apologizing: Dear God, as we are asking you to deliver us from bloodshed, from evil and to restore peace in the world while we do nothing, whose business are we spreading before you? Will you forgive us? Will you steady my steps and give me another chance?

After a huge breakfast, my sister stuffed my pockets with vitamins, and pills for any possible ailment which could afflict me, and I stepped out of my home. In less than an hour I entered the realm of Caesar, the empire of fear. Already in front of the building there were long, snakelike lines of "volunteers" ready to enter the vestibule and be registered. The lines were arranged in alphabetical order, and soldiers walked in between the lines keeping them in order. Everything was superbly organized, and a great many uniformed men saw to it that everything went smoothly. There were the black uniformed SS men, some brown shirts, the soldiers, and men in different uniforms which I never saw before. As I finally came to the "B" desk in the vestibule my portfolio already awaited me. At first I was fingerprinted, then I stepped aside and had my picture taken, then I was weighed and sent for a physical in an adjoining room with strict instructions to return to desk "B." Until recent years when I read Thomas Keneally's *Schindler's List* I did not understand why that day we were weighed and had a physical examination. Indeed those who were underweight or who suffered with some disease were eliminated from the process and were sent somewhere else. After the physical we did not get our clothing back and walked naked, to the starting point desk. I had never seen so many naked men and women before and I felt embarrassed. Desk "B" appeared very far away. I did not know what to do. Many of the naked men and women looked grotesque as they tried to cover their nakedness with their arms and hands. They did not want to see anybody and their heads were hanging down. I presumed it was a posture which was expected as a sign of submission and humility. Walking with my head up, noticing that some of the uniformed men stared at me, I felt as an exhibitionist. Suddenly there was a great commotion and for the first time I noticed Tom, the son of the new owner of our house. He suffered a massive epileptic fit, pushing everybody around, falling and then banging his head against the wooden floor. I thought that if that was what he had been instructed to do by the medium, he played the role magnificently, and convincingly. The officers were ordered to take him out on a stretcher and to my knowledge he was sent home.

At desk "B" I was issued a Kennkarte with my name, photograph, finger prints and above all, my number. I was told that later on I had to keep the Kennkarte in the pocket of my uniform. Then I was given a cobalt blue plate with my white number. The plate was the size of a saucer. A string was attached to this identification number, and I was to hang it around my neck. The officer at the desk spoke loudly to me, telling me that I had to memorize my number, that from that moment on I did not have a name, I was known only by my number. When my uniform would be issued to me, the number had to be attached to my right breast pocket.

I entered the arena of naked men and women, the blue plate with white numbers hanging around their necks. We were to march round and round the immense hall, and sing a new song they taught us, about our great march against England. It was a swinging melody, easy to sing, each line followed by a refrain with a most emphatic "gegen Engeland." Obviously a song about the Soviet Union at that time was not yet in the Nazi repertoire. During our marching, I exchanged glances with a number of students whom I knew. It also occurred to me that in that multitude, the olive skinned gypsies of both sexes were noticeably handsome. They were not at all self conscious, they had beautifully built bodies, and even in that scene in which people were reduced to animals, they maintained a certain dignity and even managed a smile, showing their pure white teeth. At last the parade was over. We were divided and half of us marched into another hall. Then in each hall began the horrid process of counting off by ten. Only the uniformed gods knew the exact meaning of the count off. I got a lucky number but Vrana whom I saw from a distance obviously got number ten and went out to go to Berlin or Kassel. When you get a lucky number you would think that you would go out singing but it is quite otherwise. You walk away morally beaten, your heart revolting against this kind of lottery saying to yourself: At least, if

I could say that I am better than those who went to Berlin and other deadly places to face horrid danger and possibly death, but I am not. What does it mean? How do I deserve to walk on this earth? There is no answer. Many people ask in which camp I spent these years, and I really do not know. I started in a big foundry near Prague where I had to learn to carry heavy buckets full of red hot liquid iron, which we poured into forms for wheels for tanks. The buckets were always carried by two men. The two handled buckets were extremely heavy and the hair on our arms caught on fire from the heat of the iron. We looked like the slaves from the frescos of ancient Egypt. The first few days I was so exhausted that in the evening I literally crashed on my bed in my brand new, stiff dungarees and all. I showered late at night when I regained some feeling in my body.

In those days I often recalled one of my happy outings in the pre "total engagement" era. A few of us students went to the annual St. Matthews carnival. There were the usual attractions: chambers of horror, the bumper cars adventures, the circus, nothing new but we were attracted by a little booth with a big sign "Your Future Foretold for Five Crowns. Madame Bonnet, Very Discreet." The curtain was drawn and a sign which was pinned to the drapery said "Do not disturb, Madame Bonnet at work." We were giggling and determined to have some fun, we decided to have our future foretold. I remember the scene distinctly. The tent was almost dark, and the fortune teller with a deep voice played her role to perfection. She asked me to close my eyes and to give her my right hand. She touched that hand gently and hissed "Your heart is goooood but oh, that hand has never worked, it has never worked, it's s-s-soft. It will be raw, I s-s-see blisters. Hah, Ha, Ha! I s-see blisters-s! You will get used to it. We all get used to it. Don't I know! Ha, Ha Ha Ha . . ." We laughed all the way home, imitating Carmen "This hand has never worked!" I thought of Carmen and I felt that in her laughter was a bit of compassion for the idiots who bring up their children as if they knew that only certain people are meant for hard work. I could hear the hissing voice of that woman "your heart is good, but oh my God, your hands are soft, they never worked!"

The combination of a good heart and soft hand was not exactly advantageous in the involvement of the total engagement of the German Reich. Of course, the Czech foremen responsible to their German lords appointed seasoned workers to teach us this work. Many of them spent years working in the foundry. Even in normal times the pay for foundry work was good, but the dust and stench in the foundry were incredible, and before too long everyone coughed as if stricken with tuberculosis. These older men who knew more than their foremen about the foundry coughed and coughed. I expected them to be tough on me, after all, they had their chance to get even with the children of the bourgeoisie, the years of depression were not so far from many of them, but I was deeply touched by their gentleness as they taught me to carry the buckets, although for the first time I had no name, I was just a number. Yet these workers, some of them ex-convicts, treated me as a fellow human being, they seemed to understand the unfairness of the situation, and gladly helped me to endure. At the same time I felt a deepening sense of separation from the people who were supposed to be my friends. There were a great many people who simply could not cope with the new reality, and in every free moment they were either arguing about who caused our lot, or complaining, or daydreaming about what they would do after the war, when their material possessions would be returned to them. For the first time in my life I was nauseated by the people among whom I grew up but whom I really did not know. They incarnated all the niceties and cultural embellishments. I am sure that they considered themselves Christians but their guiding principle simply was self interest. When I was beaten for the first time, and collapsed, there was nothing astonishing about it, but what was astonishing was that an unknown woman at noon brought me my food, and a cup of cold water. As she bent over me, trying to force some nourishment into me, my friends were returning from their break, and obviously for their benefit, she said ever so loudly, "It's a rotten world baby, when a young man like you must wait for help from the former queen of the red light district. Are you not ashamed cowards?"

I could see the little characters of Dostoevsky coming to life all around me, men and women who would never talk about religion, many of them people of very doubtful reputation, yet as if in the awareness of their need to be forgiven, to atone, they were always there in the hour of need as angels of mercy. Often I thought of Jesus and his admiration for the least of men and women who love much because they were forgiven much, the last, who will be the first in his kingdom.

I yearned to talk with someone about it, and although I was never alone, I was extremely lonely. What bothered me most was that in the multitude the Christians were hardly recognizable. I was constantly scolding myself for detesting the Nazis, for the Nazis openly confessed their faith in Hitler and in his doctrines, and they lived according to their confession of faith. I had no right to judge them. To deal with a Nazi meant to expect the Nazi behavior. In the same way I felt in my young, troubled soul, that one had the right to expect at least more than average from the confessing Christians, and I simply did not see it. It hurt, yet I knew that in that crowd there ought to be many who would be kin in spirit. How would one recognize them? I often prayed for the eyes to see. As I mentioned before, this was an empire of fear, and *fear is a dreadful enemy of faith and courage.* First of all, we were afraid, above us were the docile Czech foremen whose duty was to interpret for us the tasks dictated by their German superiors. The foremen literally trembled whenever a Nazi officer appeared in the shop, and to every order they responded, "Jawohl!" They were responsible for the quality of our products. If we produced defective wheels they were charged with sabotage by their Nazi superiors who had to blame somebody. There were many people in uniforms all around us and much heel kicking, the SS men, the policemen, the soldiers, and on and on. All these men had one thing in common, the fear of being sent to the eastern front. The guards and SS men had to prove their importance in the plant even if they had to produce stories of incredible sabotage. I could not believe how many people under the cruel pressure of these men confessed to being guilty of crimes they had never committed. In the headquarters of the labor camp or factory fear managed everything in a frantic tempo. Since Hitler was a victim of illusions, and his collaborators were afraid to tell him that his expectations of foreign labor output were unrealistic, fear paralyzed every office, especially when the raw material was slow in coming, and when hours of labor were lost by air raids. Everybody was afraid of everybody else, at times the informers were precisely where no one expected them to be. Everyone's leading desire was to keep above the muddy water of suspicion and to survive.

I was just getting a bit used to the work in the foundry when I was promoted. An officer came to tell me that it was a shame not to use my intelligence and that I was promoted to operate a crane in the cavernous hall where tanks were assembled. I really think that this promotion was intentional, it was not hard for the foreman in the foundry to observe that I had no technical ability. I never worked with a crane and from my childhood on I have suffered with a haunting fear of heights. My new job was to transport huge machinery from one side of the hall to another, according to the needs of the workers. I was given a manual, which I did not have a chance to look at because they immediately led me to my future assignment.

A man of my intelligence would catch on very quickly, I was told, I would learn by doing, the main thing was not to slow down the production. The foremen could not tire of bowing, smiling and agreeing with such remarks of the German officers. I was petrified. Yes, I noticed that crane with awe whenever I passed through that plant, but had no idea how one gets into that tiny cabin. At the same time, I almost had to laugh, and kept saying to myself, "If Germany is to be saved from defeat by people like me, the war must be lost!" My fellow workers shared that feeling. Any news in that immense factory traveled fast, and when I entered the huge hall my many friends among the workers clapped, and they saw in me the symbol of the coming freedom. "Here he comes!" they shouted in laughter, and the commandant remarked to me, "I see that you have a great many friends here. They will make your job much easier than it would be otherwise." Indeed by then I did have a great many friends among the workers, in fact some of them were with me in the newly organized Bible study group. There was cheering, and I must admit that I did quite a bit of clowning, in all that laughter completely forgetting where I was. The foremen were embarrassed and immediately shouted their commands for everyone to return to his task at once. Shortly the German officer smiled saying to me, "Here we are. Up you go!" To my horror I saw the straight ladder to the third floor where one was to make the step into the cabin of the crane. I was petrified, my stomach was turning, my body was trembling. All my life I have been afraid of heights.

"Up, up, up!" yelled the German officer, "or should I come to help you?" Yes, the machines were humming, there was the usual sound of hammers, but I could feel the eye of every worker on me and I appreciated that. Praying every step somehow miraculously I made it, and stepped into the cabin, swearing that I would never go down. Many workers looked at me and gave an appreciative smile. Hurriedly I studied the buttons on the dashboard, and just as I wanted to verify everything in the manual, I heard some workers yelling, tapping their hard hats, obviously using some code which I did not understand. Finally they pointed to a medium size wheel which had to be moved. The foreman below shouted "Slowly! Slowly!" and then in German, "Langsam, Langsam!" The German officers studied me. I was extremely lucky, and I started reasonably well, and then I was slowly moving to the end of the workshop. I surprised myself. Then everybody was advising me what to do, and along with a big applause actually I moved that thing without any major catastrophe. I could not believe it and was delighted when the foreman, and the officers left.

Shortly I realized that operating a crane could be extremely busy for a short time, and then one had to wait and wait for the next call. What a bore! Then it occurred to me that this was possibly the only job in the whole plant in which one could do quite a bit of reading during the work hours.

Soon I was called to move a monster, something between a small tank and a military truck. The fellows down below were joking, and singing, unquestionably I was the amusement of the day. I bowed to everyone, and I congratulated myself, and while the monster was being hooked nobody was working, everybody was watching the sensation. We were a noisy bunch, and I fully entered the celebration mood.

"Ready?"

"Ready," I responded. My start was not too good, and the fellows stepped aside laughing and laughing. I came to a quick stop, and the monster started swinging, then I lost my nerve, I did one stupid thing after another, the monstrous thing was swinging with a ferocious power. Still laughing the workers ran in all directions away from me, meanwhile I was causing considerable destruction, until there was a horrendous crash. The alarm sounded and the Gestapo, and officers were running in and toward the crane shouting "Sabotage! Eine grosse sabotage!"

"DOWN! DOWN! DOWN!"

As I stepped out of the cabin my legs felt like rubber. Oh to climb down into the hands of the crucifiers! I was shaking.

"Come on down!" "Hurry up!" "Do you understand? Come on down!"

"I can't," I cried, "I really can't."

I heard quick steps on the metal ladder behind me. One of the workers could not tolerate that sight any more and took enormous courage in not asking for any permission. He knew that I was at the end of my strength and ever so gently in a soft voice called to me "Zdeněk, this is Tony! Don't be afraid. I shall help you down. Come on, I am right behind you!"

At last I was in their hands, until they were done with me and I knew no more.

When I regained consciousness I wanted to believe that this was just a horrid nightmare but as I opened my eyes, to my horror, they were all there laughing, as if they wanted to say, "So, you thought you were in heaven but we are there, there is no escape from us, understand?" This was one of their famous tricks. I am positive that at least some of them remembered from their youth the one hundred thirty ninth Psalm and the words "Such knowledge is too wonderful for me . . . where shall I go from your spirit? Where shall I escape from your presence? If I ascend to heaven, you are there, if I make my bed in hell, behold you are there also" (Psalm 139:6-8). With all their might the Nazis wanted to prove that they were inescapable, the masters of heaven and earth; but as it is often the case, they left the scene too soon, and as soon as they left, as one was still lying in the dust, one could see the shadows of life and mercy coming lovingly to wash off the blood from the wounds and to force a cup of cold water to one's swollen lips.

Being charged with sabotage I went first to solitary, then I was often working, having no idea where, since we were transported in closed cattle trains. At times I was back near Prague. It really did not matter, wherever I was, there was the same monotonous work, the same food, the same tricks, the same fears, the same yearning. Whenever we worked outdoors, however, we hoped that the job would last a long time. After being in a foundry, or in a factory for twelve, fourteen hours a day, one easily forgot the glory of the outdoors. The most beautiful orchids could not be lovelier than a field with patches of yellow dandelions, in spite of all the misery of the war time, the birds were still singing. Joyfully we stripped and worked half naked, letting the warm sun tan us and let us forget the frozen misery of winters. More than once there were such surprises as an overflowing cherry tree in the midst of desolation, waiting for us to harvest it, and when we worked on the roads or near the roads, more than once, out of the passing trucks came bags with bread and pastries. The first time I caught one of the bags which were tossed to us, I was happy and surprised and I asked my buddy, "Why do they do that? It's so wonderful of them!"

"For goodness sake," he replied, "have you looked at yourself lately? We are not exactly a sight for sensitive stomachs!" These were formative years for me. Very often I was lonely, or better said, homesick for the beautiful, but then I had to scold myself for there was beauty, splendor, magnanimity and goodness where I was.

*   *   *   *   *

In the post Victorian era all the way through the thirties it was considered in poor taste to speak in the first person, and to share one's feelings. When one yearned to share a concern or a dream, it was a good idea to start with such a sentiment as, "It is often said that . . ." or to quote an author of distinction. We are indebted to Hitlerism and Stanlinism for overcoming this privatism, and becoming more open and human than we would be otherwise.

When our resources are depleted and we find ourselves in total helplessness, religious questions easily come to our lips. Do you believe in a good God? How can God be good and allow this misery all around us? Or how can we doubt God when Tony defies all rules and goes to help you as you try to come down from the steep ladder. What is the meaning of life? What is the meaning of our being in Hitler's service? What does it mean to be really human? One question was popping after another, and these questions certainly helped us to find one another.

From the point of view of religion we were a strange lot. There were a few fundamentalists who were so busy praying that they could not help anyone in need. They perpetuated the pathological, lazy eschatology which said that Hitler was bound to be victorious, that the world was coming to the end, that nothing could be done except to prepare one's soul. The Roman Catholics were perplexed, saying: how can we pray without the rosary and the missal, how can we even think without the directive of a priest? The liberals were saying, how can we pray when we do not know how and besides we are not so sure about God allowing bad things to happen to such nice and educated people from good families like us. Luckily there were also those who could never define their faith, who believed and yet were haunted by the awareness of their unbelief. They were forcing us to think. Indeed, as the time was passing by, we discovered a church among us, a group of believers who believed that God believed in us far more than we ever believed in him. I cherished the immense spiritual liberty of slaving for Caesar, and singing the praises of the psalms at the same time. It was Christianity without any ecclesiastical trapping or church crutches. We were meeting as rememberers. We had to start with that which was in our memories. Most of us, very fortunately, were the products of Sunday Schools of the era when memorization was encouraged. It was a group effort but it was amazing how many hymns, psalms and Bible narratives we could put together. We certainly had enough material to think about and to study. At the same time we were surely renewed by the awareness of our individual heritage. As I struggled trying to recall the words of the forty second Psalm "Why art thou cast down, O my soul? And why art thou disquieted within me? Hope thou in God: for I shall yet praise him who is the health of my countenance and my God." It was the last verse of the Psalm. I could also remember the opening verse, "As a heart longs for the flowing streams so longs my soul for thee, O God," but I could not remember anything in between the first and the last verse. At the same time I could remember my Grandmother Novotna, who was educated in Herrnhut, standing by my bedside repeating the whole Psalm from memory, often giving me a choice of repeating it in Czech, German or French. My friends shared similar recollections, and we felt we were reclaiming a forgotten treasure.

We studied the remembered passages of the Scriptures, and as the Holy week was approaching it was only natural for us to celebrate the Holy Communion together. A barrel was our communion table, a tin can a chalice. "In that night in which our Lord was betrayed, he took bread and when he had given thanks he broke it and gave to them . . ." It never occurred to us that we were doing something wrong or unorthodox. After our heartfelt prayers there was not any placid "passing of the peace," but big hugs and the assurance, "I love you, I shall be by you no matter what." There was something holy in that group, and perhaps it is only natural that after these experiences I have never felt comfortable with much liturgy. Yes, I can take the bulletin home, and really pray the words of the liturgy, but in worship, the hurried responsive prayers and reading have appeared to me as a spiritual pingpong and filled my heart with a deep spiritual home sickness.

Very often I recall that group of young men and women who so earnestly tried "to be," men and women, all wearing the same dirty blue dungarees and matching jackets, the cobalt blue metal plate with white numbers attached to their breast pockets. Men and women whom Hitler tried to reduce to numbers and yet who were so alive in their individuality! I remember their smudged faces, the different sets of eyes, their first names, their voices. What has happened to them all I do not know, most of them, I presume, were swept away by the stormy winds of that era, as tiny crumbs fallen from Herod's table.

In the winter of 1945 we could hear the sound of canons from a distance. Many whispered about the approaching end of World War II. There was no sign of any end to German supremacy around us. The blind cruelty of the Nazis seemed to grin at us from every corner. When I heard that Father's best friend, Consul Jiri Sedmik was executed, I was truly shaken. He and my father were like brothers, his daughters were at home in our house. We all loved Sedmik. No matter how busy life was, those two would meet every week. My heart was bleeding for my father. It was strange that the German propaganda repeated over an over again that Sed-mik was beheaded at Plotzensee. Obviously Goebels decided to do everything possible to frighten the captive nations into blind obedience.

At that time in our small group we were studying the story of Mary and Martha, and above all we talked a great deal about Lazarus. One in the group remembered Eugene O'Neil's play, *Lazarus Laughed*. He described the play splendidly for us. When Jesus brought Lazarus back to life, our friend was telling us, the people were frightened. Lazarus walked around the stage saying, "I am alive!" and they were running away from him, wanting to put him back into the grave, and Lazarus was aware that people were more afraid of living than of death. Of course, we spent a great deal of time with the words of Jesus, "I am the resurrection and the life . . . He who believes in me though he were dead yet shall he live."

One day as I was working, I was thinking about those words. In one corner of the huge workshop the foreman was slapping a woman worker on her face. I was pushing a heavy cart full of debris outside. It was a very cold but bright February afternoon. Near the dump, at a distance, the Nazis had a few of their victims on their hands. Slowly pushing my cart I heard myself saying "I am death, and he who believes in me though he were alive is dead." This Gospel in reverse filled my whole being. Everything was becoming "Either or." If I survive, do I want to perpetuate this kind of civilization, life which is equal to death? I cried, as I yearned for Life with a capital L. Without Christ there was nothing but death. My mind was made up. Suddenly sirens began to howl. A huge air raid was upon us. As always we all ran out to the fields outside the camp, but already during the air raid, inch by inch I was crawling toward the fence, I started my journey home.

WAITING FOR SPRING TO COME

Frederika von Stade likes to sing Samuel Barber's hauntingly beautiful song, "Why is the summer so short? Why is the winter so long?" a melody which always comes to my mind as I think of the last, stretching months of winter, 1945. It was a brutal winter, and there was no way of escaping it. The window panes, shattered by air raids were replaced by cardboard, the minimal coal rationing was slow in coming. It was a winter of darkness with almost daily, unexpected outages of electricity. Central Europe was discovering the charm of dining by candle light but there was little but potatoes to eat. The women literally spent hours standing in snake like lines in front of grocery stores, and often came home empty handed or bringing home something which they had never intended to buy. There was no use making any shopping lists. One could easily go to get a liter of milk and come home with a bottle of rum, or a pair of slippers. The energy level was low, and patience was running out, the one warm room, the family living without any privacy, the constant repetition of daily problems, fears and struggles did not make for peace. I was less than twenty, and I felt already old and exhausted; my dreams were limited. My family, eating a bit of hot potato soup in the family circle, and a hope for some wonderful sleep in my own bed, a sleep without any yelling, any alarms, without the stench of humanity, and the dread of tomorrow, led me home.

If I had known then what the people of the allied countries took for granted, namely that the final victory over Hitler's Germany was only a matter of weeks or months, I would not have believed it. It was beyond all my imagination that the Czechoslovak government in exile under the leadership of President Edward Benes was beginning to close its offices in London, and was getting ready for the triumphant return home via Moscow, where this government of the people, yearning to be free would get instructions from Stalin and his cohorts. The diaries and testimonies of the Czechoslovak political leaders who were taking this journey home through Moscow all witness to their apprehension about the future political rearrangement of Central Europe. Much depended on which army would be liberating Prague and a large section of Bohemia. The Americans or the Soviets?

We now know that the big powers basically gave Stalin a free hand in Europe, we know also that Eisenhower was trying to slow down the march of Patton's armies, and had no interest in liberating Berlin and other strategic centers on the premise that it was prudent to do no more than was expected, and the American presence in the great centers of the defeated territory would only mean an increased burden for the USA, feeding the hungry, taking care of the refugees, of the homeless, *ad infinitum*. Eisenhower actually ordered General Patton to slow down his march against Hitler. All of this and the rest was totally unknown to us. The Reich's Minister of Propaganda, Joseph Goebels, succeeded to a considerable degree in a total denial of the situation. The BBC broadcasts were so jammed that no one could hear any good news, and Prague became a veritable fortress. Tanks were stationed at every square, soldiers overladen with automatic guns paraded the streets, the city was overcrowded with Germans pouring in from all directions, and then continuing on their journey toward Carlsbad. These multitudes of Germans played their role magnificently, nobody would ever guess that they were desperate people, ready to pay any price to be captured by the Americans marching from the East. They understood what John Carson in one of his late, late shows summarized by saying, "The American Indians have been the only people who have not profited by being defeated by the USA."

At the same time the sovereign leader of Prague, SS Gruppen Führer Karl Hermann Frank made far reaching preparations for the final siege. Never mind Hitler's order for "Operation Scorch the Earth," as other Nazi leaders, Frank wanted to save his own life. His first objective was to scare the Czechs to absolute obedience, and mercilessly he ordered mass executions of whole families in which someone had offered help to an escapee or to any enemy of the Reich. At the same time many important Czechs were brought from concentration camps and became Frank's personal prisoners. He was planning to exchange them for his freedom to run to the Americans, or to shoot them and himself. One would think that if the Germans knew that their defeat was inevitable they would try to make a few friends among the Czechoslovaks. Such was not the case. Their last gestures were the gestures of threat and terror. We shall be glad to pave the streets of Prague with the Czech skulls!

In this situation of horror and utmost isolation people were sustained by stories of those who swore that they heard the bombardment, and the canons of the approaching liberating armies. These accounts were shared with the pathos of the Bethlehem shepherds who in the region of Herod the king affirmed that they had heard the angels sing announcing the *kairos*, God's redemptive intervention into history. A friend told me that when he heard the thundering sounds of "Stalin's organ" for the first time he fell down on his knees and praised God! From the perspective of more than fifty years the paradoxes were too strong for fantasy, but in the last months of World War II we were Don Quixotic, and while our leaders in exile worried about the growing power of the Soviets, we, who lived in those months and years in Prague or goodness knows which town or place of the German Reich, could care less who would finish Hitler, as long as he was really finished, and we had a chance to survive. Thus Stalin was no longer the bloody bear of the Revolution, he was a good bear who was only after Hitler, and otherwise did not mean any harm. The seven long years of Nazism did not mellow us, our vision often became distorted, as William Blake put it:

> This Life's dim windows of the Soul
> Distorts the Heavens from Pole to Pole.
>
> We are lead to Believe a Lie
> When we see not through the Eye.
> *Auguries of Innocence* [6]

By the time I came to the quiet residential streets near my home, it was already dark. I was surprised by the deep darkness of the blackout. Only once in a while did I notice a tiny light of somebody's flashlight. The fresh snow on the unswept sidewalks luckily softened the sound of the wooden soles of my clogs. It was slippery and I kept walking close to the fences of the houses along the street. All kinds of fears went through my mind, but I tried to walk nonchalantly, quietly whistling an extremely popular "cowboy" melody of Czech edition with lyrics which seemed especially poignant that night, "Long is my way home, and deep is my yearning... Hola, Hola Ho, Hola, Hola Ho." A perfect foxtrot easy to walk to.

Exhausted, my feet frozen, I turned the corner to "By the Royal Garden" Street, and here was my home, number one hundred forty five. Everything looked normal. Excited, renewed in energy I raced the five flights up. The lights were on in the main entrance hall with its frosted glass, wide doors. I rang several times my usual ring, two short, one long, expecting a royal welcome, but instead the housekeeper came to open the door and greeted me as an apparition, "Oh God, No!" she cried, letting me in and crying again, "Oh God, not you, That's all we need! I know it's horrid of me, but please Zdeňáčku go away. Your Mother is dying, and now if anybody finds you here, we are all lost . . . I just can't take any more! Last week they shot a family on this street because they helped somebody. God, I'm scared, I can't help it, I am scared!" Fortunately, my oldest sister Vera stepped out into the hall, shortly followed by my sister Bohunka and my father and we fell into each other's arms. "My prayers are answered," Father was whispering, telling me about Mother's serious illness, her horrid pain, and her constant worry about me.

Quickly, I slipped off my clogs and noticing that my heavy socks were covered with ice I removed them too, and hurried to Mothers bedside barefoot. She was lying on a sofa in the corner of the room, and in another corner there was an improvised bed, made of eight chairs pushed together, and covered with a mattress, obviously for the care giver. Mother breathed heavily, her eyes were closed. She was dressed in an old black quilted robe and was covered with a light blue blanket. She moaned in pain, but as I came closer to her she opened her eyes, and recognized me at once. She smiled, and then realizing that I was not a dream, tears came to her eyes, and she motioned to me to come nearer. I was supposed to control myself and not to upset her but I rushed to her burying my head in her arms, unable to stop crying.

"Are you hurt my little one?"

"No.""

"Just think, how happy I am. Now I know that you too are well and alive. It's a great blessing."

She caressed my hair and I did not want that wonderful feeling ever to stop, and also I did not want to lift up my head and see her tortured face. "You must do something for me," she said turning to prose. "Of course, what is it?" "As you know, Dad hates my plants here, especially the orchids. He calls them 'Mother's lettuce' but would you believe those orchids, in toughest times bloomed most profusely, and in a way, they were more faithful than some friends. Imagine, orchids, in this room, in the middle of a war! You must water them regularly but not much . . ."

"I shall try."

"What about you Zdeňáčku?"

I told her about my thinking of ministry. She smiled approvingly, "I am not surprised, it is like that immortal sea. A bit of the sea has been in you always. Immortal sea! If I could only remember who wrote about it. Was it Longfellow? The immortal sea! Once a bit of it is in your heart you always come back to it, you cannot be happy outside of it although that sea may be at times very rough . . .Immortal sea. . . I just hope that you will be a good minister. We seem to be choking by mediocrity. Since so many wonderful, talented people were liquidated, that will be the greatest danger for the nation: mediocrity. I hope so much for you that you will be happy in it as we have been . . . brothers, sisters in every village."

Vera came in bringing a basin with water insisting that I soak my feet. Later, Dad and Bohunka came in bringing supper and hot tea.

"That boy could stand a bit of some spirit in that tea," Mother remarked. Father smiled and said, "It is already in it."

I did not need any urging to step out of the basin. The aroma of the food filled the room and I moved to my place at the table. Seeing the plate full, I looked up beggingly at my father. He understood, and trying hard to control his emotions, in trembling voice he offered a prayer in the name of him who in the night of treason and death took bread and gave thanks for it. That night my mother died, and a great deal of me died with her and had to wait for resurrection.

Mother was literally gone from our midst. When we quieted down we gathered at the dining room table each standing at the usual place, my father at the head of the table, my sisters at his side, my place was on the right of Mother's empty chair. We stood there quietly, as if listening to the ticking of the Grandfather clock. Father cleared his throat, and in his enormous knowledge of the Scriptures he started his prayer with a biblical quote "Father, the crown has fallen from our head . . ." Those words spoke to us so deeply that I can still remember the tears which were dropping on the leather upholstery of the dining room chairs making an awkward sound. After the prayer we sat down to consider what to do next, and I dared to ask about the indictment of our housekeeper. Am I endangering the whole family? What do you want me to do?

Father measured his words, and affirmed that everything was in God's hand, and that after the funeral we would have to find some place for me. Meanwhile I was to stay at home, but everybody agreed that I had to attend the funeral service. Then Father remarked that he knew of a wonderful place for me, that he hoped it would work out and that we would talk about it later.

Father announced that Mother wanted to be cremated and that it had to be a very private service in the crematorium, just for us, our relatives and only the closest friends. I asked that the announcement which was to be sent to our friends informing them of Mother's death start with the words, "The crown has fallen from our head" and also I requested that professor Urbanec would play the organ. In turn I was asked to select the hymns, and my sisters asked me to set the table for the relatives who would come after the funeral, and also I was to polish the silver. Suddenly I felt so exhausted that I dragged myself to the improvised bed in the corner of the dining room promising to participate in all planning lying down, and I slept for twelve hours.

A few miracles happened in those days. First of all my sister Nadia arrived. She wore a black Persian lamb coat and ever so typically for her she remarked on her arrival, "It was so lucky that I had this black fur coat. I could not get into the passenger train, so I traveled in a wagon with coal!" Also later on, my brother Blahous arrived, from some camp in Hungary where he served as a medic, and thus for the first time in years we were together. There was an enormous amount of love and understanding in the house.

As I was polishing the silver, I had plenty of opportunity to think about my mother. Although we were trained in household tasks, Mother always checked on everything, even whenever we went somewhere as a family, be it church, a lecture, dinner, concert or opera, Mother looked us all over, adjusted our ties, put gloves into our hands, looked at the skirts and hats of my sisters, and we all growled, especially the men, yet we all submitted to her, knowing her philosophy: If we cannot escape criticism, let the people critize us about that which matters and not about such trivialities as gloves, ties and hats!

Mother never dictated her views to us, but her views were well known to us, and all of us strong headed people actually sought her advice. She has been my mentor all the days of my life, and long before I read Berdyaev, and the Russian prophets, she introduced me to the idea of the aristocracy of the spirit, aristocracy based not on wealth, the academic or social standing but on the spiritual condition of one's heart. Her heart was always in command of her reason, and she was an aristocrat. There was nothing studied or rehearsed about her. Her manners, her love of people and wonderful humor and the ability to laugh at herself and her folly, were all an outcome of her spiritual condition. As a Mother of five children at times she had to fight to have a block of time for herself, and indeed for a few hours every day she was not available, it was her time to read the Scriptures, to read her books, to write a few letters. She actually locked herself in her room. By the standards of today she died young, at the age of fifty four. Undoubtedly, for years she burned the candle at both ends, she could not tolerate the thought of being too busy for her family and friends, too busy to write letters or to visit them. For her the people who were too busy to be human she felt nothing but pity.

I cannot remember her ever reading a fashion magazine, the idea that someone would dictate to her what she ought to wear was foreign to her.

Hating to be a center of attention, even when she had a new

dress, she wore it a few times at home so that no one would tell her, "Oh, I like your new dress!" Her elegance was subdued, understated. When she wore some special dress, she wore it as a matter of course, as something to which she was daily accustomed, but strangely enough it was precisely her unassuming quietness which gave her a definite authority, and many people, especially the University students came to her to open their hearts. Her laughter and appreciation of everything beautiful were contagious. For her, life was too short to clutter it with ugly things, her practice of Christian faith was a constant and exciting undertaking. Before every communion service, she reminded each one of us children to prepare ourselves for the service by seeking reconciliation with those whom we had hurt, and by some practical deeds of kindness and mercy. We knew that she was very much involved in such a preparation for the Holy Communion herself. It really hurt her when she saw people arguing, hating each other, and coming to the Lord's table as if it were God's main business to forgive us. The question of the practical consequences of our worshipping, of our praying, and pious talking was constantly on her mind. She was loved by most ordinary people and felt at home at their tables, and equally she was admired and respected by the famous and well to do.

With the exception of one young conductor she felt no hostilities. Of course, we laughed at her, and made her feel very guilty but she never attended a concert when this man conducted the symphony, she simply could not forgive him his treatment of her friend, a young pianist of great talent who made her debut with him conducting the performance of Beethoven's *Emperor Concerto.* Mother had some reservations about the conductor allowing her friend to make a debut in such an ambitious work.

Her friend played brilliantly but suddenly she paused, and collapsed. Everybody in the concert hall was stricken with panic. The conductor was mad. He took the score into his hands and with all his force tossed it on the floor and walked out. I do not know the details, I do not know whether Mother's friend had a heart attack or an attack of utmost anxiety. Her career as a concert pianist was finished that night but she became an exemplary piano teacher, and the conductor became famous in spite of Mother's dislike for him. Mother not only could not forget this man's inhumanity to a fellow artist but also she had definite reservations about an unfeeling man playing Beethoven! Years later when I was ministering a large church I realized that I was my mother's son, for I was truly nauseated by a musician who specialized in character assassination, and in plotting shady deals and yet loved to conduct Handel's *Messiah*. For Mother everything was connected. There was no Christian faith in the church if the same faith did not rule in a factory, office or at a high tea. In the realm of arts she liked to see the same spiritual connectedness that she saw in Albert Schweitzer, who was literally praying, and not performing when he played Bach. As a teenageer I was captivated by Rodin's bronze door, and I studied its monumental details with immense interest. I remember Mother cautioning me in my admiration for Rodin, saying, "One never knows whether the praise should go to Rodin or to the poor woman who truly loved him, for years slaved for him and provided for him and whom he refused to marry." One memory went through my mind after another and I fully realized that in Mother's life there was something of God's grace. I could not cry for her. I was glad that she was no longer suffering, but also I had a distinct feeling that Mother's sensivity was not for the era we were entering, that she was spared great spiritual suffering. Everything within me called me to give thanks for the way she lived, for the way she died but I did not know how, I was just hoping that in due season I would learn her way of being grateful. I never paid much attention to the churchy words "communion of saints" but now I believed in them, and yet before I finished polishing the silver, I thought that I knew Mother better than ever before.

As is often the case, a secret becomes general news. Of course, the people in our apartment house knew that Mother had died. Father's colleagues and students told one another, and when we arrived at the crematorium about half an hour before the service the big hall of the crematorium was full. We gathered in a small anti room which was filled with the most awful funeral pieces from relatives and friends, mostly evergreen wreaths with gaudy ribbons and horrid paper flowers—the only flowers available. I was asked to choose the piece which was to be attached to the casket, a hopeless task. Just at the last minute, my childhood friend, Vlastik and his mother came bringing a most beautiful bouquet of lilies of the valley, my mother's favorite. How and where they got the flowers I shall never know but it was the most beautiful thing one could imagine. That bouquet was attached to Mother's casket, and the rest of the "floral tributes" were placed in the background of the stage, yes, stage, for the service in the crematorium has a great many elements of drama. The casket rests on a very tall dais. On each side of the dais is "the honor guard" of candles in towering candlesticks. At the end of the service the dais with the casket slowly moves into the fire and the curtain closes.

As we entered the packed hall, professor Urbanec played magnificently, but nothing could surpass the enormity of the congregational singing! There were two ministers and I do not remember anything they said but I do remember a tremendous sense of peace.

After the funeral we shook hundreds of hands, and I was glad that I remembered most of the people, especially of the university professors so that I was able to address them by title and name, just as Mother had taught me. I was also glad that I was largely spared the usual platitudes. It is just amazing what nonsenses people tell you as they try to comfort you. It pleased me no end to see two of my professors, one tolerated me in Latin, and the other was despairing over me in trying to teach me mathematics. Considering the circumstances all people who came to the funeral took a courageous step by standing by us in our sorrow. Everybody knew that we were not exactly the favorites in the eyes of the Nazis, and we were grateful. Well, here was the professor of Latin telling me that time will heal everything, and already then I knew that time was static, healing nothing, just turning young fools into old fools. The professor of mathematics to my embarassment spoke about my mother "up in heaven." The new owner of our house, the spiritualist Mrs. T. topped it all. She embraced me tearfully and whispered into my ears, "Last night, I talked with your mother. She is so happy for you! Shortly you will travel to a far away country, and a great future is ahead of you! You must believe it, my dear!"

The last in the line was a young, attractive man of my age. He came, put his arms on my shoulders and said "You must be exhausted, we do not mean to do that to you. God bless! I am Mirko Harych, a future student of your Father. I have always wanted to know you, and we must get together soon!"

That was my first meeting with my truly best friend, Mirko Harych, a man and an artist who appeared in my life just when I needed him and he needed me, a man who gave true meaning to the word "friend."

As soon as the relatives left after our lunch, Father informed me that I was expected at the church at Zizkov, which was willing to take care of me.

*   *   *   *   *

The Zizkov church is indeed so hidden that it took me a while to find it. The sanctuary is actually built in the courtyard behind an apartment house so that it cannot be seen from the street. The apartment house provides the housing for ministers, custodian, the church offices and there are also a number of meeting rooms. The greying, kindly minister, Mr. Lanstjak received me most warmly and immediately began to speak about my mother and her funeral. He did not ask me any questions but gave me the keys to the church and then proceeded to give me a tour of the establishment. It was after the office hours, and no one was around. The hub of the offices was a large room with several desks, and at least two mimeograph machines. On each desk there were stacks of paper waiting to be collated. Mr. Lanstjak was justly very proud of this office and of the fact it secretly provided printed curriculum for the Sunday schools in the whole city and beyond. Since the universities and theological schools were closed by the Nazis, Mr. Lanstjak in collaboration with the former professors of the theological faculty, in this office, printed text books in the Old and New Testament, Systematic Theology and Church History to be used by students who were planning to become ministers and who were anxious to study at home. Before I knew it, I had a pile of these books in my arms.

Mr. Lanstjak obviously had great skills in organization, and the sanctuary witnessed to his gift in making every bit of space serve several purposes. The sanctuary was not pretty, it appeared

cold and severe. It was not old, the furnishings were functional and
certainly of this century. As most sanctuaries it had a balcony on
three sides. On the balcony opposite the pulpit was a small but fine
pipe organ. What was unique was that the balconies could be separated from the sanctuary by the means of roll out steel screens. It
was not attractive, but since the congregation was small, the balcony provided plenty of good space for the Church School children.
Immediately it came to my mind that this would be an ideal place
to have a gathering of friends some night. Behind the organ was a
tiny room with a wide bench "Just right for your nap," said Mr.
Lanstjak in jest, but nothing could appeal to me more than that, I
felt totally exhausted. I explained to Mr. Lanstjak my need of a bit
of solitude and of some rest. He seemed to understand. I thanked
him profusely, and shortly I was left alone on the balcony. Soon I
discovered an enormous echo from every step, every cough, but it
did not bother me. I stretched on the wide bench with a musty velvet covered cushion and within minutes I was sound asleep.

The idea of sleeping and spending my days in the attic behind the organ actually appealed to me but Mr. Lanstjak adhered to
the Calvinistic work ethics, and could not tolerate any laziness under the roof of his church, and shortly I became involved in the
production line in the main office. At first I felt a bit uneasy, not
being sure that I could even sign my name. A young man, named
Joe noticed my hesitation, "It's not easy," he said, "but you will be
amazed how soon everything will come back to you."

"How do you know?"

"I felt just like that when I came back from Dachau," he replied. Beside Joe, there were several secretaries, another young
man, and the biggest desk belonged to the minister of visitation
and pastoral care, Mr. Kubat, a blessing incarnate. He looked a little bit like the angel from James Stewart's remarkable film, "It's A
Wonderful Life," an angel who was still earning his wings. Mr.
Kubat was brought up in a monastery, and before his conversion to
Protestantism he studied for the priesthood. He retained many usages from his Roman Catholic past—never accepting the idea of
calling Mr. Lanstjak by his first name, always addressing him as
"Father Superior" or worse yet, "His Reverence."

Every day, rain or shine, he would come to the office singing, truly rejoicing in a new day. He would go to his desk, and first glance at his liturgical calendar, and the name of a saint for which the day was designated. A short homily describing the saint followed. We learned a lot and laughed a great deal. Mr. Kubat noticed that I was always in a hurry, and dubbed me "a colt of God," a name which stuck.

Mr. Lanstjak had his office outside of the main work room, and only once in a while did he step out to check how the work was going. Usually he brought out more and more texts which were to be reproduced. A great many visitors went through our room, and of course, first of all they stopped to visit with Mr. Kubat first. I marvelled at his ability to make everybody feel good and important. He knew everybody and their respective families, and had plenty of time for everybody, inquired about this or that family member, recalled the funeral of some grandmother and then he said, "Well, may God bless her soul," it was coming straight from his heart. This man with thousands of stories in his heart was a delight, but to the great displeasure of Mr. Lanstjak, Kubat certainly was slowing down the production and was not paying attention to deadlines. One could easily sense Mr. Lanstjak's frustration. Mr. Kubat was never in the office in the afternoon, that was his time to visit his patients in hospitals and suffering parishioners, as he called it "my sacred time with the lambs." Daily he reported to Father Superior on the condition of his lambs: a litany of human needs.

Once we were extremely busy, I guess it was before some holidays, and although I used to take a lot of work to my place on the balcony and do collating until late, there was no way the work could be done in time. Mr. Lanstjak came out and begged Kubat to stay in the office in the afternoon. Kubat was shocked. "Your Reverence," he said, "you know I would do anything to help you, but I cannot give up my sheep. They are counting on me, they have been waiting for me, they are human beings, this is only paper." Lanstjak walked away without a word. For the first time I witnessed the constant conflict between the structure and the spirit. How many times in the course of my long ministry I remembered Kubat with envy, as the church principalities constantly seeking "restructuring" were pushing us to spend more and more time on the phone, at meetings, at the fabulous machines in our offices, and at times I was near tears, thinking of my lambs. Perhaps my father was right in his exagerated statement, "Once you have a phone, typewriter, a mailing list and mimeograph machine the soul of the church is in danger." Oh the good old days! Now we have such fabulous machines that the church secretaries get out at three, when we call on the phone we get the monologue answering machines. We print more than ever before, producing new litanies of "innovative" worship services, the church bulletins are like books—words, words and more words, announcements and then they are brought to our attention as if we could not read—and what about the little lambs, the desolate ones, the forgotten ones, crying in some pit? The psychiatrists, counsellors and social workers in unison speak to us about the immense loneliness of men and women and young people. We do not seem to be among the healers. Obviously, Kubat had a formative influence on me in his adament obedience to his calling to be a shepherd, a pastor and not a chief executive.

One day just when we were extremely busy, I had to excuse myself to attend the commital services of my mother's ashes in a columbarium of a church on the other side of Prague, but I promised to return and finish my work in the evening. This time there was truly only our family, and my uncle, brother of my mother. Dr. Novotny led the services. Of course I knew that Mother would be eventually buried at the graveyard near the homestead, but the columbarium left me cold. It looked like a slick post office with boxes of marble on the walls, the only difference was that here the boxes had names and not numbers. The urn with Mother's ashes was put into one of these boxes. The whole service seemed to me cold and perhaps unnecessary.

As I hurried back to finish my work I heard a voice, "What's your rush?"

It was Mirko Harych. I explained to him that I was on the way from Mother's commital service. He offered to walk with me.

"By the way, are you going home or where?"

"I am on the way to Zikov church."

"Do they have a midnight mass or what?"

Of course, I had to explain the situation to him, and he

walked with me all the way to Zikov church, then he helped me with the collating until it was finished. We shared a sandwich and then Mirko sat down at the organ console.

"What do you want me to play?"

"Oh, Bach's *Toccata in D Minor.*"

"For that you have to wait, I am still playing it with minor success only for myself, but one day I shall play it for you."

Mirko played beautifully and the whole evening was magical. We had so much in common. Both of us were planning to study theology, both of us were scared to death of taking exams in Greek and Hebrew, both of us loved art and literature, both of us loved to laugh. A beautiful friendship was born, and Mirko stopped by almost every day.

By the back door of the church a white patch of snow drops announced the end of March. Spring was in the air, I was energized and bit by bit more daring in coming home until I once again occupied my own room. The household was abnormally quiet. Father was back at the homestead, my brother was shipped to some camp again, sister Vera worked impossible hours in the laboratory and my youngest sister Bohunka, who was engaged to our family doctor, suddenly decided to get married. It was a small wedding but without Mother it appeared a huge undertaking. One of my mother's last joys was the celebration of Bohunka's engagement. I was happy for her, although my new brother in-law was more than twenty years older than she was, I hated the thought of her leaving our home. She was always so much fun, and I was possessed by fear which never materialized, namely, that she would become a boring matron, "a doctor's wife," who would be associating with all those "old people" the age of her husband. I missed her terribly.

If there were a way to measure the temperature of hope, it was by observing the mood of our housekeeper, Anna. The same Anna who gave me such a hysterical welcome when my mother way dying, was now singing, and in every spare moment was sewing, making the flags to welcome the liberating armies. In her imagination she visualized our house on the V Day bedecked with buntings and flags. A huge Czechoslovak flag was to hang from the center window, and on each side of that window were to hang the flags of the Soviet Union and France, on the left on the other side the flags of Great Britain, and the United States. Her bedroom looked like a sewing room of the United Nations. Proudly she showed me the first finished products, the Soviet and French flags. It was a major achievement. The flags were made of old sheets and it took several dyeings before the white sheets turned reasonably red or blue. In my wishful thinking I thought that Anna's flags represented the era of dying nationalism. "Why did you start with the Russian flag, and why did you make the hammer and sickle black? They are suppose to be yellow." "I know, I know! I made the Soviet flag first because it's the easiest, and the only yellow thing I have is my good blouse which I refuse to sacrifice, but look here!" With immense pride she showed me the stripes of an American flag, "Good Lord," she sighed, "Just think Mr. Zdeněk, forty-eight stars and thirteen stripes!"

"Are you sure?"

"Of course I am sure, here it is in the encyclopedia. Some woman named Ross made the first flag. I guess she had nothing else to do, but it's chic. No one can deny that it is the nicest looking flag, don't you think? Well, as I said I must let something go, if I am to finish these in time, but it's important, our house must look nice. I can hardly wait to hang these flags and see the German bastards running. Excuse me, Mr. Zdeněk, you know what I mean."

Suddenly I was no longer a boy, not even a teenager but Mr. Zdeněk, a man to whom Anna was frequently turning for advice about household matters.

Mirko, who was strong in his socialist views, was always laughing when he came and Anna welcomed him saying, "Mr. Zdeněk is waiting for you." He could imitate her perfectly and although he knew the way we thought and the way we lived, he poked fun at me, "Wait, when the Bolsheviks will come, Comrade Bednář, you will be just one of the people."

"I am one of the people, but I certainly would resent the idea of everybody considering me his or her kin. Relationships cannot be dictated, you know that!"

"Well the Early Christians called one another brother and sister."

"Of course, but they had a common denominator in Jesus Christ. It was their choice."

"The communists have a common denominator."

"Yes, and I know what that common denominator is."

"Oh, Zdeněk, listen to me. The Soviets sacrificed more blood in this war than any other nation. . . . You simply cannot expect them to sit back, and let the Western powers treat them as inferior and dictate to them. Their hour has come."

"For goodness sake Mirko, you sound like the spineless Mr. Weigle downstairs. He used to crawl here, now he tells me he is very optimistic, for the hour of the people has come. He tells me that as if I were subhuman!"

"Listen, you better be careful what you say in front of Mr. Weigle, you have a big mouth, did you know that?"

"Be careful! Over my dead body, I have had enough of these long years of being careful, of whispering, you know that. How do you even dare to say that to me?"

One thing led to another and there was a total war on the top floor of one hundred forty five at Royal Garden!

"Cool it!" Mirko shouted and walked out of the room. I thought he stepped out to have a cigarette but he was gone for a long time. No, he did not go away for I did not hear the distinct sound of the closing of the front door. I was furious, unhappy, yet wanting to take a few words back. I heard some clatter from the kitchen. I wanted to step out but preferred to stay hurting in my room.

When Mirko returned it was like a scene from a grand opera. Anna opened the door for him and disappeared, but here was Mirko ceremoniously carrying a large silver tray, with a bottle of wine, two goblets and a plate of sandwiches. "What's going on," I laughed, "and where did you get this?" "I bribed your friend, Anna, I say friend! I told her that you were very blue, very upset, and very unreasonable, and do you know what she said? She said, 'That poor boy has every reason to be blue.'" And then she said to me, "be a good friend to him, he needs you!" I think she was listening to our argument, or she was divinely inspired. She gave me the bottle of wine and as in warning she said to me, "And let me tell you, he is just like his mother, every inch a democrat."

"Don't you feel better already?"

"No."

Mirko put the elaborate tray on a side table and proceeded first in prose and then in poetry, transforming my room into the court chamber of King Arthur. It occurred to him, he said, that we never sealed the covenant of brotherhood, and totally succumbed to the manners of the street.

He played his role so marvelously that I was choking with laughter, but he did not blink an eyelash, and ceremoniously poured two glasses of red wine. He clapped his hands "Music please!" and he walked toward my ancient phonograph and turned on the first record at hand. It was a collection of great opera choruses, starting with the stately chorus from *Nabakov*.

"A most unfortunate selection," remarked Mirko, "enough of Babylon!" Then he recited from memory or from his imagination the ritual of brotherhood. I stopped laughing, for some of the words spoke to me. "Please rise and take a goblet in your right hand. Make three steps forward."

I found myself in the middle of the room facing Mirko.

"Raise your glass!" he intoned and began to recite in Latin a page from Cicero, the only Latin text he knew by heart a passage from Cicero's *On Friendship*.

"Tonight we want to affirm the bond of true brotherly friendship, the covenant of love and loyalty. Zdeněk, I care for you as if you were my brother." Astonished, I repeated my version of the promise. Still holding the glasses in our hands, we made a few steps clockwise, our arms at last were intertwined and we drank from each other's glass.

That night we talked about many important things, about the events that shaped us, about the sorrows that burdened us, about the hopes we had. Although Mirko behaved like a cavalier, he came from a very poor family. His father was severely handicapped, his mother a woman of enormous faith kept the flame of love and hope always alive in their tenement apartment. Mirko served some time in a labor camp near Kassell, and was sent home.

"I shall tell you about it. Soon you will come to visit, but don't expect it tomorrow! I mentioned to Mother that I would like you to come to visit and she nearly fainted, saying 'Oh my dear, we simply have to get some new draperies, and this and that before he comes.' It's always like that. The fear that we would be rejected because of our poverty is fierce. It does not bother me that I am broke, or that I wear second hand clothing, you know that, but with my parents it's an obsession. They are so ashamed of living in that house, that they are almost afraid to step out. Imagine if somebody at church would find out that we live in a human jungle. I would give anything to get them out of that house. I guess, you don't know anything about things like that."

"No, I don't, but at times I am also afraid of going out because I am marked. Wherever I go people immediately associate me with my family, expect a definite way of thinking, speaking, a definite behavior simply because I am Bednář."

"I have never thought of that . . . Zdeněk, I am sorry about our argument tonight. You must be very patient with me, because I have too much to do, too much to think about, and I am upset."

"Is it about Alena?" I asked. Alena was his girlfriend, a beautiful, gregarious girl from a prominent family, whom he loved very much. Recently she was a constant source of anguish for him. Alena and her family simply could not accept the idea that Mirko would study theology. Day by day Alena came up with a new argument against Mirko's dream of being a minister. For her it was absurd. Her latest plot was to make out of Mirko another Chopin, promising her Father's willingness to support him if he studied at the conservatory. Mirko did not change his mind for a minute.

"Is it Alena?" I asked again.

"No, Alena for a change is behaving, even her mother yesterday was quite civil. Perhaps that family smells something . . . I don't know, I don't know," he sighed. "I have dreamed about surviving Nazism and the war, about being a part of the forces which would bring the end to Hitlerism and now. . . now I am scared."

"Scared of what?"

"Zdeněk, suffering does not necessarily improve our character. Starvation, horrid injustices and humiliation, seeing loved ones being treated as cattle does not make people refined, many of them become as blood thirsty beasts. All right, you want to know why I am upset. Here it is: I am scared of the victory . . . I do not think we are as yet ready for democracy as you perceive it. I know how much Masaryk and his thought mean to you. His concept of democracy is an ideal, and we are not ready for it."

Mirko elaborated his thoughts, I listened to him carefully, and some of his thoughts did not seem to me original. Of course, at that time I had no idea about Marxism but in retrospect I realize that already Mirko was active in the underground movement and struggled with the Marxist dialectic. "If people are not ready for democracy, and I think you may be right, then our goal is very clear. If we have to wait for people to be ready, and wait for some kind of development, you and I may just as well forget our sense of calling. When on earth do you think people will be ready for Jesus Christ?"

"I realize that . . . don't torture me, or I will start repeating nonsenses. All I ask of you is to be patient with me, and to understand that in the next several weeks I simply will not have time to come here as often. I shall miss coming here. It's strange, I have learned so much from you in such a short time. You and your family have changed a great deal of my thinking . . . It's too late now, one day I shall tell you about it."

"What can I do for you Mirko?"

"Just pray for me every night that I may not lose my soul and . . ."

"And what?"

"You must know that I do not want to lose you as a friend."

He gave me a big hug and walked away.

Father returned from the homestead at the end of April bringing not only some butter and eggs but also the incredible news that according to the British broadcasts the war was over, the world was getting ready for the V Day celebration. The big question was what the Nazis intended to do with us. In Prague everything looked normal, only the security seemed to be tighter than ever before. Every morning when Anna came home from the grocery stores she brought another piece of news. Once she announced that the Nazis poisoned the water, and that we ought not to drink any. "Everybody talks about it," she said, "so there must be some truth in it."

Meanwhile Father silently studied the maps and as a way of encouragement was telling me that according to the broadcasts he heard the army of General Patton and also our Czechoslovak divisions under his command were approaching the former Czechoslovak boundaries at Carlsbad and at Pilsen, about one hundred twenty miles away.

In Prague it was still impossible to get any foreign news. Our days seemed terribly long for we really did not dare to go out. For the first time in ages we had plenty of time to talk one with another. Father was full of energy and appeared to be in excellent health. The reopening of the University and of the Theological School was foremost on his mind. Since the University was closed by the Nazis for seven years, he felt that not a day without learning could be lost. According to his figuring our losses in learning were enormous, and he was worried that our people would not be up to the great tasks and struggles which were ahead of them. His first task would be to put the faculty together, but his biggest undertaking would be to put together the essential library. Luckily with the help of the former librarian, the theological library was dismantled and the most valuable volumes were stored at a church center in Prague before the University was closed by the Nazis. Father had no illusion that any University could function without a library. He elaborated for me what enormous advances were made in the field of learning during the seven years abroad, and that we would need to get acquainted with all the representative thinkers and scholars of that era. I think Father was already mentally making a list of individuals and universities which could help us.

For the first time I had a chance to ask some questions about my postwar education and my matriculation at the University in theological studies. For a moment or two Father thought about it and then he spilled it out in rapid succession: First you have to finish your undergraduate studies which were interrupted by the Nazis. It is my feeling, that in the same way as after World War I, you will have an option either to go to school or simply to appear for qualifying examinations whenever you are ready. The requirements in each discipline will be given to you, all you need to do is to study and prepare yourself.

"In what?"

"You have to take qualifying examinations in Czech, then in Czech and world literature, Czech history, World history and in Latin and one other language, you can always take German."

The front page of the University Matriculation Certificate signed by Zdeněk. Under the photograph, at the bottom right signed by his father, the dean 1936-1948.

"And what then? What do I have to do to be admitted for theological studies?"

"Well, I hate to tell you," he said with a smile, "but it is a prerequisite that you pass examinations and prove your reading competence in Greek and Hebrew."

That was enough to discourage anybody. Just the thought of studying textbooks was frightening for me because at that time I was still suffering with incredible sleepiness. I would start reading a book, and in a few minutes I was sound asleep. I was anxious to see Mirko and tell him about the requirements, hoping that we could study together. He came one afternoon and as soon as he exchanged greetings with my Father, he offered to play a game of chess with him. Shortly afterward he glanced at this watch, and hurried out, obviously late for some appointment.

Very hot, unseasonable weather arrived, and all the lilac and chestnut trees started blooming at once. One morning Father flew from the small radio in his bedroom into the living room saying, "Turn on the radio, the broadcast station is in our hands and there is fighting in the streets!"

Anna, father and I stood at the radio hungrily listening: "Attention! Attention! The Czechoslovak revolutionary forces under the command of the National Revolutionary Council led by Professor Albert Prazak, after heavy fighting, at last overcame the Nazi forces and the Prague Radio Station is in our hands! Long live a Free Czechoslovak Republic! Long live the Courageous Soviet Army and our Allies! All citizens are requested to await further announcements. Heavy fighting now wages in the narrow streets near the Old Town Square. Let's be prepared to defend ourselves and our city!"

"I can't believe it," cried Anna, "at last, at last! Oh goodness, the flags."

"Yes, the flags!"

Father had no idea what we talked about until Anna came in with an armful of the flags of our allies.

"Beautiful!"

We started hanging the flags, first the Czechoslovak, then the American, then the Russian and suddenly, we had no idea what was happening, but bullets were whizzing by, and I shouted, "On the floor! On the floor! They are shelling us! Dad, hide yourself behind the piano!" The Nazis, hidden in the bushes and among the trees of the park decided to put an end to our flags and to us. They shelled the house mercilessly, the walls in the room were like a sieve, and the chandelier was hit and glass shattered in a thousand pieces. Then nothing, but a complete silence. All three of us on the floor did not dare to move.

"What now?"

"Don't get up! Let's move on our stomachs to the hall!"

Planes passed over our house at a very low altitude, and shortly the whole house shook, the noise of explosives was incredible. We thought that we were being bombed while in reality we were staggered by the detonations of Molotov cocktails used in fighting a block away. Anna began screaming, "I don't want to die! I don't want to die!" I slapped her face, and then I was apologizing to her while we went to join others in the basement shelter. Our heroism fizzled already during the revolutionary overture.

The basement was full of people who were excited and profoundly shaken at the same time. Although we lived in a large apartment house, we knew everybody by name, we knew something about everyone's vocation and family, but it took the Tillichian shaking of the foundations to bring us all together in one place. We were not there for a cocktail party but to share an enormous uncertainty and anguish. It was a first class sensitivity training session decades before the term "sensitivity training" was even born. As the occupants of the largest apartment in the house, of course, we had the largest cellar located at the very end of a long corridor. We invited everyone to move in to make the long corridor less congested. The only light was provided by kerosene lamps and the cellar was extremely musty. Father opted to sit at the very end of the shelter. I have no idea what was going through his mind but I think he wanted to be as far away as possible from the people who at every detonation screamed, "Virgin Mary, Mother of God have mercy on us, and intercede for us and our sins." As the detonations were increasing, there was a common cry, "Jesus, son of God, have mercy on us!" He swallowed hard, he knew that this was no time or place for any sermonette yet the constant invoking of God, using religious expressions as magic formulas, the breaking of the third commandment by people who had no idea that such a commandment even existed was painful, and nauseating for him. Fortunately, he had the ability to ignore the happenings around him. He seemed lost in deep thought, I think praying for the beloved nation.

There was no electricity in the basement, and we sat in those long corridors and cubicles using kerosene lamps and candles. The bulkhead door and also the front door to the cellar were wide open, letting in some fresh air and light. There was a woman who simply could not tolerate the confinement of the cellar and insisted on sitting day and night by the door. She was of dark complexion. Her face was lined with wrinkles, her dark brown eyes were accentuated by beautiful white hair. In the thirties her husband volunteered to fight Franco in Spain and he never returned. She was a devout communist of the old school always giving the principles and ideals preference to party loyalty. There seemed to be some connection between her sitting with eyes closed at the door of the cellar, perhaps thinking of her husband, and the approaching day of vindication, and my silent father at the very end of the shelter. Her name was Jane Kopecka. Our only source of information were two radios, plugged into the outlet somewhere in the vestibule of the house with the help of many extension cords. Unfortunately the news was not good, and the original fanfares turned to a despairing cry, "Prague needs help! We need ammunition, we need guns. The Nazis are waging a major offensive!" This kind of news was totally un-understandable to all the people in the shelters of Prague and filled their hearts with anguish. Patton's army and also our Czechoslovak division were only a couple of hours away from Prague. We heard nothing. There was no answer to our pleas. Every week during the war years there were several air raids in Prague, for that was the place where the pilots were simply unloading, and now when we desperately needed air protection, only German planes were constantly terrorizing us.

There was heavy fighting in the streets of our vicinity, and the sound of continuous explosions. On the second day, the radio announcements were calls of despair. The Germans, according to the radio destroyed the main section of the ancient Old Town Hall, and were guilty of monstrous atrocities on women and children in the outskirts of the city, "We call for volunteers, all men over twenty volunteer now! Report to the nearest school building. All teenagers are encouraged to help the Red Cross. All churches are used to help the wounded!"

Suddenly I realized that I was the youngest in the shelter, a baby not yet twenty. There was another young man, in his thirties, whose wife was extremely pregnant. That man was ever so eager to volunteer, but his wife and his mother-in-law were so hysterical that he did not dare to move an inch. Whenever the announcer on the radio said, "All men of honor help . . ." these women shouted, "What do you know about honor, the first honor is to take care of the baby!" The call to help with the Red Cross came just in time when I was getting suffocated by the atmosphere in the cellar. Quickly I was figuring out the best way to get to St. Anthony's church. "Don't go on the street, take a short cut by jumping the fences behind the houses!" somebody was advising me when we heard a definite thud in the vestibule: the first wounded collapsed. I rushed to go to the vestibule. Mrs. Kopecka, sitting by the door of the cellar gently touched me and decided to go with me. She was very arthritic, and leaned heavily on my arm.

A young man with an automatic pistol lay face down in a pool of blood in the middle of the vestibule. With all my strength I turned him around. He was still alive, breathing heavily. Out of nowhere Mrs. Kopecka brought a small pillow and I put it under his head, but I was petrified by the pistol. I never held a pistol in my hand and was ashamed of myself. Mrs. Kopecka read my mind, took the pistol in her hands with the expertise of a veteran revolutionary, "Empty," she whispered. "Poor darling used his last one . . .and those scoundrels are still nowhere with their help! There is no need of this! There is such a thing as a drop off, and after all our crying nothing as yet has come!"

There was nothing we could do for this young man but to wait for the Red Cross ambulance to pick him up. As we were told on the radio we were to place something white on the front door. Mrs. Kopecka went to her apartment and brought a white pillow case, which I attached to the door. We both knelt by our patient. I washed his forehead with cool water, unbuttoned his shirt, held his hand. He took a sip of water and said, "Thanks." He was in horrid pain, then he quieted down and whispered, "Priest!" Bewildered I looked at my companion, and she shrugged her shoulders, and then gently caressed his shoulder. Feeling nothing but helplessness, knowing that the young man was dying, I put my finger into the glass of water and then with the water on my hand I made a sign of the cross on his forehead. Shortly afterwards he died. Mrs. Kopecka closed his eyes for which I will be forever grateful to her. I felt enormous kinship with her, and it crossed my mind that I would like to be called "comrade" by her. She obviously expected the young man to die, for with the pillow case she brought also a sheet. Without a word I covered the body of our unknown soldier with the sheet. Mrs. Kopecka was still kneeling by his body, and it was extremely difficult to help her up, after the long time she spent kneeling on the hard tiled floor of the vestibule. When at last she was standing up, she looked at me approvingly with her brown eyes and kissed me. We hurried downstairs, the detonations seem to be in the proximity of the house. We were also anxious to hear the latest news. It was an appeal to all citizens, "Attention! Attention! We urge all citizens to assist our fighting forces by building barricades across the streets. Your help is urgently needed."

The last time I thought of barricades was when I was passionately reading *Les Miserables*, a book which left a permanent impression on me. In the days of advanced means of warfare, of German tanks and planes, the idea of building barricades seemed to me a desperate measure. Nevertheless everybody, without any hesitation was out participating in the project. I guess there was also help from neighboring houses, and some men acted as though they had years of experience in such tasks. Out of nowhere there were crowbars and we dug out the cobble stones. Meanwhile the women and the rest selected an incredible amount of things which could go on barricades. One could hardly believe the number of old fashioned, ornate, upright pianos being wheeled into their last gallant position. Some men cut trees which were placed on the barricade. At the end we built two barricades on our street and we were pleased with ourselves. At last we felt we were doing something, that we were a part of the desperate struggle.

Although I had some doubts about this way of fighting, the barricades gave our forces good places from which to throw Molotov cocktails and behind which to hide, and astonishingly enough the barricades complicated the assault by the German tanks.

The street was unusually quiet, and although the hot May sun was luring us to the exit of the shelter, with the exception of Mrs. Kopecka, who always rested in a chair by the door, most of us obeyed the command of our weary bodies, and rested in the compartments of the shelter. It was so quiet, so incredibly quiet that one could dream of some tomorrows. Those who wanted to talk, whispered. Many slept, and the silence was accompanied by tonal variations of snoring. Suddenly we were all awakened and stunned by a gun shot, followed by screaming in the shelter. A German officer was infuriated by the solid baricade in front of our house. He entered the shelter. To give himself the necessary authority, he shot Mrs. Kopecka, who was resting in her chair by the door. Then came his command: "Walk out with your arms up and dismantle the barricade you have built. I give you a very short time," he yelled, "understand?"

At the end of the long corridor in our shelter, we knew only that something terrible was happening, and that a German soldier was in our midst.

"What did he say?"

"Raise your arms and get out and remove the barricade!"

"Jesus."

"Mary, Mother of God!"

As we walked through the corridor one after another with our arms up, ready to get the officer's kick, we realized that gone was the quietness, that in the street there was heavy fighting between the Germans and our revolutionary forces.

As we approached the entrance to the shelter with our arms up, the officer kicked the dead body of Kopecka to get it out of the way. We walked toward the barricade in a shower of bullets, being caught in the crossfire between the Nazis and the Czech volunteers.

We were so proud of the barricade we had built, it was the only concrete expression of our opposition to the Nazis. We had no idea that while we were dismantling the barricade under the cruel supervision of Nazi officers, the people in the West were dancing in the street, celebrating the conquest of the German Reich.

When we returned to the shelter, it seemed to us unbelievable, miraculous that none of us was shot. It was May 8, 1945. Gone was the screaming and invoking of Mary and Jesus. Even the unsolicited military advisers were silent. The radio announcer urged us to be brave and courageous.

"We are betrayed," a voice cried in the corridor.

"Yes, our dear allies are nowhere again!" other voices joined in.

The echo of these voices went through the long corridor. By the time the news reached our compartment, the conclusion was an anguish which was paralyzing every heart: we are forgotten, betrayed.

Later, on that desperate evening, came a special, joyful announcement: "Marshall Stalin gave special orders to his armies to hasten to help Prague." Who could ever comprehend it? In several hours the announcement came that the Soviet army indeed crossed our boundaries. We burst into a spontaneous applause and embraced each other. In the morning Konev's armies entered Prague, the Nazis capitulated, and ran. Many tried to prolong their lives and their hostilities by hiding. It is not an exaggeration to say that the young Soviet soldiers were greeted as liberators and saviors with bouquets of lilacs.

At last we were able to step outdoors. It was a glorious May day. Excited but also exhausted, we were cleaning the debris in the corridor of the shelter, and just as we were ready to go upstairs Mirko appeared, unshaven, with the gear of a soldier and a red arm band on his right arm. We fell into each other's arms. "I was so worried about you, it was bad only three blocks away from you, Zdenácku," he smiled. "We are alive, we are free!"

"Long live Stalin, Comrade Harych" chimed in Mr. Weigle as he passed by. I froze.

"Good morning, Comrade."

Mirko looked at me beggingly as if he were saying, "For goodness sake, Zdeněk, shut up!"

I obeyed but as I looked at Mirko, I noticed on his shirt a pin with a red star, hammer and sickle. I do not know why, but impulsively I removed that pin from his shirt. "I think we have had enough of people who feel the need or perhaps obey the order to parade their opinions in pins and badges. Please never wear this in my presence."

Mirko swallowed, looked in another direction, and put the pin into his pocket. He felt deeply hurt. He fought for us in blood, he made his way through Prague to see if we were safe, ready to help us, and a matter of a pin was most important to me. He realized that without the Soviets we would have been massacred. He saw in the outskirts what horrid things the hysterical Germans did to our children, cutting their throats! Mirko realized that I was not comprehending that we were a part of the Soviet orbit.

No, I did not realize it, and did not want to accept it. The scene over the pin cast a long shadow over our friendship, but Mirko remained faithful and true in those difficult days, and indeed never wore his party identification in my presence.

Slowly we went upstairs, and we could not believe our eyes. When Mirko saw the smashed chandelier, the walls and the ceiling all marked by bullets, he embraced us, saying, "The Lord was surely watching over you." The bullets with which we were showered were some kind of special or more deadly bullets than ordinary bullets. I was more concerned about the new reality, the broken window, the plaster all over the floor, dust covering the furniture, the chandelier gone.

*   *   *   *   *

As Anna, Mirko and I were cleaning, or at least trying to establish some order in our apartment, we were quietly, in our separate ways thinking about what had happened in the previous days and nights. To this day I am not sure who is to be really blamed for the incredible anguish, and sense of being abandoned, betrayed, but I do know that in those fatal days between May 5 and 9, while the world was already dancing in the street, celebrating the triumph over Hitler, the fate of the former Czechoslovakia and my own fate was decided. The historians and political scientists debate about it, and after the distance of more than fifty years we have more and more documents from which to draw our conclusions. At the Yalta Conference, before the end of World War II, Churchill and Roosevelt gave in to Stalin's demands. He wanted to get Berlin and he got Berlin, and the leaders of the Western world also agreed that the so called Eastern Europe lay within the vital interest of the Soviet Union. Of course, the armies do not necessarily progress by the agreements reached by leaders far away. The exhausted armies of the Soviet Union were much slower at that period of the war than expected. On the other hand the armies led by General Patton were actually asked to slow down as they were approaching the boundaries of Czechoslovakia.

General Eisenhower was a strict constructionist who refused to sacrifice another American life. He proceeded strictly by the orders sealed at Yalta. One does not know what knowledge he had about the post war plans of the Soviet Union. After all, at Yalta, Stalin charmed Churchill and Roosevelt, who understood that the Soviet Union had to be counted on as a new super power. From the military point of view Eisenhower adhered to his principles, foreign affairs were not his department. It is tragic that more than decades later we learned that Eisenhower was not as insensitive as it seemed, that he actually obeyed the communist dictates about the assistance to Prague. Most unfortunately his good will, or his willingness to help Prague at that time, was kept as a deep secret, and to my knowledge Eisenhower never mentioned it. From the human point of view, the behavior of the Western powers was impossible to understand. In Prague innocent people were bleeding, being at the mercy of insanely furious Nazis. These freedom loving people called for help, for military supplies, and they met nothing but silence. The refusal of the USA to give the Czechoslovak people some explanation was really playing into the hands of the Communists. In the first election the Communists fully exploited the fact that the Soviet armies alone came to help Prague. Even those who had strong reservations about the Soviets, were biting their lips. People who were in a desperate situation could never comprehend why the American forces, stationed so near, did not come to help, and why at least the Czechoslovak divisions, stationed with the Americans, were not allowed to assist Prague. At the end, these Czechoslovak soldiers were extremely bitter. How could one explain to the parents of those who fell on the barricades, fighting so to speak with their bare hands against the Nazi tanks, that it was necessary because our friends were obeying the decisions made at their meeting at Yalta! Indeed, it seemed to me that we deserved some explanation of the truth even if that explanation would have caused great displeasure to the Soviets.

President Edward Benes is often criticized for returning home via Moscow, where to a considerable degree he gave in to the Soviet demands, but by that time the realms of Soviet interests were already well defined by the Yalta agreement. He could have given up, stayed in London and let the Communists and the Soviets take over Czechoslovakia. He risked his life on the idea that perhaps the democratically thinking people of Czechoslovakia would be strong enough to achieve some balance of power with the Communists. Nobody can criticize him for taking this risk especially when we consider his ill health, but exactly like Churchill, or Roosevelt, Benes did not understand that the fate of his nation would not be fought in Prague but that it was already mapped out in Moscow.

The recently published memoirs of Dr. Prokop Drtina, who for years was the private secretary of President Benes, and who served as the Minister of Justice both in the Czechoslovak Government in exile and in the fatal postwar years, put the 1945 Prague crisis into new light. As the Czechoslovak government in exile traveled home by special train, the news of the fighting in Prague arrived. At the same time the Communist members of the government were alarmed by the report of the fast movements of the American armies not only toward the borders of Czechoslovakia but also within its territory. In his words: "Although we were concerned about the uprising in Prague, we were rejoicing about the entrance of American troops into Czechoslovak territory. Our Communist colleagues expressed great concern about the possibility of an American occupation of Prague while we were in Moscow. Now as we received the news of American forces already being in the Czechoslovak territory the Communist leaders were depressed, furious, stricken with panic. It was very obvious to us that our Communists had far reaching plans for using the protection of the Soviet troops to establish their revolutionary organization. They were anxious to be in the Czechoslovak territory first, before anyone else, to establish their political base. It was understandable, their anguish was justified, but in their anguish and in their zeal they went much further than anybody expected, **and were instrumental in their intrigue to stop the Americans from entering Prague Their leaders, Gottwald and Fierlinger**—who was destined to be the premier of the new Czechoslovak Republic—**turned to the influential Soviet Ambassador Zorin, and urged him to intervene with Stalin and ask him to reverse the course and for the good of all, not to allow the Americans to come to Prague before the Soviet troops!** That was the basis of the celebrated decision of Stalin to order generals Konev and Rybalkov and their armies to hurry to help Prague"[7]

Dr. Drtina writes that although this story of Gottwald's and Fierlinger's intrigue was well known in the government circles it appeared to him too daring and too sensational. He was more than surprised when Fierlinger in 1966 published an article about the Prague Uprising and unashamedly admitted that while he was in Kosice early in **May, 1945, the Soviet Ambassador Valerin Zorin delivered to him an urgent message from General Eisenhower who was offering immediate help to Prague provided it met the approval of the Czechoslovak government. Fierlinger reported** (undoubtedly after a consultation with Zorin) **that he *rejected* that offer.**

The Czechoslovak government and President Benes were unaware of any American offer of assistance to Prague. If General Eisenhower dealt through Valerin Zorin, this infamous Soviet Ambassador obviously never bothered to speak with the President. It was mighty convenient for him to deal with Fierlinger, the premier of the provisional government whom he had known for years from his stay in Moscow. As Prokop Drtina writes: "Until I read this testimony of Fierlinger in 1966, although I was a member of the Czechoslovak government, the story of Eisenhower's offer to help Prague was a revelation to me."[8]

When we consider the character of people like Gottwald, Fierlinger or Zorin who later on appeared on the stage of Czechoslovak history as bloody agents of Stalin, unafraid of any shady deal, and the character of General Eisenhower, it is easy to see the truth: before the Czechoslovak government arrived from exile and Prague was "liberated" by the Soviets, the Czech and Slovak communist leaders stood in the way of the well being of their country.

Their only interest was self promotion in the framework of the Soviet plans. At the same time one wonders why the United States remained silent and did not tell the Czechoslovak public this all important truth, especially when for years the Soviet propaganda fed the Czechoslovak people with the assertion that in the critical hours they were deserted by the Western powers.

In my own reflection as I was sweeping the floor of our living room on that first day of our new liberty, a total confusion ruled. I could not comprehend the American silence, and my mind was full of suspicions and fears, overflowing with questions for which there was no answer.

Father was basically optimistic. President Benes was on his way to Prague to lead a decisive struggle in behalf of democracy, in which all of us have to help him. Father was ready but at the same time he expressed some anxiety about my sister Nadia and the homestead, because that part of Moravia was occupied by the ill fated army of Marshall Rybalkov. When Father stepped out, Mirko winked at me and said, "We need to get out of here, offer to go to Vir. I shall go with you!" I did not hesitate for a moment, and Father was happy to hear that Mirko was willing to go with me, and give Nadia any help she needed. Next evening Mirko and I boarded the night train toward Vir. We carried empty suitcases in hopes of bringing back some food. The train was jammed but we were as excited as little children taking their first train ride.

TO WALK AGAIN

The train was jammed mostly with Russian soldiers. After much pushing, inch by inch we made it to the corridor. Justly many passengers cursed our suitcases until somebody grabbed them and tossed them on the top of the luggage shelf in one of the compartments. It was beastly hot, and everyone was gasping for a bit of air. The trouble was that all the windows were not only painted from the recent black out days but also that they were hopelessly stuck. Since we could not even see outside through the painted windows the stuffiness seemed doubly intolerable. One strong man after another tried to open at least one window without any success. The Russian soldiers thought these efforts were quite funny and then one "tovarish" decided to show us how they do it in Mother Russia. He took an empty bottle of vodka and then skillfully smashed one window after another. His skill was in fact that the broken pieces of glass flew outside on the platform. By the time the train pulled off, we were pushed in one of the compartments. Mirko whispered into my ear, "Put your wrist watch in your pocket."

"What?"

"Put your watch in your pocket."

Just when I though that Mirko was totally out of his mind, I noticed in the corner of the compartment a jolly Russian soldier with a number of wrist watches on each arm. We tried to be friendly and congratulated him on his loot. He told us that he had many, many more watches, that wherever he went he scared people to death by saying, "Davaj časy!" (Give me your watch.) Proudly he told us where he got each watch. The most beautiful watch with a few diamonds was from Dresden.

"What will you do with all the watches?" we asked.

"Oh I will give them away to family and friends. Some I will sell, some I will exchange for a bigger clock." Then he turned to Mirko and asked, "and where is your watch?"

"No watch." said Mirko with a deep sigh, trying Czech, Russian and German trying to say, "Me, very poor."

"Here, take some," said the soldier, pointing to his arms. Mirko hesitated, "Come on, I am telling you, it's no problem for me to get more, all I say is, 'Davaj časy!' " He removed a simple looking watch with a black leather strap from his arm and gave it to Mirko. Mirko blushed, stuttering, "Spasibo, spasibo," and as we both looked at the watch, we could not believe our eyes, it was a fine Bulova watch, an unheard of luxury! At first Mirko tried to put the watch on his hand but then he said to me in a low voice, "I better put the watch in my pocket before someone else comes to me and says, 'Davaj časy!' This will be a perfect gift for my dad, he never had a decent watch."

The Russians were also very generous in offering drinks, and their supply of vodka seemed limitless. The trouble was that one could hardly refuse them because every drink was introduced by some toast. There was a definite gradation in the toasts. We would start with a toast to "dear mother Russia," then to Marshall Konev and on and on until we toasted Stalin. Everybody was reasonable happy, and ready to sing. Thank goodness, most of the Czech passengers knew the Russian favorite, "Volga, Volga, sirokaja." The Russians could sing the many verses of the song beautifully and with real gusto.

This was my first encounter with Russian soldiers, and I could not help but like them and feel a genuine pity for them. These soldiers were members of the Rybalkov army, and were obviously shipped out of Prague to the country. Here their behavior would not be as strictly scrutinized. Many of these soldiers were teenagers when they fought at Stalingrad. When I looked at them, I thought it was very doubtful that they would ever be reunited with their loved ones and friends. Nobody could possibly imagine the immense suffering these men had endured at Stalingrad and then in their march on Europe. Many of them were illiterate, as some of them later on remarked. Stalingrad was a good way of solving the Soviet problem of illiteracy. They refused to be praised for heroism, explaining, "Behind us were men with guns, if you stepped back you were shot, there was no choice, at the end, one was glad

to take the risk of going forward through the horror of Stalingrad."
In comparison with the defeated Nazi soldiers, these soldiers were
in rags, and were totally uninhibited. To the shock of the people in
Prague, on their first hot day in Prague, they stripped themselves
naked and enjoyed a wonderful swim in Vltava in down town
Prague. Obviously, they did not have a change of underwear and
frequently on a sunny day one could see them doing their laundry
in a brook or river. Then they just waited, and waited for their
clothing to dry. Of course, this was in their much deserved postwar
period. Their officers allowed them to have a good time while they
themselves enjoyed life immensely.

It was quite obvious that for them to be in a land which was
almost untouched by bombers or tanks, was a big treat. As liberators they helped themselves to whatever appealed to them. They
were feared by the tavern keepers and others as death. It was interesting to observe what they were looting, it showed their sense of
values. They loved everything glitzy, loved jewelry although they
had no way of distinguishing the genuine from the fake. Clocks,
watches, typewriters, cut glass vases were their treasures, but also
they hoarded yardage of materials for dresses. On the other hand
they did not mind taking a huge oriental rug from some villa and
using it for camping. They sat on it and built a fire in the middle of
that rug, having no idea that it was priceless.

The Russians got off the train at the first or the second stop,
and we were actually able to sit down, and the slow moving train
soon rocked us to sleep. Because some of the rail road tracks were
damaged or were just temporarily repaired, the journey which included numerous long, long stops, took us twelve hours and then
we had to walk eight kilometers to the homestead. I felt totally re-
juvenated, admiring every hill, ever tree. This was Mirko's first
trip to the homestead, and he patiently listened to me as I recalled
the memories these places evoked.

Once in many years there is a May which is just right for
the fruit trees at the homestead. This was such a year. There was
no better time to show Mirko the homestead. Every tree, every early apple tree looked like a white-pink bouquet. The lawn in front of
the house was literally covered with the purple, fragrant English
violets. When I saw the orchard from a distance, I almost started

running for here it was in all it's glory, too good to be true! We walked through the orchard. Father's bees were busy, and the lilac hedge at the entrance of the front garden was full of blossoms.

"Unbelievable!"

"If one could be another Monet!," we exclaimed. Ruzena spotted us from the window of the workshop and ran to welcome us. There was no end to hugging and since I introduced Mirko as my best friend, he also got a kiss.

"I knew that someone would be coming. All beds are made!" cried Ruzena.

"Of course, I am very sad, only now do I realize that it is really true," she started sobbing, "that your dear mother will not be coming again."

Ruzena's husband, followed by his daughter, Bohunka, and the apprentices from the workshop all came to welcome us.

"What about Nadia?" I asked.

"I knew you would ask. She is fine. Would you believe she was anxious about you and she also needed to have a check up on her diabetes. She was here this morning, she had a chance to go to Prague by car with somebody, and she just stopped here on their way. It's a shame but she will visit with your father and the girls, and you will see her soon, now you will be coming often."

On the way to my bedroom, Mirko noticed the doors to my father's study were ajar and he spotted our ancient, ornate harmonium. Nothing could possibly keep Mirko from trying to play it at once. One had to pump it with his feet, and some of the keys were sticking. He started by playing, *Jesu Joy of Man's Desiring*. It sounded quite awful but Mirko was thrilled. "This is fantastic, this is really a museum piece and I think I can fix it."

I knew then what Mirko would do.

We changed, opened the windows of the bedroom to watch the incredible beauty of the blooming orchard. Right in front of us was the old pear three. It was leaning, every year we thought that we would not see it again, but there it was covered with blossoms. "Under that tree Mirko, my great grandfather proposed to his bride. She was a Catholic, and he fell on his knees and begged her to turn Protestant."

"You cannot possibly mean that you had a Catholic in your

family! That's a scandal!"

"Yes we did! As I said he begged her to turn, and she said to him, 'Joseph let me be me.' It must have been a scandal when they married, and do you know what? Years later, secretly, without saying a word to her husband she walked to the next village of Rovecne to take instructions from the Protestant minister, and when she was ready, she joined the church. Is it not marvelous?"

"So this bullheadedness is in your blood."

"Oh Mirko, I am so glad that you had the idea to come here. I really thank you. I feel like new here. I do not know how to say this but this is the place which is dearest to me, the dearest place in the world. If I ever found this place and the orchard ruined, I think I would stop being a Czech. It means so much to me and I am glad that you are here, because now you too will be able to say, 'Let's go to Vir.' Are we not lucky to be here?"

"We are lucky, and I have so much to tell you. In Prague we are always in a hurry."

We heard Ruzena's voice, "Everything is ready."

We hurried downstairs and Ruzena had a nicely set table with a veritable feast for us. Piles of scrambled eggs, her home-made bread, jams and jellies, bits of the best she had, a pot of fragrant coffee. It was like a dream. Mirko volunteered to offer grace. As we inhaled the marvelous aroma of the coffee, Ruzena exclaimed, "It is from your mother's supply, just a bit left for tomorrow. She would be so happy to see you here. Bless her . . ."

We ate with gusto, while Ruzena informed us of all the happenings in the village. Somehow she wanted to bring up the subject of my mother again in her preamble and asked, "Zdeňáčku, did you stop in the bedroom of your mother?"

"No, no, not yet," I stuttered, "somehow I am afraid to go in. I am still expecting her to arrive any minute, and now, to see her bed, the closet with her dresses . . . I realize that as yet I have not accepted it. Why do you speak about Mother so much Ruzena?"

"It will never be he same here without her," reasoned Ruzena, "never, but let me tell you Zdeněk, that after the hell we had been through, first after the murder of the Ohlers and now with the Russians, night after night, I thank God for taking her. I want you to know, Zdeněk, that her death was an act of mercy." She was wiping the tears from her eyes, as I was biting the knuckles of my right hand, not wanting to say anything, my face was twisting as I tried to hold back my tears. I felt Mirko's hand on my shoulder, "Come on, you must eat."

"Yes, Zdeněk, you must eat, we can cry later," said Ruzena and continued, "I can hardly wait to talk with your father and to hear his views, but you can tell him from me that the best thing that ever happened as horrid and painful as it was, was the occupation by the Russian army! After seeing the Russians in action, we all know what the Soviet paradise must be like. Even the party members, the old Bolsheviks are disgusted, the great liberators came like thieves. You should see them!"

"Did they take anything here?"

"For heaven's sake what is here to take?"

"I would know of a few things here to take." said Mirko.

"Well, these gangsters do not go after paintings and feather-beds, they want silver, gold, the cash, but our dear Bohunka, thank God, stayed two days in the hayloft and they did not find her. Yes, I know that you will say, and I agree with you, war is war, those people went through hell and without them the Nazis would not be licked, but this is something else, they came here not only as thieves but as barbarians, after every woman in the village. Here is our Tony, one of the best men in the workshop. You know that he is a member of the Communist party, he has worked in the underground, he probably knows about the plot against the Ohlers more than anyone else. His father, the old Stehlik is an old time Bolshevik. Well, Tony's girl, Bozenka, a sweet girl . . they were planning to get married this summer. She was raped by so many of them and so mistreated by them that she is in the hospital in terrible shape. There is another girl, Jirina, you remember her, she is another one. After she was raped, she came out of the hands of the Bolsheviks totally insane. She does not know anybody, she is afraid of every human being now. The only time she is at peace is at the sunset, when she sits by the waterfall, singing, watching the birds, and the deer. Go and ask Tony about the Communists, and he will tell you that if the elections were held today, thanks to the Russians, the Communists would be lost."

One story of the Russian cruelty followed another. This was devastating news for Mirko, from the lips of an ordinary woman who would not hide her leftist feelings. I tried to change the subject. We spoke about the loveliness of the orchard, and the promise of the harvest, and about what Ruzena could secure for us to take to Prague, some eggs, some flour and especially butter or lard. I left some money on the table.

"When do you leave?"

For the first time I realized that we really had only one day to stay, while I wanted to stay forever. "What about today? What would you like to eat?"

"I shall tell you what I would really like on a day like this. I would like to take Mirko on a hike through our woodland, and then up to the hills and have a picnic."

"I knew it, I knew it!" she exclaimed. "I can read you like a book, and I have a few sausages for you to cook on the fire. I shall fix a picnic lunch for you, indeed there are not many days like this!"

Mirko offered to help Ruzena, and I disappeared to roam through the house alone, thinking of Ruzena's narrative. Of course I remembered Jirina from the summer dances, such a gentle soul. At harvest time she always wore red poppies in her hair and looked like the goddess of harvest. Now she is afraid of every human being, because of the Russians, she prefers the realm of nature, to the human family. Dear God, what on earth is happening to us when such gentle creatures as Jirina prefer deer, bears and all creatures of the realm of nature to us human beings, made in your image?

I entered my parent's bedroom, a large room with two windows commanding a beautiful view of soaring mountains above the river Svratka. The room looked exactly as I remembered it, as if Mother and Father were to return any minute. On Mother's bedside table was a stack of letters, weighed down by a small worn out Bible. As I took the Bible in my hand I noticed that the letter on the top of the stack of letters was my last letter to her. I was tempted to open it and read it, but I resisted, fearing that I did not tell her in that letter how much I loved her. Maybe I did, but I doubted it.

It was obvious that Mother and Father read the Bible every night, because there was a Bible also on his bedside table, and both

Bibles had book marks at the same place, at Isaiah 40. I took Mother's Bible in my hand and I noticed that her bookmark was an old silk red ribbon with the embroidered words, "Thy Will be Done." I stared at Mother's bed, holding her Bible in my hand, wanting to take it to my room and to read for myself the pages which she read before she left that room for the last time. "It will never, never be the same again" echoed in my mind, and I cried for myself. The world without Mother appeared to me frightening, I knew I had to learn to walk alone.

As I opened the door of the room, the Bible in my hand, in the hall, Mirko was waiting for me, giving me a hug, but also growling, "For goodness sake, let's get going, the mountains are awaiting you and besides before the sunset I want to convince that Jirina, or at least you, that although I am a Communist I am human."

I left the Bible in my room, and hurried out whistling a melody from *Il Trovatore* about going to the mountains, a melody which is contagious, and which both of us whistled for a long time.

Quite obviously Mirko got acquainted with Ruzena, and won her heart. He carried our picnic basket and a blanket. "A good, remarkable, and very perceptive woman," Mirko interrupted our singing, "I just wish the election were tomorrow, but in six months God knows what people like Ruzena will say ."

I was so preoccupied with my own experiences and thoughts, and by seeing the beloved landscape that I was not really listening to Mirko. We walked up and up, suddenly we came to a clearing from which we could see the beautiful panorama of the river and the village, dotted with the white of the blooming fruit trees. "This is the place for us to rest, to talk and to eat."

"Which first?"

"You Mirko—you want to tell me something."

"All right, but I warn you, after I talk to you, you may not feel like eating! I am a member of the communist party, and I have been working with them in the underground perhaps because no one else asked me. It may well be that I am a communist first of all from selfish reasons, but do not think for a moment that I am ignoring my religious convictions, just the opposite. I wish for others what I wish for myself. I know that it is on the agenda of the communist party to nationalize education. Unless that happens I simply cannot go to the university and plan on higher education. I cannot ask my parents to go into more debt because of me, they have already borrowed for my piano, and my organ lessons. My dad is handicapped, he should not be working anymore. Every day he comes home exhausted, and he cannot afford the medication he should be taking. I know the communists will give us socialized medicine, and the people no longer will be punished for being ill or old. The nationalization of the heavy industry should pay for these. I do not doubt that in the process some big mistakes will be made, but I really believe that it is the way to progress. Freedom means a great deal to me, you know that, but there are certain liberties which are only for those who can afford them. Would you believe that my mother was at the National Theater only once? She would dearly like to go to see an opera or some fine play, but she cannot afford it, that realm of culture is only for those who can afford it.

"I also wish for us and for our children a chance to live in peace. No matter what, the Germans will always be our neighbors. Two horrid wars within twenty years. I do not want that for our kids. After our experiences with Munich, although the Western powers have paid dearly for their mistake, I am not so sure that we should put all our cards into their hands, in fact I wish that we would not need to play any politics, that we could be neutral but that cannot be done. The Soviet Union will also play a big part in the postwar world now whether we like it or not. I am not as stupid as to think that Stalin fought this war out of the goodness of his heart. He will want plenty in return for every sacrifice of his people. I think president Benes is perfectly prudent in his pro-Soviet policy. Nobody can accuse him of being pink, in his thinking. He is permeated by Western political thought, but in his pro-Soviet policy he is simply pragmatic. I cannot and will not believe that Benes has given up his ideals but I believe that he is convinced that in this half of the twentieth century we shall deal with a completely different Communism than in 1918. That has been for me almost decisive. From the point of view of classic communism, religion was regarded as the opiate of the people. All my friends in the party know that I want to study for the ministry, the issue of religion has been widely discussed, not once have I witnessed any hostility toward the church or Christianity. They plan to guarantee religious freedom, otherwise I would not be a part of it. I am a librarian in my party district. On the shelf there are volumes on Marx-Leninism but there are also volumes by Albert Schweitzer, and they are read. They will be pushing for a complete separation of Church and State, as your father has always wanted. It may well be that the Roman Catholic Church will lose some of its immense real estate, but the communists are ready to guarantee religious and civil liberties. Before you say that I am a complete dreamer, I judge the Communist party by the people who belong to it and by the people who cooperate with it. The recent Prague uprising certainly was a result of Communist plotting, but the Communists asked professor Prazak to lead the national Revolutionary Council, although he is not a member of any party. They recognize that he is a highly respected and admired intellectual of rare integrity. Count the people of enormous integrity who have been cooperating with the communists both in London and Moscow, and in the underground work here. I just refuse to believe that president Benes would be willing to cooperate with scoundrels, I think he believes that in the spirit of democracy we may easily coexist with the communists in our state, and that the democratic forces in our state will be strong enough to balance the power. That's what I want to believe with all my heart, my role in the Communist party is not to agree with them on every issue, my hope is to exercise as much influence as I can."

"Are you saying that our communists will be Czechoslovak Communists, adhering to some principles of their own, rather than being a part of the world communist movement?"

"Absolutely, after the fiasco with the Russian army, they would not have a chance. In fact this will be a very tough election, the Soviet army has not helped."

"What do you mean tough?"

"I mean that if the reactionary forces use dirty tricks against the communists, the communists will be twice as nasty. I think also that we have a tremendous chance to help the communists to trust us, so that we may have some influence on them."

"Mirko Harych, are you saying that all brilliant men and women should join the Communist party to influence the Communists, to convert them to the principals of democracy?"

"No, I am not saying that, I am saying that if you are patient with me, trust me, and not suspect me of being a bed fellow of Rasputin every time I go to a party meeting, and if you consistently help me to understand the democratic principles, I think I will be able to change the views of at least a few people."

"All right, Mirko, I shall try. Actually your exposé was not bad, and since you are an idealist, I am going to support you in creating a new type of Communism. Correct? Now I am starved, let's build the fire."

"Wait until you see what Ruzena gave us! It's incredible! There is even a bottle of wine! By the time we shall cook it and eat it, it will be evening. Do you know the way home?"

"Yes, I know my way home.""

Indeed, after we ate a fabulous dinner, and came down from the mountains to the main road it was dusk. Then we walked a few kilometers through the village toward the homestead. I knew every farm house along the way from my childhood. Lights appeared in one house after another, the milking was done, only here and there the cats patiently waited in front of the stables for their share of milk. As we walked through the almost quiet village, we talked together about our common reading of Dostoesky's *Crime and Punishment*. We both loved Sonia, and hated Roskolnikov, hoping that some beautiful Sonia would appear in our lives.

It was a memorable day and a special evening. When I recall Mirko's reasoning, I realize that this was the reasoning of the great majority of the intelligentsia at that time, a great hope for some refined communism with liberty and justice.

As we were approaching the homestead, I was limping, and we both realized that we did not sleep much on the night train. Ruzena awaited us and asked if we wanted to eat something! Then she brought this and that which ought to be packed, and reminded us that we had to get up early in the morning to catch the train.

Upstairs I discovered that I had a first class blister on my right foot. I started to pack, and typically for Mirko, he just realized that he had forgotten all about the harmonium. We both needed to be alone. I enjoyed listening to his playing as I packed, and reflected on the wonderful day. I was already in bed and almost asleep when Mirko returned. The Bible retrieved from Mother's bedside table was on my bed. "Look, Mirko what I read tonight, and there is a notation I cannot understand. Read it." Mirko sat down on the edge of my bed and read the last verses from the forti-eth chapter of Isaiah:

> Even youths shall fain t and be weary, and the young men shall fall exhausted. But they that wait upon the Lord, shall renew their strength: They shall mount up with wings as eagles, they shall run, and not be weary, and they shall walk, and not faint.

"Have you noticed the numbers?"

"What numbers?"

"The tiny numbers, one, two, three."

"Oh yes, is it the writing of your mother?"

"I don't think so . . . I am not sure, but the numbers help me to comprehend it. One: in emergencies we shall fly, we shall be good Samaritans. Two: We shall run, but ultimately we shall learn to walk . . . We must learn the patience of walking. Am I a victim of imagination? According to our thinking it should be in reverse, we start with walking."

"It's much easier to go fast on a bike than to go very slow-ly."

"What do you think?"

"I am too dead to walk anywhere, but I think it's true, we have to learn to walk."

"But not just now."

"Exactly. Good Night and God Bless!"

PRAGUE INTERMEZZO

Prague was in turmoil, the streets were being repaired and cleaned to welcome the provisional government formed by President Benes. This government was already in Slovakia and just awaited a signal from Prague to arrive. We studied the make up of this government with great interest. It was much larger than the pre-Munich governments, and there were a number of deputy ministers. The Premier was Zdeněk Fierlinger, a personal friend of Benes, a member of the Social Democratic Party. He used to be our ambassador to the Soviet Union, and after Munich he opted to stay in Moscow. President Benes obviously was under pressure to include the Czech communist leaders who spent the war years in Moscow, and also some Slovak Communist leaders, therefore the communists occupied almost a majority of the cabinet, but other parties were represented, and there were also a few nonpolitical appointees among them, Jan Masaryk who was to serve as our foreign minister. General Ludvik Svoboda, was nominated as a Minister of Defense. He was not a member of the Communist party, but since he stayed in the Soviet Union during the war years and led the Czechoslovak units which were a part of the Soviet army, his pro-Soviet leaning was not any secret. A great many people in this government were not known to us at all, but we were delighted to see two Roman Catholic priests, and such seasoned and trusted politicians as Dr. Prokop Drtina, our Vir neighbor, Dr. Jaroslav Stransky, and of course Jan Masaryk. We were encouraged to see the people with their expertise and character in leadership positions. We knew them personally, and had no doubt that they would not serve in a government about which they had some great reservation.

We were told that the government would arrive on a certain date, and then the date was postponed for security reasons. We were also told that Jan Masaryk would not be coming because he had to be present at the signing of the United Nations Charter in San Francisco. President Benes who was also already in Slovakia was to come later when the Soviet occupation army would consider Prague reasonably safe. Day by day there were still some skirmishes with the Nazis who were either found in their hiding places or who were trying to escape to the Americans.

President Benes spelled out in detail the political procedures. This was a provisional government, with a provisional presidency. As soon as the political parties were organized, their deputies would elect a new president of the Czechoslovak Republic. Later on, according to the directives of the parliament, general elections would be held, and taking the results of the national elections into consideration, a new government would be formed, and it will replace the provisional government from exile.

I was always a political animal, and I studied these procedures with tremendous interest, excited about having a chance to participate in the building of a new State. Since May 9, 1945, when the representatives of the National Revolutionary Council and the representatives of the Nazi State signed the terms of peace, the National Council, limited in number, was in charge of the affairs of the State in this critical period. Undoubtedly the Council was in touch with the government which was stuck in Slovakia, and, at times, received direct governmental directions, yet there was great confusion. Considering that until May 9, everything was in the hands of the Nazis or their collaborators, the transition of power was accomplished effectively in a few days without any major upheavals. The underground movement leadership which worked together with the National Council achieved a considerable victory. After the Nazis left, the streets in Prague were in total disrepair, full of debris left from the barricades, unpassable, yet telephone and electricity were restored within hours, the Post Office started to function, and above all, the train and bus transportation, and transit of food supplies were quickly restored. The cafés opened, and jazz bands never tired of playing "Sentimental Journey" and "Alexander's Ragtime Band." The people on the National Revolutionary Council worked hard, and everyone had tremendous respect and admiration for its chairman, professor Albert Prazak. At the same time dark forces were also at work. There was a tireless witch hunt of collaborators, who were put together with the caught Nazis in internment camps to await the trials by the People's courts."

Many people returned from concentration camps and found no one from their families alive. Some, in their despair, volunteered to deal with the collaborators, and it would be abnormal if some vengeance were not involved in their behavior. The term "People's Court" was known to us only from books describing the life in the Soviet Union. It was a foreign and imported idea, representing a perversion of justice. At the same time the newspapers carried stories of such collaborators as actress Lida Baarova, the famous mistress of Goebels, and of her sister. President Emil Hacha who gave in to Hitler's demands and indeed fully collaborated with the Nazis, although extremely ill, was taken out of the Lany castle to an ordinary hospital room and was guarded by police although President Benes sent orders to Prague, that Hacha be left to die in peace at Lany. It almost seemed that certain people, who for a few days rose to power, wanted to use that power to the fullest and to settle old conflicts before the arrival of the government. We did not doubt that the people's courts would be out of business the minute such jurists as Dr. Drtina and Dr. Stransky assumed their responsibilities, and we could hardly wait for the government to return.

One day, shortly after our return from Vir, as I was going home, I saw a commotion on a little square a few blocks from our house. A great many people stood by, and I went to see what was going on. The captured Nazis and some Czech collaborators were brought here to repair the pavement of the square. They worked in a sort of a pit. The members of the National Guard, men in their twenties, were in charge. What appalled me most of all, were the people who were just standing around and watching the horrid spectacle. Some shouted, some spat on the prisoners. Most of the workers, men and women had swastikas painted all over their arms and legs. I stood there only for a minute, my stomach was churning, and then something stabbed me. No, I was not mistaken, there was Vicky, my first love from the eighth grade, serving her sentence. There was no mistake, the same dark, almond shaped eyes, her beauty not diminished by this suffering and confrontation with justice. "Father in heaven," I cried to myself, "don't let her see me!" I ran and ran as if I were escaping from a crime I had committed.

Of course I knew that Vicky, under the influence of her beautiful mother absolutely refused to suffer for such "stupid things" as nationality, democracy or principles. "Well enjoy your principles and suffer, I don't have any, except that I know that I refuse to starve and to be without things which make me happy. Why should I allow the Nazis to hate me, when they can love me and share with me their power and what they can buy." Vicki and her mother did not waste any time, for one could see them parading with the Nazi officers from the first day of the occupation, always chic, elegant in movement. Even in that pit, when people were spitting on her, Vicky was easily recognized by her elegance. I had always known that people like Vicky would one day get it. Nobody can guess how many people she and her mother betrayed. The word harlot in the case of Vicky was an understatement, nevertheless I hoped that I would never see her again and I was totally unprepared for this kind of justice. I was accusing myself for overreacting, and there was no one under the sun I could speak to about my anguish.

Shortly after I came home that fateful day, I wanted to rest for a while, but somebody was ringing the front door bell and I hurried to open the door. There was dear Jozka, the former fiancé of my sister Bohunka, a man who was reported lost in action on the Czechoslovak broadcast from Britain. Several people swore that they heard that dreadful news, and here he was, dressed in the smart uniform of an officer of the Czechoslovak Army organized in Great Britain.

"Jozka!"

"Is that you Zdeněk?"

We fell into each other's arms. Then his first questions was, "Bohunka?"

I wished to be dead but I had to say it, "Jozka, she is married, but it's all a horrid misunderstanding . . ."

'What about my parents, my sister and her boys?'

"Sorry Jozka, they . . . they are all gone."

"Sorry to disturb you," he wanted to run away.

"No, no Jozka," I cried desperately, "I am only a boy, or at least feel like a little helpless boy, for I do not know what to do or what to say, except that we have all loved you, your family, and those wonderful boys. Please," I sobbed, "come back and talk to my father!"

He stepped back, gave me a big hug, and then walked in to talk with my father. He stayed for a long time, and when he was leaving, I was delighted that my Father offered that I go with Jozka to Vir, the very next day. It was important, because Jozka's parents, his sister and her two boys were living in hiding in a small house behind the homestead until they were dragged away. Their last possessions had to be there, and perhaps at the house those who witnessed the departure of Jozka's family would be able to give him some important information.

Jozka was to pick me up with his military car the next morning. As much as I tried, I could not sleep, I was dreading the long trip with Jozka. How can one comfort a man in such a sorrow? How can Jozka survive it? At the same time I felt that someone had to tell my sister Bohunka, she must be told, and Jozka and Bohunka must meet. No one else can do this but my oldest sister Vera. Suddenly it occurred to me that she was not much around in these busy days. Late at night I heard her coming in, I jumped out of my bed, stepped out in the hall and motioned to her to come to visit me. Her usual good humor was gone. She looked dreadful as she sat down next to me on the edge of my bed. Whispering and not wanting to wake Father, I told her about Jozka and the urgent need to tell Bohunka about his return. "Dear God, why is so much happening to us?" she cried, "and where do we find the strength to go on?" She could not be comforted and at last she told me of her own anguish. For years Vera was in love with a Russian nobleman called Lord Peter. He was only a teenage boy studying at an academy for white cadets when the Russian revolution came. His family was eliminated by the Bolsheviks, and Peter alone ran and succeeded in escaping to Czechoslovakia. As other Russian nobles in Prague he supported himself by doing odd jobs, hoping that one day he would have Czechoslovak citizenship and that he would be able to study at the university. Although poor, he was very much a part not only of the Russian elite in exile but also of some of the Czech noble families. He was an entertaining, cultured, and captivating man, but he was a product of his society, a dreamer who needed an endowment so that he could pursue his interest without needing an income. My Father was dead against that relationship. Then the Nazis came and for seven years the question of the marriage of Vera and Lord Peter was not even brought up. Then came our liberation by the Soviets and the fear this refugee nurtured in his heart for almost twenty five years was justified. Although he was a member of only a minor Russian nobility, he was in danger. Prague was full of stories of the horrid fate of the Russians who fought in the ranks of a certain General Vlasov against the Nazis. Vlasov was a part of the Czarist regime. His followers by the order of the Soviets were brutally shot. That story which at first seemed fantastic later on was proved to be true. Vera knew that Lord Peter refused to fight against the Nazis with the Vlasov army, because he had some personal reservation about the Vlasov movement, but she knew that he fought at the barricades. She was distressed that she did not hear from him, he was not at home, he simply disappeared. As a last resort, Vera went from church to church where they still kept the unclaimed bodies of the fallen which were to be buried in a common grave. This was a horrifying experience for Vera although her worst fear was ungrounded, Peter was not among the dead,. The Soviets were merciless, but at the same time they were also pragmatic. We talked about many important things that night. I loved Vera with all my heart. No one deserved a bit of happiness more than she did yet her dream of marriage with Peter was a distant, and very dim possibility. Nevertheless she perked up when I assured her that after all his experience Lord Peter was too smart to fall into the hands of the Soviets, and besides he was a Czechoslovak citizen, and he was smart enough to fight on the barricades, which meant he was trusted by the revolutionary guards. It is just amazing what comforting ideas come to one's mind late at night! Vera went to bed renewed in hope, promising to tell Bohunka about Jozka.

I tried and tried to sleep, but the ghost of fear haunted me. Suddenly I realized that in a few days I would be twenty, and I felt as helpless as a little orphan. Also I realized that in all the business of the days I was not able to see Mirko. We were supposed to meet the following day at "our" café but I would be in Vir, and there was no way of notifying him. We had so much to talk about. The two experiences of the day were not leaving my mind. Seeing the captured Nazis and collaborators repairing the pavement of the street under the supervision of the revolutionary guards, being watched by blood thirsty men and women, and then seeing Jozka, who fought in our army and endured horrible hardship and came home only to find out that his beloved was married, and that all the members of his family were murdered by the Nazis seemed too much to bear. The second scene helped to understand the first but it was not easy. I dreaded the coming day, and I prayed not only for the strength to cope but also for some ability to give Jozka just a spark of hope.

Jozka drove the military Citroën insanely fast and we made the trip to the homestead in record time. Naturally, Jozka wanted to know every detail of every visit with his family. He laughed when I described for him his sister Hanna often coming to our house for supper in disguise as a poor peasant woman with a heavy shawl wrapped around her head. He seemed to be grateful knowing that his family was loving, joyful, and enjoying each other until the day when they were separated and taken away.

The house where Jozka's family spent the last months of their lives was the last house above the homestead. We knew the owners of the house well. To my knowledge they had no children and were always looking for new ways to make money. The house was well kept, and was surrounded by a lovely country garden. Whenever we had an overflow of guests, they always stayed at this house.

When we arrived we were welcomed tearfully. There was coffee and pastries, and countless stories of little incidents from the life of Jozka's family and especially about his much loved nephews. "We never dared to let their rooms, I have not dared to touch it, everything is exactly as it was when they left. The Lord knows that we had an opportunity to rent that room, but we would not do that. It is a horrid, horrid tragedy."

"May we go in their rooms?"

"Of course, of course." We were led to two or three adjoining rooms. I know that one of these was used as a dining room. In

each bedroom was a desk. I wanted to leave Jozka alone and to visit at the homestead, but Jozka begged me to stay with him. We entered the first room. Without a word Jozka turned to the desk. He
never thought of the idea of finding anything, and did not bring
along even a briefcase. I rushed to the homestead and brought back
a suitcase. This was terribly painful for Jozka, and he was glad to
put all the contents of the desk into the suitcase, and to have an opportunity to go through everything when he was alone. After a
while he was ready to leave.

"What about the dressers and the closets?"

He frowned but went through the dressers. I opened the
closet, and there was an array of Jozka's mother's dresses. He was
still looking through the dressers.

Standing in front of the open door of the closet I had a very
uncomfortable feeling. I stepped back, and there I saw the face of
an extremely curious woman at the window looking from outside,
anxious to know what we were doing. I was furious, so furious that
I stuck my tongue out at her, and then hurried and closed the curtain. In that moment I was very much ashamed of myself, and furious at the same time. Why do people love to watch tragedies? Nevertheless, I must register here that the woman was extremely noble,
and unlike others never reported me for anti-socialist behavior.
Jozka did not want to look at his mother's dresses, but she was of
the generation of my mother who liked to wear pins with certain
dresses. Indeed there were some fine amethyst and garnet brooch-
es.

"Take them."

At first Jozka hesitated and then put them into his pocket.

We drove home in silence. The paper boys in Prague were
shouting "Extra, Extra!" announcing the special edition of papers
and describing the arrival of the government in exile to Prague.
The arrival of President Benes was scheduled for May 16. Something of excitement and tremendous hope was in the air. Even Jozka sighed in relief, "At last!" We parted in front of the house and
he promised to call within a few days.

Upstairs our home was in a state of celebration, and panic.
The University was to open and Dad was working on his address.
At the same time there was an all out search for his academic

gown, the hood and also for his tuxedo, his tail coat, the white kid gloves, top hat, and all the accessories needed for big occasions. Several receptions were to be held, plus the opening of the National Theater, and the first concert at Smetana Hall. By the time we found the tuxedo and the tail coat we were just about overcome by the fumes of turpentine and moth balls, After seven years, the horrid smell permeated the fabric. I presume the same tragic comedy was going on in many households, and learned men and women were consulting each other on the most pressing subject, how do you get rid of the most awful smell of moth balls?

Although I dreaded my birthday, it turned out to be a week long celebration. The day before my twentieth birthday, Father and I walked together for the opening of the University. Although I still had all the qualifying examinations ahead of me, I was considered a student. During our walk we had an interesting conversation. Father was extremely happy and proud that I was going to study theology, but at the same time he was obviously worried that my expectations were unrealistic, that my sensitivity and my frankness would complicate my life, and gently he warned me that the theologians are also sinners and at times they appear to have hearts of stone. He shared with me some of the deep hurts he had experienced during the years of his deanship.

It did not occur to me that this was the first big celebration for Dad without mother sitting in the first row, without her reading the speech first, without checking on everything. Perhaps I made a mistake in not sitting with the family, but it seemed to me only natural to sit with Mirko, with the students. I have forgotten the pomp of university celebrations, but I felt goose pimples seeing the familiar faces of the gowned professors and when the crier shouted, "His Magnificence, the Dean!" Dad looked resplendent in his gown with ermine, and heavy gold chain which Charles IV presented to all deans in 1348. Dad was deeply moved, he worked terribly hard, nobody but the family knew how hard he worked to have the library and everything ready for the opening. He deserved that standing ovation. Suddenly I felt uncomfortable, and sheepishly I looked at my sisters in the front row, wondering whether or not it was proper for me to applaud my own father, and for the first time I had the uneasy feeling that I was not one of the students, that I was Bednář's son. I thought that father spoke extremely well and had an appreciative audience. After the ceremony Mirko and I decided that we simply had to go to a café for a little visit. First of all we discussed Father's lecture and then quickly we turned to the subject of our place in the student body. Unashamedly, I told Mirko how happy I was to have him there, that without him I felt terribly isolated. I shared with him that my former friends were somewhat distant ever since they learned that I would be studying theology. I could almost feel their shaking their heads and saying "What a shame, such a good kid. We used to have so much fun, and now we cannot even talk with him, after all he is a Holy Man!" On the other hand, at the university I felt not only labeled but at the same time most of the colleagues were so somber that they did not appeal to me. If the psychology was right in affirming that the outward appearance was witnessing to the inner state of men and women, then the future theologians seemed to me beyond hope. Mirko could not stop laughing and at the same time sincerely confessed that he felt exactly the same and thanked God for me. I felt as if they all looked at me saying, "Here is that Communist, Harych, and now he is chummy with the Bednářs! And look at his suit! A debonair summer suit as if he were going to a garden party! My circle of friends has also narrowed, on the one hand because of my decision to study for the ministry and then because of my being a member of the party. Of course the party members let me know that I am entitled to my religious views, but at the same time there is no doubt that they feel I am slightly out of my mind." We laughed, and were so glad in having one another, but at the same time we admitted that we were scoundrels, that we were so afraid of blending with the multitude of somber men and women that we were determined to stick out as worldly debonair. Mirko was a good politician and immediately started making a list of students who were at least slightly interesting and whom we wanted to know. I even made a plan to invite those on the list for a light supper in the near future.

    Our main concern was our need to study and to prepare ourselves for the examinations. My problem was not only that I was hopelessly busy at home, but primarily because I just could not concentrate, the happenings of each day were occupying my mind.

"Well, if you are planning to wait for some peaceful times, you are kidding yourself. What we need is discipline, and some structure. Both of us perform better under pressure, then let us set up the dates or approximate dates of the exams, and just to be sure, let's go right from here to the University and schedule the exams!"

I decided to take Czech literature in three weeks, Czech history and world history in another three weeks, then Latin and German. We figured that this schedule would require at least six hours of studying a day. We decided that we would examine one another weekly. Another monumental decision was to go to the university and to secure a tutor in Greek and Hebrew. We were planning to start with that at once, and then we planned to go to Vir and to spend the whole of August studying so that we could present ourselves for the qualifying examinations at the beginning of September before the opening of the fall semester, when we would start with our regular lectures.

"Let's go right now to sign for it." Mirko was enthusiastic.

"I think I am overtaxing the Lord, but I will do it, just let me have another cup of coffee, and then we shall go." Just at that moment my uncle, professor of Practical Theology, Dr. Adolf Novotny waddled in. He was my favorite uncle who possessed a tremendous sense of humor and an extraordinary intellect, a man who was never bluffing. Well, Uncle Adolf smiled broadly and went straight to our table saying, "May I join you, I need to talk with someone under sixty!" He talked quite a bit about Dad's lecture, and we told him about our fabulous plans of study. He laughed and agreed that discipline was needed, but he warned us that we would not make up for the lost time enforced by the Nazis for a long, long time. He was terribly worried, he said, by the wide spread illiteracy especially among the new politicians, and urged us to spend more time on world literature and world history not because of the exams, but for our own sake. "Well, our Masaryk used to say that people have leaders whom they deserve. I would think that today he would say that illiterate people elect illiterate leaders . . . I have been thinking a great deal about that during the last seven years. Did the German people deserve Hitler and why? No nation had more prophets of great depth than Russia, and why did the Russians turn to the German thought of Marx? It is all staggering. And you know . . . when I saw you, I expected you to argue about politics!"

"Professor Novotny, may I assume that you also know that I am a member of the communist party and therefore you assume that Zdeněk and I spend every moment fighting or arguing?"

"I would not be surprised, after all he is the son of my sister, and I would welcome it. There is no friendship, no dialogue without an argument. . . and let me tell you, Mirko, I have nothing against intelligent, knowledgeable communists with whom one can talk."

"What do you mean?"

"Well I have spent a great deal of time studying Karl Marx. There is a lot we can learn from him. After all, he was a Jew, and converted to Christianity as many others, for the sake of their safety, but Marx as a young confirmand delivered a very interesting little sermon. So I have been studying Marxism and what happened when this totally foreign thought was introduced in Russia. There are so many questions I have and I cannot find a single communist who would be willing to discuss them with me simply because most of our communists have absolutely no idea what they are talking about. It is not unreasonable for me to ask you, young people what you think of the anthropology of Karl Marx! Do you believe with him that human beings will become more responsible, more human if they are materially more secure, or should we say, that bread is more important than grace?"

Mirko especially was fascinated, and raised a number of questions, but Adolf stood firm in his question: "Have you ever studied Karl Marx?" The indictment was awful, "You would not like it, if we taught you just what someone thinks of Jesus, you insist on going *ad fontem* yet here you are, just quoting what people of doubtful knowledge say about Marx-Leninism. I think it is fair on my side, to say read Marx and Lenin. Study them, and then let us talk about them, but do not talk to me about Marx-Leninism because you read an article in the communist papers!"

"Professor," said Marko, "I cannot thank you enough. If we studied Marx as seriously as you suggest, would you be willing to discuss it with us?"

"Of course, at any time, gladly, although it really belongs to the department of philosophy, or to Dr. Hromadka. It will be very interesting to see what Hromadka will have to say, but I am ready to talk with you and to learn from you any time.

Uncle Adolf lit his pipe, cracked a few jokes, and we told him of our fears of theologians. He told us several delightful stories, and asked some gutsy questions of us. He was one of the people one could never fool with phrases. It was a magical afternoon, and as we were leaving, both of us were saying to ourselves: If this is academia, we love it!

Mirko promised to come the next day to help me to celebrate my birthday.

As it turned out, we celebrated my twentieth birthday most memorably for two days! According to the family tradition, I opened my presents, and we celebrated around the breakfast table, and then I had a special lunch with Father. Everybody was shocked that "the little one" was already twenty, but nobody was more shocked than I myself. Already I understood that time was static, that it was not changing anything by itself, and I was haunted by the realization that I was twenty, and that I had accomplished absolutely nothing of significance. Just at that time, at the urging of my friend, Vlastik, I read the life of Galois, who as a mathematician was most creative at the age of 18. It was of some interest to me that Verdi got a second wind after eighty, but how could I forget the unmatched, vibrant melodies of the young Mozart in his *Requiem*? Obviously I was not meant to compose *Magnificat* or *Requiems*, but I did not know what I was meant to be, my mind was swirling with ideas and thoughts. Hitlerism really left a deep mark on my soul, I felt like a crumb fallen from the table of the mighty, and as I was starting to study for the qualifying examinations, I was surprised by my own exhaustion, and I was worried, really worried that I would not amount to anything. From the point of view of today those worries seem ridiculous. At that time I desperately needed someone to tell me that first of all, I had to be a good, honorable and loving man, I did not have such a someone. Mother would have been able to verbalize this, Father was not, he took it for granted. From childhood on, I often heard the expression "the buried talent" a horrid indictment. Indeed, the parable of Jesus about a man who buried his treasure, not realizing that to take the gift of God, this one life with all its possibilities and to present it without any interest as an achievement, meant an invitation to rebuke. That story has never been totally out of my mind. Our family certainly was not unique, the proper families of that era had tremendous expectations of their sons and daughters. Any moral failure was a black spot on the family reputation. One always lived in terror of being a shame to the family. Advanced degrees, and fine career developments were marks of belonging to distinguished families.

In those days I dated, or better said, escorted, a number of attractive girls, the more decorative the better. Some thought of me as a budding ladies' man, the truth, however was, that the minute we started to talk about that which really mattered to me, about principles, about faith and truth, I was alarmed and like Cinderella, I ran and ran before any midnight at which relationships are sealed, I ran and ran back to my realm. What bored me most of all was the monotony of questions repeated by so many: Does religion, the truth, the spiritual orientation really mean so much to you? Why? They do not seem to bother anyone else!

I fully realized on my twentieth birthday that God gave me a very special gift in the wonderful friendship of Mirko Harych. During the lunch Father was in an excellent mood, and we discussed plans for the following day. We had reserved seats for the parade welcoming President and Mrs. Benes home. Since enormous crowds were expected, and many people planned to spend the night in the streets to get a good view, we had to get up early and occupy our reserved seats long before the stated time. Then Father surprised me with a special gift: Would I like to accompany him to a special gala concert in honor of the President? I was thrilled, for the concert was to be conducted by Rafael Kubelik, the idol of my adolescence, back from his years in exile. At last, at last, my tuxedo would be able to make its debut!

Mirko came early announcing that he was taking me to celebrate my birthday. "You are very, very lucky my dear Zdeněk, I am loaded! Three funerals in a week! The old Urbanec does not want to play at funerals of ordinary people anymore. They are now mine! Did you hear, they are mine!," he enthused. "Just think, if this keeps going, I shall be solvent! One thing really surprises me, and that is that the Protestants are so cheap! Give me the Catholics anytime. They are used to paying."

Our first stop was at the columbarium. Mirko left me there alone while he went to their nearby apartment to get something. There was nothing morbid in our stopping at the columbarium. I would not have wanted it otherwise. To this day in Central Europe the people do stop at the graves of their loved ones and friends at special days of the year. It was good for me to have that moment totally alone, to reflect on the rich heritage my mother left for me. I was anxious to tell her that we were all fine, and that the day of her dreams, the day of the arrival of the Benes' was upon us. A procession of events went through my mind, I laughed at our efforts to manage the household. I wanted to tell her that hardly a day passed by without our saying "How did Mother ever do that?" Our admiration indeed grew day by day.

Shortly Mirko was back, carrying a small picnic basket. Although I was in a section of Prague which was not familiar to me, I knew we were walking toward the river Vltava. In a small harbor we rented a row boat. It was a gorgeous, hot day, not a cloud in the sky. On the other side in the shade of the blooming chestnut tree Vltava was deep blue, but all around us it was touched by silver. Mirko secured the picnic basket, we stripped ourselves to the waist, and happily we started rowing down the stream toward downtown Prague. Before too long, the magnificent panorama of the old Prague was unfolding in front of our eyes. The multiple shades of greens in the palatial gardens, the splashes of the purple lilac, the silhouettes of small churches and historic buildings, the towering, bright green dome of St. Nichols Church, and the Prague castle with the gothic towers of St. Vitus cathedral on the top of the hill. We could feel Smetana's triumphant music on Vysehrad and Vltava, everything around us was singing! "For seven years we have dreamed about this, and here it is! Prague is ours again! We are alive! How on earth do we deserve this? How is this going to be safe in our hands?" Mirko stretched his arms and yawned, "Before we become sentimental and philosophical, we better eat."

Mirko knew Vltava by heart and we found a perfect harbor not too far from another renting place where we would leave the row boat and go to another attraction in the birthday celebration.

Mirko set up a beautiful picnic lunch with wine glasses and all. Everything a true sacrament of love. Since I was still captivated by the view all around us, and we admired one building after another, Mirko remarked, "You should see this at night! I am taking Alena to see the fireworks tomorrow night. If we could get a row boat it would be sensational."

I felt greatly relieved not only knowing that things with Alena were under control but also because I was terribly embarrassed to tell Mirko that I was going to the gala concert. It was a new, and a very unpleasant feeling for me. When I finally told him about that he laughed and said, "Now you know how I feel when I have to attend meetings with the comrades! That's funny, from now on, a few times a week you will be occupied with the upper crust, and I will be with the scoundrels, and then when we shall get together and compare our notes, we shall come to the conclusion that the Lord distributed sin pretty equally! The day after tomorrow is the opening of the opera. Did you know that?"

"No, I did not. What are they playing?"

Libuse.

"Strange, that Dad did not mention it."

"Well you can just as well count on it."

"Did you know that I have only one stiff shirt? And how do you know that the opera is opening?"

"Mother is going. I mean she is not to attend the opera, but whenever there is something special Mother and her best friend stand in front of the theater like in a dream, studying every gown and then they talk about that for months. It is the funniest thing. These women do not have a penny to spare, they certainly do not envy the rich and important, but they assume they have the right to say who is chic and who is not. It's almost as if they were saying, 'We deserve a good show'!"

"This year they will see the Communist women for the first time."

"Tell me about it, I shall hear about it for weeks! I expect them either to wear flounces made out of the fatigues, or sheer glitz! One thing is sure, not a single fur piece belongs to them."

Mirko glanced at this watch, "Well time to go back to formal."

We cleaned up after the lunch and put on our shirts and ties, and rowed to a nearby station to debark. Mirko looked at me and burst into laughter. I got a first class sunburn, and Mirko predicted that I would be peeling before the concert. After we returned our row boat, we walked rapidly for what seemed miles to St. Nicholas Church. As we entered the nave of that awesome baroque church no one was in sight but an old grandmother kneeling in prayer in one of the back pews. Her hair was covered in a black silk shawl with a long fringe, and one could hardly see her. Then we noticed a young boy in a wheel chair, "It must be her grandson," Mirko whispered, "they are here, whenever I come to practice." The boy wheeled himself to the high altar. He lit a candle, and watched it for a long time. It was his candle among many. He bowed his head in prayer, because he could not kneel. I was hurting for that boy, almost feeling his feverish prayer. "Please God, make me well." After all these years I can still see that boy vividly on the screen of memory and thinking in terms of today, considering our own spiritual condition, I keep wondering, and wondering what it takes to make the high altar 'handicap accessible' for the lame humanity.

"Well, come on!" Mirko led the way up and up, the narrow spiral staircase to the choir loft. Still puffing, I looked at the huge organ, it's silver and gold gleaming pipes, and the frame bedecked with cherubim and seraphim.

While Mirko was getting ready at the console, removing his shoes, I sat down on one of the pews near him where I could watch even his feet. "As yet, I do not own a pair of organ shoes, but it is just fine, although Urbanec maintains that it means a lack of class, but when I sit at a console like this, I always recall the fine scene in which God calls the young man Moses, saying to him 'Moses, Moses, first take off your shoes for you are standing on holy ground!' . . . Now, listen Zdeněk, this is my birthday present for you!" He paused for what seemed to be a long time. He looked down very close to the key board, and then up to the ceiling, and started playing. It was Bach's *Toccata and Fugue in D Minor*.

Heaven was very near, every tone seemed to speak of the

majesty of God and of the glory of our belonging to him. I felt goose pimples all over my body, marveling at Mirko's footwork, his timing, his passion, his crescendos. When he finished he gave a victorious smile. He knew he played well. "I did it! I never played it better before!" Deeply moved I rushed toward him to thank him, and to give him a big hug. He was slightly puffing as after running a marathon. Still sitting on the bench, he was telling me that there was something demonic about playing that piece. He described his asking for permission to practice on that organ. "The first time I came to practice here, I was excited and then I was scared to death, afraid of even touching the keys and disturbing this awesome silence. Nothing but perfection belongs here. Then I recalled the legend of the Master builder of this church." He gave his name, spoke slowly, without any pathos or exaggeration, as a natural story teller.

"This poor man had the dream of building this church which with its green dome would put a permanent mark on the landscape of Prague. He designed its daring vaulted ceiling. He did not trust anybody with the work. With a few close friends he supervised the laying of every stone and brick, until it was finished. The people came from far and near to see it. The only remaining problem was to remove the scaffolding in hopes that the immense structure and the whole dream would not collapse. In the legend the builder is so petrified that with his own blood he signs a contract with the devil. He is ready to give his life, his everything for the glory of this building. When the scaffolding was removed, the prelates applauded and the choirs sang, 'Te Deum,' and the builder was found dead."

"Yuck!"

"No, it is not at all yuck, every artist, every minister, everyone involved in some creative activity, every politician, and when you think of it, everyone yearns for a bit of praise, and at one time or another, has to deal with the temptation of glory. For me the story of the temptation of Jesus is tremendous, for the temptation of glory, of popularity is so overwhelming! So here I sat, the score appeared as a super-structure, and I wanted so much to please you, I wanted so much that you would believe in me, just a bit. You told me you heard your mother playing it, you heard Urbanec perform-

ing it, in your subconscience, you certainly heard Schweitzer playing it. I wanted very much to give this to you, and yet ten days after exhaustive rehearsing, I almost gave up the idea, and wanted to
postpone it for a year. Then I came here just to give it another try. I
bowed my head and found myself saying 'Dear God have mercy
on me, this was written for you. On every page your servant J. S.
Bach reminded himself and all who play this, that this is for you,
printing so clearly the words, "*Soli Deo Gloria!*"—and here I am
killing myself to please people, to win their hearts. With a bit of
confidence in me, so please God, please, help me today to play this
as it was intended to be played, for you alone! And would you believe, for the first time, I really started playing it'!"

It was a magical moment, and anything I wanted to say
seemed unfitting, cheap. "Mirko, you really have made this day
special for me, and without you it would have been awful . . . when
you played, ever so brilliantly, I could not believe that this petite
man at the console was my friend, who is good to me, on whom I
can always count. How do I ever deserve you? At the same time I
must say, that if you failed, if you messed up that piece, I hope
very much that you do not believe that it would change an iota in
my friendship for you."

Mirko understood but quickly changed the subject. "Wait,
here are you presents!"

First, there was a lovely silk tie, which I had admired in a
shop window on Prikopy a few days before. Mirko gently reminded me that he wanted to use that tie for some special dates. Then I
was given two compositions with the words of a famous Czech
poet, Jiri Volker. In the late forties, the so called recitatives, the
reading of poems with the accompaniment of piano, or string en-
semble was very popular. Once Mirko asked me to be the reader of
one of his recitatives at a big gathering of his friends. He said that
he liked the shading of my voice in reading the poem, what he did
not know was that I was simply terrible in counting. It took us
hours of rehearsing!

I like the poetry of Volker very much. What surprised me
was that both compositions dealt with death. The first one, written
in pencil and which for years was hanging in my room started with
the words, "When I die, nothing will happen, nothing will

change. . . ." Mirko and I never discussed the subject of death and dying, or of eternity, and here were two recitatives dealing with death. I thanked him, and promised to study the recitatives that we would perform them together but I could not avoid the question, "Mirko why all the emphasis on death? Are you afraid of death and dying?"

"Terribly, abnormally, more than you can ever imagine, but then death is a part of life, is it not?"

He paused and then softly recited the text of the second recitative:

> Sweeten not, O priest, your sermon with
>   talk of paradise,
> angels and blessed souls.
> Sing not, O choir, over the grave a canticle lack-luster
>   with dole.
> Sing rather as gardeners at seed time sing.
> If I weep, I weep not for the dead, None there be
> If I suffer, it is grief for the living, that suffers in me.
> Only the coffin we bury.
> Only the name we bury.
> Of hearts which lived righteously . . .

There were still more small presents to open and it was getting late.

"The old dean will have a fit."

"Yes, he will."

We hurried out of sanctuary.

"Where are you going to watch the president tomorrow?"

I told him, but there was no time for teasing. He whistled and summoned a taxi to take me home.

"What a day! Thanks a million!"

"Look for me in the crowd tomorrow, I shall be waving a big flag! Will call you soon?"

*   *   *   *   *

The excitement of welcoming Dr. and Mrs. Edward Benes after seven years of their second exile, and his horrid humiliation at Munich, was beyond imagination. Everybody was out and the streets along the scheduled presidential motorcade were a sea of happy people. Benes was vindicated in his political thinking. We were grateful to him, and felt that as long as he was at the Prague castle there was hope for democracy in Czechoslovakia. The communists knowing the enormous popularity of Benes joined the crowds in enthusiasm and praise. Benes was to arrive by train, his car was to go down the Wenceslaus Square, then on National Avenue, and then along the river to the Old Town Square, where he was to be officially welcomed and deliver his first address at home. After that the President and his wife were to return to Prague castle.

Since the Republic was occupied also by some American forces, the parade was to include the Soviet, and American units, as well as a unit of our soldiers who fought along with the British and American forces. When we heard the twenty one gun salute, and realized that it was true, that Dr. Benes and his wife were actually in Prague in that very minute, we were overcome with emotions. The crowds fell silent, counting the gun salutes and then everyone burst into a deafening, "Hurrah!"

The parade was marshaled by several Soviet generals, followed by a huge brass band and an elite, foot stepping Soviet unit. The members of the government followed in their limousines receiving a heartfelt ovation. The president's car was approaching, but ahead of him was the band of the USA unit, and Prague went absolutely bezerk. For the first time in my life I heard a band playing, "The Stars and Stripes Forever," and here was something which the Prague people had never seen before: a drum major! An immense, black, god-like man, twirling his baton with absolute authority. The contrast between the military unit of the Soviet Union and the American representation was incredible. The first one was a unit of robots without any expression, the other was a unit of elegant, smiling, individuals, marching in perfect discipline, yet their humaneness was not removed. Behind them, ever so fittingly, was the open limousine with Dr. and Mrs. Benes. They were standing, and received a truly royal welcome.

At the Old Town Square President Benes spoke brilliantly, according to his custom, recalling to us the great chapters of our history, and the humiliation of Munich. He thanked our allies,

Roosevelt, Churchill and Stalin, and reminded us of their enormous sacrifices for our freedom. Then he quickly turned our attention to the enormous struggles at hand, struggles from which no one was excluded in building a true democratic and just State. The speech ended in a call to rededicate ourselves to the principles of T. G. Masaryk and to the idea that the principles of democracy could not be translated into reality without a commitment to spiritual principles and to that Truth which makes people free. It was one of those moments in my life when I was tall, very tall in gratitude. We came home happily exhausted, each seeking a bit of solitude. I could not believe that before too long we had to start dressing for the concert. For the first time I realized that social life can be extremely tiring. My sister Bohunka, who was to go with us to the concert arrived toward the evening. My sister Vera who opted to go to the opera the next night was hemming her gown, not a minor task for a scientist who had no domestic abilities! The house was resounding with laughter when Ruzena came to announce a new crisis. No it was not the plumbing, the electricity was fine, there was no leak in the roof, it was much worse! The Russians were coming! Yes, we were asked to provide some homely hospitality for some Soviet high officer and his orderly. To this day I do not know why we were elected for this high honor when so many splendid villas were left vacant by the Nazis. My sisters decided which room would be best for them, and somehow refused to believe that any Russian would feel too happy among us.

Fortunately, as yet I was not peeling, but the contrast between my red face and the starched white shirt was too strong and I had to submit to a "tone down" administered by my sisters. Bohunka wore a brand new dress that evening made from Mother's old dress, and looked extremely chic. The dress was a sleeveless, dark blue, silk sheath. She wore long white gloves, had several beautiful white and pink camelias by her neckline. Her beautiful blond hair was tied into a chignon. I could not help but admire her aloud. She was beautiful, and Father and I approvingly smiled at the prospect of accompanying such a lovely woman to the gala. At the same time I was puzzled. Such an elegance does not just happen. Everything was planned. Bohunka that night wanted to be beautiful, and to hold her head high. In that effort she succeeded beyond measure. Even the fact that she did not wear any jewelry that night was a policy statement. Many of the Communist woman looked like Christmas trees. When Bohunka stood next to Father in our box she look regal.

Before the performance, we greeted a number of people whom we had not seen for years. Many returned from exile, others returned from concentration camps. That itself was very emotional. Of course, a great many people inquired of my mother, and nobody believed that I was the little Zdeněk. Father was busy greeting old friends, and meeting some of the new people in our political life. What was upsetting me was, that so many of these people were white haired, and appeared tired. It troubled my soul. Here was the gathering of the survivors of Nazism, a gathering of the best men and women we had, and on whom we could count. So many of them showed signs of weariness, yes, they were old enough to retire. The President was over sixty, and we expected these men and women to help us make a new beginning. Next to them the new Communist leaders with the exception of the senile Minister of Education, Dr. Zdeněk Nejedly, represented a young front. For many of the Benes' colleagues, very tragically, this was the second time, that they were called to build a democratic state from ruins.

The lights blinked and we were summoned to our seats, which meant that President and Mrs. Benes were arriving. We entered our box just as Rafael Kubelik appeared on the podium receiving a tremendous ovation. He motioned to the orchestra to be in readiness to welcome the President. All eyes were set on the presidential box. At last Mrs. Benes and her husband came in. We could not tire of applauding. Kubelik motioned to the orchestra to sit down, raised his baton and led it in a stirring rendition of our national anthem. Most of us unable to control our emotions, could not sing the swelling melody.

> Where is my home? Where is my home?
> Streams are rushing through the meadows,
> Mid the rocks sigh fragrant pine groves,
> Orchards decked in Spring's array,
> Scenes of Paradise portray!
> And this land of wondrous beauty
> Is the Czech land, home of mine!
> Is the Czech land, home of mine!

Kubelik and the orchestra were in excellent form. Obviously the maestro wanted this concert to be a celebration of the Allies.
He started with the first part of Smetana's *My Country*, and he concluded the concert with an electric performance of Gershwin's
Rhapsody in Blue. It was a daring, and a wonderful step. I was fascinated. Bohunka and I exchanged a look, as the saxophone was
whining through the venerable Smetana Hall. I did not dare to look
at my father. As most of the old audience, he associated the jazz id-
iom with cafés. Bohunka and I just about cracked up laughing
watching the prim and proper people around us as if they were subjected to nothing short of torture, for the sake of international relations. On the other hand, the Communists in their boxes were politely smiling as if they were saying "Only the Americans can
come up with something like this!"

The applause was tepid, but then came the bravos of the
young from the second and third balconies, and personally I knew
in that moment what recording I would buy for Mirko for Christmas.

What a day! We came home talking about our experiences
over and over again. Happily we shared the conversation over a
glass of wine.

Father noticed a stack of paper on the side table, "Goodness, we have been so busy celebrating that I have not even read
the papers!" He said it with the sadness of a school boy who suddenly realized that he had not done his home work. Late as it was,
and against all his principles, Father started to read the papers. It
was a must of his days.

Recalling that period, I see now, that it was not easy to get
used to freedom of the press. Suddenly, instead of one ultimate expression of truth spelled out in "Der Neue Tag," which no one
bothered to read, there were at least half a dozen papers according
to the political affiliation. The Communist paper, "Rude Pravo"
was the most prominent. The Social Democrats were publishing
their papers under the title, "The People's Democracy." The middle of the road was well represented by, "The Free Tomorrow" and
"The Free Word," and there were such "non political" papers as,
"People's News." Father subscribed to them all, and although it
consumed quite a bit of his time, it was fascinating and important.

Father was an editor of a journal, and we were all diligent in clipping articles and thoughts for him to which he was to react. Some of these papers were only a few days old and already in their editorials, they were fighting other papers. The war of words was on. At times it was all down right disgusting but in the diversity of the printed word there was also a sign of hope. The Communist, "Rude Právo," however, seemed to set the tone to which other papers were reacting. "Rude Pravo," for instance, was the first paper which published an appeal to speed up the proposed transfer of Sudeten Germans as a response to constant sabotage by the former Nazis in our lands. There was an extensive coverage of the proceeding of the people's courts, and also the newly born United Nations received an unusually large coverage, hailing the bold Soviet demand that the Charter of the United Nations would include the ultimate promise that this body would never interfere in the internal affairs of any sovereign state. The editorials recalled the horror of Munich when other nations dictated our policies. The principle of nonintereference at that time certainly sounded noble and rational, yet the minute the Charter was signed, the Soviets were ready to use it for their conquest of the world. They never invaded any country, they were always invited to invade and to assist the threatened democratic forces, and at the same time they invoked their obedience to the UN principle of not interfering in the internal affairs of any sovereign state.

Of course, in that era, before television, the papers often summoned the best writers and experts in the field to respond to this or that published by, "Rude Pravo." The debate was lively, summoning, not allowing anyone to be neutral. Since the Communist press, and the communist representatives led a definite offensive they introduced a new vocabulary which like measles spread in all papers:

Peoples Republic: We are not just a democracy, but a democracy in which the people rule. The word "people" depended on a variety of definitions. Quite obviously other democracies as France or Great Britain were not quite kosher, they were governed by other species than people.

Reactionary: The old fuddy duds, and the young people misled by them, who oppose any revolutionary process, the greatest enemies of the people who try to stop progress and to betray the blood of the Soviet soldiers.

Collaborators: Everyone who in the past associated with the enemies of the people. (Watch out! The street and the party determine your pedigree).

Workers Brigades: The people who with some help of the Party, volunteer to build houses, to cultivate the fields, etc., in their free time. This is strictly voluntary but attendance is taken according to the party affiliation.

Social Realism: The only true art form, developed primarily in the Soviet Union which portrays life and history "as they are."

Some new word was added to the political vocabulary every day. This was an era before television and when radio was not used for political purposes. The pen and the typewriter were enormous weapons, and this was a time of great journalists, when people often read the editorials before reading the news.

Father folded the papers and said with a smile but also with a concern, "Well, thank God Benes is back, we have his leadership, but a horrendous struggle is at hand." Everyone at home understood.

THE WAR WITH INTERRUPTIONS

There is a great fallacy which suggests that after a good sleep everything will look brighter and that our fears will appear ungrounded. Being a night owl, my morning hours are not my best, and everything unpleasant seems exaggerated. After the exhilarating day of welcoming the President and his wife home, the glittering concert, the wonderful reunion with old friends, and the intoxicating hope for the future, the presence of the Russians in our house appeared unbearable. Typically, by the time I got up, Father had gone to the university, Vera was in her laboratory, and Ruzena and I were left with the invasion. Actually, just one very pleasant orderly, named Boris, moved in, and then some committee came to inspect the premises. One good thing about this affair was that the big dining room was plastered and painted in absolutely record time. Later on, our dear Boris, one day appeared with a huge, monstrous Victorian chandelier, the most awful thing imaginable. When he installed it, he was not only admiring it but was also beaming with pride. It was made of a shining, hammered brass and it featured two layers of lanterns with frosted glass and fluted rim. Obviously the Communists and the Soviets had access to enormous store houses with stolen goods from the former Nazi villas, the confiscated properties of the reactionaries and from homes of the Jews who were eliminated. According to Boris, quite a few new comrades were choosing the furnishings for their flats in these vast centers of loot. Thus we had a stolen, ugly chandelier in our dining room, and I was mad. What was funny about it was, that I was not as upset about Boris bringing a stolen chandelier, but that he had no taste, that instead of stealing some nice crystal chandelier he came with this shiny contraption, meant for a third rate dacha. I called my sister Vera at once, only to be told that she was busy working on some experiment with cobras. When she called

Zdeněk's father presenting honorary degrees. The historic gold chain which he is wearing is one of those which Charles IV presented to each dean at the founding of Charles University in 1348. Dr. Františec Bednář is also wearing hoods of honorary degrees received from St. Andrews and Paris.

me back, she advised me to calm down, and to understand that at present no good chandeliers were available. That did it. All my frustrations came to the boiling point, and I called the dean himself. His kindly secretary did not have a chance with her usual chit chat, and here I was telling my father that I had had it, that I had no chance to study without constant interruptions, that it was most unfair to expect me to run the big household and study at the same time. I went on nonstop for several minutes, ignoring every nuance of the fifth commandment of honoring my father. Against all his customs, he let me yell at him, he did not tell me that I was rude, nor did he tell me that I ought to count my many blessings; he did say that indeed, it was too much for me, that he had discussed the matter with Vera and that we would have additional help whenever guests come, but and there was always a but, "But Zdeněk, if you think that you will ever find time just for study without any interruptions, you are living in an illusion. You must learn to live with interruptions, to cope with them without cursing them . . . actually some of the interruptions are good for us, they give us other dimensions, they make us more human than we would be otherwise, and you must remember that it is you who is putting this tremendous pressure on yourself, you do not have to take all those examinations so soon. What's your rush?"

"Oh Dad, I don't know why, but I just cannot wait another day, I have so much to catch up on, and I have to get through the University as soon as I can, and go on."

"And do you realize that you will have the whole household to yourself for more than a month? Imagine the studying you can accomplish!"

"Where are you going, or what's going on?"

"Well, I am getting an honorary degree at St. Andrews University together with the Norwegian Archbishop Bergraff, and then I have to stay in England, since I was asked to be a part of the commission preparing the coming first Assembly of the World Council of Churches in Amsterdam in forty eight."

"Great! Well, see you tonight!"

This was about the third or fourth time that Father dealt with me as with an adult and not as if I were a little boy coming to kiss him good night. I could not get used to that. I felt like calling

back and apologizing to him, but here was my first, blessed interruption, the tall, skinny, blond, blue eyed Boris, the orderly of an
officer, whom I never met. I really do not think that any officer
ever lived in our house. It may well be that after he saw the bedroom which was reserved for him, it was not what he wanted, but
his orderly, Boris, awaited his arrival for what it seemed months. It
was all very Russian, we had no idea who would come when, and
above all, we had no idea when they would move out for good.
The presence of the Soviet troops in Czechoslovakia certainly had
far reaching influence on the first election in which the Communists received the majority vote. Once I asked Boris about their departure, and I realized that I touched a very sensitive subject. As
many of his friends, Boris had no idea whether any member of his
family was alive. For the first time in his life, in Prague he lived in
a free society. It worried him because some of his friends who returned to Russia from places such as Prague, were under suspicion
and were shortly eliminated. Therefore, Boris joyfully announced
that he would like to stay in Prague forever. I still feel guilty of
toasting that sheer human desire.

    Boris was an interesting young man, planning to study at
the Moscow University. He had a marvelous knowledge of Russian
literature, and I am forever indebted to him for helping me to learn
Russian, and above all, for helping me to understand the spirit of
Russia. No teacher could possibly interpret the passion of Push-
kin's "Onegin" as Boris: Interestingly enough, he, a Bolshevik, saw
something tremendous in Olga's ultimate rejection of Onegin. It
was because of Boris that I started to study Russian literature very
seriously. When Boris dramatized for me the great scenes from Karamazovs, particularly the scene in which Father Zossima bows
down in deep compassion in front of the rebellious Ivan, the open
enemy of God, I was deeply moved, for Zossima was bowing
down before the great suffering which was still ahead of Ivan.

    "Do they teach that at the Moscow University?"

    "Of course not. We read that on our own."

    "Well, what do you say of Zossima, and his conviction that
Ivan would not escape dreadful suffering?"

    "I believe that this suffering is unavoidable. Are you asking
this because you have noticed the icon, hanging on my neck?"

"I have noticed it. May I see it?"

He unbuttoned his shirt, "My grandmother gave it to me. I believe it has protected me all the way from Stalingrad."

"It's very beautiful. Is your Grandmother still living?"

"I don't know, I doubt it."

"What does the icon mean to you?"

"I really do not know. At times I believe that God believes in me. I do not know why. Now so many, many things do not make any sense to me. We have a great deal to talk about. Shall we drink to it?"

I have no idea what Boris was doing during the day. When he was at home, he loved to sit in the kitchen and observe the cooking procedures, once in a while he worked in the garden, always looking to be of some help, and then eager to get a bit of love and praise. Boris was a magnificent interruption, and he disappeared from our household just as quickly and mysteriously as he appeared.

*   *   *   *   *

Although my room looked like a forest of books; and piles of books marked the way from my bed to a small desk, there was just one book I really wanted to read at that time. A beautiful, fresh translation of Margaret Mitchell's, *Gone With the Wind* and I really had to discipline myself to keep away from its pages, and to concentrate on Czech literature. This was in no way a review— many volumes I read for the first time and with a great benediction. Along with a note book, I also kept a sort of journal in which I jotted down some questions for future consideration. I have always loved books. To this day some books are like old friends. I know the color of their bindings, I know exactly where they are, and I turn to them often. Some of the books which I read at that time were added to the ranks of my friends, while many books in the piles were just helping me to learn as much and as fast as possible, they were unfriendly textbooks, and compilations of data.

As soon as I started to read the authors and poets of the 19th century, I realized that perhaps unlike the writers of other nations, the Czech writers wrote with a holy, passionate sense of purpose; to preserve the Czech language, to encourage the common people to read. Considering the centuries of systematic Germanization, we can justly say that the Czechs and Slovaks are totally indebted to the poets, writers and ministers for the preservation not only of their respective languages but also for their perception of truth. I am particularly thinking of a distinguished woman, Bozena Nemcova, who among other works gave us a gem—a much loved book, *The Grandmother*. It is a book for everybody, the life of a noble grandmother. She lived simply but nobly in the given society. In a truly magnificent prose Nemcova describes the life of the nobility living in a nearby castle, and the life of ordinary folks in the village. The book is totally free of any effort to create hostilities. When people finish reading this book, the young and old know exactly where the nobility of the spirit rests. Similarly, Jan Neruda and others wrote masterfully about the ordinary people for the ordinary people. The readers could see themselves. It is not at all surprising to me that during those long decades of Germanization, the people literally sacrificed to buy books, and poems were clipped out of the papers to be memorized. These writers and poets did not have an easy time. Many suffered persecution, others were ostracized and starved but they had a very definite sense of mission. Similarly it astonished me when I read the many delightful fairy tales by Jaroslav Kvapil. When Kvapil submitted his beautiful story *Rusalka* to Antonin Dvorak for a consideration as a libretto of an opera, Dvorak expressed interest but asked Kvapil to rewrite one paragraph in which the desperate waterman curses God and man, saying, "You certainly do not expect me to curse God in my music, do you?"

Along with the enormous amount of reading and studying, my journal was bulging with questions, primarily with the questions of the moral, social and political responsibility of writers and poets but also of all those who assume prophetic roles as they address the people of today. During my life time I have seen the advocates of the poor, and the advocates of civil rights, of this and that cause, so that at times I have wondered who will be the advocates of the totally manipulated God as if God did not make himself ultimately known in Jesus of Nazareth? It bothered me terribly, especially during the sixties and seventies when the Marxist-

Christian dialogue was flourishing, when our churches were sending delegates to the so called Christian Peace Conference which, as
can be documented today, was funded by the Communists, and
when my colleagues behind the former Iron Curtain were telling
me that they were not interested in politics as the ministers in the
USA, that they preached the pure Gospel of Jesus Christ. We do
know now what that meant! At the same time the writers of today
taught us to assume that they speak for themselves, and that we
read their text at our own risk. I like the liberty of it, but the question of the political, social and moral consequence of what we
write and say remains.

I went to the examination in Czech literature according to
schedule. Thousands of students were involved in the same procedure, and the University had to secure dozens of examiners to accommodate the crowds. I was fortunate and my examiner was a
distinguished woman of letters. The exam consisted of a long test
and of an oral examination. I went home not only with excellent
grades but also with much inspiration to pursue the study of Czech
literature.

*   *   *   *   *

A most wonderful interruption came in the arrival of Professor J. L. Hromadka from Princeton. We were all rejoicing that
he was returning to assume his duties as a professor of dogmatics.
He came to visit Father shortly after his arrival in Prague, and we
served tea. It was a moving reunion. Hromadka was a master of
words. When he arrived, he embraced father and spoke most eloquently about my mother, about her comprehension of our culture,
and her tremendous investment in the lives of the students. As Father led him to the living room, Hromadka still had his hand in Father's arm, and was saying. "I come here with a true hesitation. All
the way up here, I kept saying to myself, how can I ever thank
František for what he had endured for our safety?" He went on and
on, and elaborated that he had no illusion about the enormity of
work which Father put into the opening of the University, organiz-
ing the theological faculty, and above all, in putting the extensive
library together again.

Father was touched. He needed to hear those words. The members of the family knew that he was literally killing himself not only in opening the school but also in keeping it running. It meant a great deal to him that the words of appreciation came from Hromadka, but Father quickly dismissed those words of gratitude with exclamation of joy over Hromadka's return, saying over and over again, "We need you! You have no idea how desperately we need you!"

It was time for me to excuse myself. Personally I must register here, that although in the coming months, Hromadka had countless opportunities to express some appreciation to Father in public, he never did so. It hurt me deeply, although Father was too much of a gentleman, and we never spoke about that.

The tea with Hromadka lasted over two hours, and as Hromadka left, I could sense that Father was terribly disappointed. Obviously Hromadka wanted to be reinstated as a full time professor with pay, and at the same time Hromadka felt duty bound to finish his turn at Princeton, and simply could not plan on being a part of the faculty until the Fall semester of 1947. Here was something typical of Hromadka. Because of his world fame, as in the days of Munich, he came to ask for help, but at the same time he dictated the terms. Father was crushed. He counted on Hromadka's help. At that time the faculty desperately needed him, and the nation needed him not in Princeton but in Prague. That was not on Hromadka's mind. He planned to spend the summer in his homeland, to give a number of lectures, to observe the scene and the prospects of the struggle between the Communist and the Democratic forces, and then to return to Princeton, and lecture on the vitality of the East and the decadence of the West.

Shortly after Hromadka's arrival, he gave a major speech in the largest hall in Prague, in Lucerna Palace, on Wenceslaus Square. The leaflet which was given to passers by on Wenceslaus Square described Hromadka as a very intimate friend of President Benes as well as of the leaders of the Communist world. In those days strange things did happen, I have no idea who published those flyers, but both Mirko and I were given one, and felt like going to a political pep rally rather than to a presentation by a theologian. To our great relief, the members of the government, or even the representatives of the political parties were nowhere in sight. That made the lecture for us doubly important. The immense hall was packed, it was a true gathering of the Protestant Zion, and Hromadka, introduced by his brother-in-law, seized the moment, and was seductively brilliant. This lecture which of course was delivered in different forms at different times and places during that summer, summarized Hromadka's basic conclusions: the world which we had known before Munich simply was forever gone. The Munich pact of the Western Powers with Hitler was only a manifestation of the mortal illness of Western civilization. Ever so masterfully Hromadka described the mood and the spiritual orientation of the West, effectively quoting the last letter of the much loved and admired writer Stefan Zweig, written only hours before his tragic suicide. He survived the years of exile, and committed suicide, simply unable to face the awesome responsibilities of the post war world, admitting that he did not possess the unusual strength needed to make a new beginning. His best strength was exhausted by the long years of homeless wandering. The hall was silent. Hromadka had us in his hands.

It must be said that Hromadka always spoke from the world's perspective. He mentioned that in such a city as Marseille there was nothing but prostitution and the black market. When Hromadka used the words, "the leaders of the world are saying to us . . . ", he put it in such a way, that one actually believed that he was a buddy, buddy friend with them.

Over and over again Hromadka warned us not to count on some resurrection of the dead culture and moral values, but to have eyes open to the enormous vitality of the political East, and above all to our own immense opportunity and responsibility in a truly revolutionary epoch of the world. Hromadka unmistakenly elaborated Jesus Christ as the new beginning, as the ground of hope, and at the same time he pointed out that God was not necessarily stuck with us, and that if we were unwilling to be the instruments of his peace and justice, God may use others to establish a just social order.

Mirko and I were deeply stirred by the address and were among the first to be on our feet, giving a standing ovation to our theological giant. There is no question that Hromadka was inspired and that he spoke to our hearts, but strangely enough, it took me years, and the help of the analytical minds of Reinhold Niebuhr and particularly of Hromadka's truly close friend, and my dear mentor, Dr. Matthew Spinka, to understand that already at that time Hromadka used a completely different yardstick for the people of the political West and for the people of the political East. He could speak convincingly about the moral stench of the Western cities, and could not smell the horrid stench of the moral deterioration of the Soviet armies along the embankments of Vltava or in any Soviet city. That was, as we shall later point out, Hromadka's tragic shortcoming in his perception.

*   *   *   *   *

Shortly after Hromadka's first appearances, Father left for his glorious reception of a doctorate at St. Andrews, and then he spent about four weeks lecturing at universities which were dear to him from his student years, and finally he settled in Cambridge. The Commission on International Affairs of which Father was a member, was meeting there to work on the position paper for the opening session of the World Council of Churches in Amsterdam in 1948. In the shambles of Europe, and throughout the world, with great joy the Christians were rediscovering the word "ecumenical." Many spoke eloquently about the scandal of the broken Christendom, but today nobody can even imagine the enormous, exhausting, pioneering work of those who stood at the cradle of the ecumenical movement. Even in Czechoslovakia, for the first time since the 15th century and the Hussite wars, the Catholics and Protestant sat together around the same tables at ecumenical work sessions. The young people from different churches traveled afar to reason together and to hope together. Even the least hamlet boasted an ecumenical council, and at least one ecumenical service a year. In those days when the Christians yearned to present a united front, my Father developed a beautiful friendship with cardinal Josef Beran whom I like to remember as a man of great humor and good will. When he laughed, his biretta seemed to dance with joy on the top of his head. A horrendous tragedy gave the World Council of Churches its birth. It seems incredible to me that in a short fifty years the word "ecumenical" has become stale. It was the painful task of the church historians to research "the contribution" of the churches of the political East, the zest of the representatives of the new emerging nations to get rid of the yoke of the European theological and organizational leadership, so that for a while the organization became almost bankrupt and ineffectual. My Father would never believe this. The world ecumenical movement was very dear to his heart, and when he was dying as a reject of the communist system and of those who not only tolerated it but defended it, he was upheld by prayers and messages from ecumenical brothers and sisters far away. The ecumenical movement is bound to come to its second, or third birth, and the burying ground of the best is not necessarily destined to be the place of its rebirth.

While Father was in England two major goals were accomplished. First of all the parquet floors in our house were stripped and polished so that they were shining as the floors a Versailles. It took a whole brigade of our theological acquaintances. The work was topped with a big party at which Mirko and I discovered that some of our colleagues could be extremely funny, that they could laugh, that they just carried the ministerial image in such a way that it was less than becoming. It was not a minor achievement, and both Mirko and I felt good about it.

The top achievement was my passing the qualifying exams in world history. For those examinations I really had to memorize and memorize, and until the day of the exams, I realized that there were definite pockets of ignorance in my mind. I was not at all sure about the Thirty Years War, I prayed that I would not get any question from American history because so much happened in such short centuries. As in the preparation for the exams in Czech literature, I kept a journal which was overflowing with questions. I was fascinated by the origins of the labor movement, by the first strikes fought not for higher wages but for the right to have the same number of candles at the funerals of loved ones as the rich. The idea that the rich would have even better chances for eternal life than the poor was too much to bear, the strike was inevitable. I was fascinated by the impact of the Black Death on the religious thought. I could see the revolutionary fervor in John Hus and his predecessors, and could not escape the question: Was John Hus responding to the economic questions from the perspective of the Gospel, or did the economic conditions give birth to the revolutionary fervor of John Hus and of his movement? And again I was turning to the question of political and social responsibility raised in the journal number one, as I was haunted by the thought of John Hus and the consequence of his preaching against the indulgences in Bethlehem Chapel. Several students took his preaching seriously and on the way from Bethlehem Chapel, as they were approached by the sellers of the indulgences, they were infuriated. They attacked the sellers of the indulgences, turned their money boxes upside down, saying, "You are a fraud! We know from Master John Hus that you are liars and exploitationers!" When those students were arrested and condemned to be beheaded, John Hus hurried to the judges and begged them for reconsideration, saying "They are innocent! It is all my fault! they heard me preaching against the indulgences. Please, I beseech you, take my life, I am guilty of the preaching against indulgences, these boys are innocent!" His pleas did not get him anywhere, the students were executed, and all that he could do was to bury them as saints in the crypt of the Bethlehem Chapel. The question of preachers political and social responsibility, and of the readiness to accept the possible practical consequences of one's preaching the Gospel responsibly, loomed big in my mind.

Obviously there were more questions in my mind than answers as I went to take the examinations. My exams were at nine in the morning. Mirko was scheduled at one in the afternoon. Upon the arrival at the University I was told that professor Somebody who was scheduled to examine me was taken ill, that another lecturer would take his place. He appeared shortly and introduced himself as Dr. Zahansky. He was an attractive young man in his thirties, wearing slacks and a rather fashionable sport coat with a tiny emblem of his membership in the Communist party in his lapel. I knew that I passed the written exam very well. In the oral examination I had no difficulty with questions on Commenius, but then came the clincher: President T. G. Masaryk, and the role of the Czechoslovak Legion in the Great Russian Revolution. I was stunned. I knew right away that to give him the answer he wanted would mean to betray the truth and my allegiance to T. G. Masaryk. I stuttered profusely, finally saying that Masaryk's objective was to liberate the Czechoslovak people, to establish an independent State, and to bring the Czechoslovak legionnaires safely home, perhaps under international protection. The legionnaires were caught in the Russian Revolution, and Masaryk certainly did not want them to get involved in a revolution of another State. My examiner was shocked, yes almost furious, and told me that although I did very well, it was very obvious that I was a victim of very dated historical scholarship. He gave me a "B" but with a collegial encouragement and warning to skip repeating the old phrases and taking the Marxist interpretation of history seriously. I was staggered. I was elated by my grade but absolutely morally beaten by the "scholarship" to which I was subjected. As soon as I came home, I placed a call to the Minister of Education, our good friend, Dr. Jaroslav Stransky, ready to report the case, only to receive the information that the Minister was on vacation until the end of the month.

In the afternoon, anxiously I called Mirko over and over again. At last he answered the phone. He sounded absolutely desolate.

"What has happened to you?"

"That idiot flunked me!"

"He did what?"

"He flunked me because I did not know anything about Lenin."

I burst into an uncontrollable laughter, but Mirko was not in any laughing mood, he was ready to kill.

"Well come on and spend the night. Bring the guitar, and you can learn to play balalaika from Boris."

"Perhaps," he said and he was at our door in an hour.

For Mirko this was a hard pill to swallow. Of course he was ready to fight it in the party, he was ready to write an article about the examinations for the daily papers, and I had to beg him to quiet down, not to take any hasty step until we could consult with Father. Mirko was ready to forget the whole world, and Boris provided for him a wonderful diversion. It was amazing what wonderful music these two could make together. Boris was a good teacher and Mirko was eager to master the balalaika. Late in the evening I just could not keep my eyes open, and went to bed, while the two moved out doors and continued in their duets until the morning hours. I tried to sleep but they were happier and noisier minute by minute, as if they were singing right under by bed. Impulsively I went to my bathroom, filled a big bucket with water and poured it over the heads of the two balladeers. Of course, they would not be intimidated, and my deed resulted in a first class pillow fight near my room, and finally in a truce. We needed that playfulness and laughter.

It took Mirko several days to recover from his academic down fall, and the celebration with Boris. I was not willing to stay another minute in Prague and was busily packing to leave for the homestead. We made plans for Mirko's coming to the homestead and for a joined concentrated study of the biblical languages. We planned to take the exams in Hebrew in September. After that we were hoping for a period of total Shalom.

My sister, Bohunka, and her husband were already at Vir. Every day somebody was arriving, the homestead was full of laughter. Although the harvest was very poor that year, the current bushes were getting red, the cherries were ripe, and the apples and pears were gently telling us that this would not be just a summer for leisure. At last I had a few days for myself, and since Bohunka was in charge of the kitchen I had no responsibility. I slept late, spent the days swimming in the river, basking in the sun and actually finishing the reading of *Gone With the Wind*. It was good to be at home, it was good to be alive.

IN PRAISE OF THE YEAR 1946

The late Henri Nouwen passionately used to remind us that we are authentically human only when we feel insecure. When, in obedience to the Gospel, we dare to go into the unknown, looking for the land of promise, the world according to God's design. Only as pilgrims, who are able to leave the safety of our positions and of our possessions, as well as the approval of society, said Nouwen, can we know the creative insecurity, and the amazing grace of having nothing to count on but God alone. Nouwen convincingly argued, that whenever we are extremely comfortable, we are in spiritual danger, and that perhaps voluntarily we ought to seek a departure from safety. He himself, of course, never settled in the ivory towers of famous universities permanently, and just when he was getting heavy doses of praise, he seemed to be on the move.

When I recall my life, especially after reading Nouwen, with a definite sense of sin, I unashamedly admit there were days and years when I felt that I had enough of creative insecurity for a lifetime, and when I yearned for days without acute anxiety. The social scientists observe the so-called self-made men and women, who finally make it and then passionately protect and defend their shangrilas of security The idea of creative insecurity is the last thing they desire, they want to rest in their "hard earned" security. Scarlet O'Hara in one of her desperate moments swore that she would do absolutely anything not to starve again. One cannot blame or judge the people who remembering the days of starvation or persecution never outgrow the fear of a possible repeat experience.

Over a decade, the members of my family wore clothing made up of old clothing. It was a great discovery for us that an old winter coat, taken apart, cleaned and ironed provided perfectly good material for a "new" coat, using the fabric on the opposite side which was not worn! Indeed we learned the art of making things out of nothing. Every year before Christmas the attic was a treasured reservoir of ideas and of materials. Oh, the precious old laces, pieces of furs, the old velvet evening coats which so easily were transformed into luxurious bathrobes. It was fun for us all to give Father for Christmas a dark maroon, brocade smoking jacket lined in a fine wool, all made from mother's old outfits. There is no doubt in my mind that in these experiences were the roots of our pathological reluctance to dump old things. To this day the children of our children mimic us in saying, "You never know when you may need this."

No, I had never considered myself a self-made man, indeed, as the days of renewed stability were returning, I cherished every day as a special gift of God, and I lived in a sense of a continuous amazement. The rationing of food was almost over, and in the kitchen everything seemed to be under control. Ironically, however, as our physical needs decreased, our eyes were opened to all the neglect of the years, suddenly we saw the draperies which were falling apart, the rooms which needed to be painted, the furniture which needed to be replaced. Indeed here was the danger of being as Martha, "anxious about many things," and not about that one most important thing, or as Henri Nouwen pointed out the danger of our spiritual hunger becoming secondary, the danger of being spiritually desensitized. Yet, if I had read Nouwen in 1946 just when we began to enjoy living again, I think I would have revolted against his idea of voluntarily seeking insecurity. Indeed, it seems to me now, that if God Almighty depended on our voluntary departure from the flesh pots of Egypt, he would have to wait eons to accomplish his purposes. Such a man as Moses, at last is reasonably happy in his new life as a refugee in the Midian hills. He has no hope for the world of the pharaohs, his hope is fulfilled in escaping that world. He has absolutely no intention of doing anything except taking care of his flocks. When God tells him that he had seen the great affliction of Israel in Egypt, that he had heard their crying, Moses almost says, "I am glad that at last you have noticed it, and that you will do something about it. It's high time!" No matter how we read that narrative from Exodus, as God calls Moses to be the deliverer, he resists the idea, he wants to protect his safety, he must be pushed against his own will into the role of being the liberator of his people.

The idea of being pushed rather than volunteering, the idea of resisting, the thought of leaving the new safety and being pushed into the insecurity of a new pilgrimage describes perhaps the life's experience not only of myself but of most of us. There are different variations of the same story which tells about a distinguished and much decorated paratrooper. A society lady asked him, "Jack, how many times did you really jump?"

"I never did jump."

"Oh, come now, everyone knows that you are recognized as an outstanding paratrooper."

"That is true," he replied, "but I never really jumped, I was just pushed twenty times!"

I hope that I am not irreverent or flip when in the retrospect of my years, I feel that I am what I am in spite of myself, that every so often my experience of the Holy was in an unexplainable, mighty push.

In January,1947, one of our most distinguished journalists, Ferdinand Peroutka, who spent years in Dachau, called us to count our blessings in his editorial entitled, "In Praise of the Year 1946." I am indebted to the memoirs of our former Minister of Justice, Dr. Prokop Drtina, for sharing Peroutka's thoughts. Yes, we did lose the election to the Communists, but considering their immense power and their treachery in using even former Gestapo men, who were promised their freedom if they issued compromising statements about the leaders of the opposition parties, the Communists, especially in the big centers such as Prague, won by the skin of their teeth. Peroutka in his article ignored the shady deals of the election but went on to elaborate that among all the nations of Eastern Europe, an American journalist painted us white, that is, as a country in which democracy had a real chance. Peroutka pointed out that in 1946 the decision was made whether we would be a democratic or a totalitarian state. There is no doubt, wrote Peroutka, that ugly totalitarianism had not disappeared, but it is important for us to see the tone of the total development, which in 1946 realized what we had hoped for, the synthesis of the new economic order with the old cultural and moral ideals of Europe. What is won, has to be defended. In 1946 at least four democratic institutions were realized, and we had better be grateful for that. First, we had a free election. Although we are still in a revolutionary mood, the nation returned to the tradition of free elections. When we compare our situation in the present election campaign with the situation in Yugoslavia, Bulgaria, Poland or Rumania, we realize that indeed we belong to the family of nations in which freedom has a chance.

The unanimous election of Dr. Edward Benes as president of Czechoslovakia, has to be counted as a confirmation of democratic tendencies, because the election of Benes also means the acceptance of his program.

The biggest triumph of the year was in the establishment of the rule of law, even when there was a considerable controversy about the trial of the traitors. It was decided in this year of 1946 that the court is the court, not an institution of political lynching. The validity of the law was placed above the noisy voice of the street. It must be recognized also that these achievements would be totally impossible if the leadership of the Communist party was unwilling to submit to the rules of the democratic procedures.

This summary coming from Peroutka, a man committed to democratic principles was most encouraging. Indeed, there was a wide spread opinion that a cooperation with the Communists was possible. We all enjoyed a definite break from the election warfare, at the same time, we had plenty of reasons to believe that the Communists would be defeated in the election of 1948.

On a personal level, 1946 was the happiest year in the post war era. The dreaded exams in Hebrew, Greek and Latin, were almost forgotten, and with all seriousness I plunged into theological studies. I carried a very heavy load but I really enjoyed these studies, although taking courses with my father was not a pleasant experience. Dad was a good lecturer. There was only one girl in our large class and I shall always remember Dad's opening of his lectures, "Miss Molnar and gentlemen. Last time . . ." As much as I enjoyed his lectures, I surely dreaded taking examinations with him. He was very much aware of it, and although I hardly ever talked with him about it, the pietists among the students treated me as an *enfant terrible* and generally made my life miserable. Nevertheless, Father was proud of me. Considering my truly brilliant brother, and sisters, it was a new experience.

Mirko and I enjoyed the flourishing cultural life in Prague. Once a week, every Tuesday, we went to the symphony, and on Saturdays we often enjoyed some great theater performance. We both agreed that we would go to every performance well prepared, that is, knowing something about the composer, the score, and the circumstances under which the music was composed. After some great performances such as Haydn's *Creation* with Rafael Kubelik conducting, we would walk for blocks without saying a word. There was, at that time, a truly remarkable crop of new Czech actors and actresses, who made some performances of the classics unforgettable for us. We fell in love with the plays of Chekhov and Ibsen but also the new production of Goethe's *Faust*, and Shakespeare's plays marked our souls. These cultural enrichments became a part of us just at the time when theology occupied our souls and when both of us jumped into the, at times, discouraging study of Kierkegaard. It was not surprising that after some performances we stopped at some cafe and talked till late hours. More than once some friends from college days joined us. We enjoyed the company of people from diverse disciplines of study so much that we formed a group and met once a month in a private room of the Hotel Belvedere to share a supper and some lively conversations. There were quite a few mathematicians and scientists in our group, balanced by a number of young artists. Of course, Mirko and I, were the only members of the group who studied theology, and what pleased us was that after the absence of several months these friends not only accepted us as quite normal, but also that they asked gutsy questions, forcing us to think, giving us an excellent preparation in apologetics.

Mirko finally resolved his continuing warfare with Alena. It was a tearful parting, but shortly Mirko struck another match with a delightful girl named Olga. The only trouble was that Olga was commuting to the University from a small town about thirty miles outside of Prague, and most of the evenings was not available.

One morning as I walked with my father to the University, he asked me whether or not I noticed on the bulletin board the announcement about the scholarship to Hartford Theological Semi-

nary in Hartford, Connecticut. He was surprised that I had no idea
what he talked about, in fact, he scolded me for not studying the
bulletin board, and then not only did he encourage me to read the
announcement, but strongly recommended that I should apply for
that scholarship, telling me that a year in the USA would mean a
tremendous enrichment for me, and an overcoming of my provincialism. I had no idea where Hartford was, I could not even find it
on my little map, and I did not want to move from Prague even an
inch. Nevertheless, when Father had an idea, he could be a pest.
Day by day he asked me about my thoughts, and about getting the
application until at last, I filled it out and sent the application, being absolutely convinced that I would not get the scholarship anyway, wanting to get over my Father's dream for me.

The summer of 1946 was absolutely glorious. The whole
family with assorted friends was at the homestead. Of course, the
center of attention was Bohunka's newborn son. My brother Blahoslav was engaged to a delightful young woman whom I dearly
loved. They were planning to get married in October. Ambassador
Cisar and his family next door to us were back again after their
years in exile; the Minister of Education, Dr. Jaroslav Stransky
again occupied his villa, and our tennis court was again the scene
of dramatic matches. In the evenings a lot of politicking was going
on, and although nobody had any illusions about what the Communists were capable of doing, there was a general feeling that democracy had a chance in Czechoslovakia.

The kitchen was like a factory for the production of straw-
berry, currant, and gooseberry jams and apple sauce from early apples. We took turns at a large fruit mill, and the whole house was
permeated with a delicious fruit aroma, cinnamon and fine herbs.
We were mighty glad when Mirko arrived, because just that year
Father's bees worked over time, and Father really needed help with
the processing of honey, a job which all of us hated, Mirko, on the
other hand, had a tremendous patience, and actually enjoyed working with the old dean who always rewarded him with a supply of
honey for his family for the winter. That year my father also had
the idea of producing fine liquors from honey and fruit for our
Christmas giving and home consumption, a project which was
largely successful except that some of the spirits in the bottles

which were scattered all over the house, did not follow the recipe, fermented much earlier than expected, and exploded, usually in the middle of the night, with the sound effects of the last offensive on the Western front, and making an enormous mess to clean. Nevertheless, Father was very proud of the ultimate outcome of this project.

As always at the homestead, our days were divided between work, swimming, playing tennis and late suppers. Usually late in the afternoon we all gathered in the orchard in the shade of the old apple trees for some libation. It was hardly ever an intimate gathering but usually a group of twelve or fifteen. One afternoon our dog interrupted our siesta with ferocious barking and running toward a man who was arriving on a bicycle at the small gate to our orchard. It was a dear friend of our family, the Postmaster, Lada Stastny, the son of the owner of the local inn keeper. Lada was a loud, rapidly talking eccentric, who "confidentially" loved to be the first to have the news and then to have a chance to broadcast the news. He sorted the mail, and when we came to get the mail, he informed us about a letter in the pile, at times embarrassing us, in front of many people in the Post Office saying, "Be careful, there is a letter from the President to your Father." Of course, our neighbor, Dr. Stransky who was a member of the government of the Czechoslovak Republic had real difficulty with Lada, because he was presiding not only over the mail which was to be delivered to surrounding villages, but the Post Office was also the telephone and telegraph office, which meant that Lada knew the content of every telegram, and most of the time he knew also the content of the telephone conversations. Nevertheless, Lada had a heart of gold, and we could always count on his help, a true lover of democracy, a student of Masaryk. Whenever Lada arrived at the homestead before five o'clock, it meant he locked the office and endeavored to deliver a telegram personally. Of course, he knew the content of the telegram, and his smile, or his serious look revealed whether or not he was the messenger of good tidings or of some bad news. In those days a telegram in most cases meant the announcement of someone's death, unless of course Lada was smiling and assuring everyone that he was bringing good news. It is reasonable to assume that half of the village already knew that at the Bednář homestead something was happening before Lada arrived. I can see him closing the Post Office, mounting his bike, meeting this one and that one saying, "I'm in a hurry to deliver a cable, yes a cable from the United States to the "little one." Imagine that! A cable to Zdeněk from the United States!" We all welcomed the smiling Lada Stastny, and invited him to join us. He was always glad to do so.

"Well folks, nothing to worry about, but I do have a cable from the United States for Zdeněk. With trembling hands I opened the beige colored cable and read aloud. "I am happy to inform you that you were granted a full scholarship to the Hartford Theological Seminary, Hartford Connecticut. The academic year begins September 15. Sorry about the delay in notifying you. It is understandable that you will arrive late. Please, cable your acceptance as soon as your travel arrangements can be made. Congratulations! Tertius Van Dyke, Dean."

I stuttered, I could not believe it. I handed the cable to my father to translate it. "It's tremendous," Father enthused. "That dean is the son of the famous American poet, Henry Van Dyke." Father translated the cable word by word. I felt devastated, I was so happy that summer at the homestead! I had no desire to move anywhere. My brother broke the silence saying, "Well congratulations! And happy swimming! How else can you get there?"

Everybody laughed. Indeed we were in a most precarious post war situation, and there was no allowance for any extras. Father was silent about that matter, but extremely happy. Mirko looked at me anxiously. He read my mind perfectly, but begged me not to say anything hastily. Later on that night, as we walked along the humming river, he assured me that if I really did not want to go, I could always break my leg at the last minute. At the same time he told me that he was planning to apply for a scholarship to Princeton the following year. "Can you imagine the ball we could have together in the United States? Just think, you will look it over, and then we proceed. Goodness knows, perhaps they would offer another scholarship at Hartford for me. Can you imagine the fun? Don't miss the chance!"

I swallowed hard, the idea of parting with my family and Mirko appealed to me as an offer to enter an international orphanage. To my total astonishment in less than ten days I received the acknowledgement that the World Council of Churches was ready to pay my travel expenses to Hartford, and that I was to start to work on my travel arrangements at once.

I had no choice but to return to Prague and join mostly foreign travelers in making the arrangement for my travels to the USA. I was somewhat surprised that Father who traveled a great deal did not go with me. Obviously he thought I had to learn to take care of myself, considering that in those days no one traveled for pleasure, I was shocked to find out not only that my earliest possible departure was in October but that also the only possible way for me to travel was to fly to Stockholm then to travel by bus to Göteborg where I had to spend several days until the departure of the Gripsholm. The voyage was to take ten days, and I was to arrive in New York on October 28. That meant that I would have to miss the wedding of my brother and that I would arrive at Hartford one month late. How would I ever catch up with the rest of the students in their studies and in English? The only pleasant surprise was that among the elegantly dressed travelers, I noticed a young man who according to his coat was definitely a fellow proletarian. It was a colleague from the University, Jaroslav Stolar, who received a scholarship to Yale. Although I did not know him too well, he was pleasant and he was dating my fellow confirmand Vera, the only daughter of our good friends.

Jarka and I sat down in leather upholstered club chairs, and discussed our problems. After looking at the map of New York and Connecticut we discovered that New Haven and Hartford were not too far from each other. Jarka was worried about how on earth we would get from the harbor, to the railroad station and then to New Haven and Hartford, but I told him that my father assured me that a certain historian, professor Spinka was to meet me in New York, and that undoubtedly he would be glad to take him along. After this conversation we decided to travel together, and we booked our journey. Jarka was a couple of years older and already was known among students as a brilliant biblical scholar who spoke to God "in his native language." Indeed his command of Greek and Hebrew were outstanding. At the same time Jarka was totally unable to distinguish Rembrandt from Picasso, and what was very dear about him was that he was not at all inhibited by his cultural ignorance. That simply was not his field. Although we had very little in common, I liked his childlike sincerity, I trusted him, and I think we were both glad to find one another as we planned to journey into the unknown. Father was extremely gentle and supportive, and asked me to make a list of things I had and of things I really needed. The self study was frightening, I was really in shreds, and did not even possess a suitcase. Even before I discussed the matter with my father, I made a list of things, including my bike, and my phonograph which Mirko quickly sold to his comrades. Just at that time the Communists began to wage an enormous struggle against other parties, demanding more and more socialization of private industry, and confiscation of the property of the rich in general. The economic situation was reaching critical proportions, and the Communists began to accuse all other parties of subversive activities, and of trying to destroy the people's democracy. I know that Father visited president Benes several times, perhaps primarily because of the execution of Monsignor Josef Tiso who was justly charged with treason. The paradox of his wearing the clerical collar and at the same time the red band with a swastika on his right arm, has never disappeared from my memory. Hitler richly rewarded him for his total collaboration. The execution of Monsignor Tiso created a great stir among the Catholics in the world, although the Pope never intervened in the case of Tiso, and to my knowledge never expressed his views after Tiso's execution. I think Father as a jurist wanted Tiso to be tried by an international tribunal. That unfortunately was not possible to arrange at that time, and the case of Tiso was decided probably more by the Slovak Communists than by the court. Although the death of Tiso in certain circles, especially among the Catholics in Canada was commemorated almost as martyrdom, we know now, what we did not know in 1946, namely that Monsignor Tiso was guilty of dragging thousands of Jews to their death, and had he been tried by an international tribunal, he would not have escaped the death penalty. I am sure that at that time there were other problems on Father's mind such as the proposed separation of Church and State. My Father always advocated the separation of Church and State, but the brewing proposal certainly meant something totally different from what we know from the practices in the free world. The Communists were first of all most anxious to confiscate the immense property of the Roman Catholic Church, and although they loudly expounded their readiness to support the people of all faiths, and made far reaching promises of religious liberties, a definite plot against the churches and religious communities spilled out of the secret considerations of the Communists, and became an object of much concern.

Strangely enough I was so preoccupied with plans for my departure that I hardly remember the political drama of those days. What surprised me most of all was that Dad was ever so understanding of my needs. Everybody in the family knew that in the war times we had depleted our resources to survive. Just securing insulin on the black market for my sister Nadia meant a fortune. We never regretted the money spent, we survived, we were alive, and we were ready always to celebrate that. At the same time, both the homestead, and the house in Prague screamed for essential repairs for which there were no funds. As far as my needs were concerned Father acted as if he printed money, and he insisted that I would buy good suitcases, that I would order from our tailor a good winter coat, a raincoat, and two suits. A woman in the neighborhood was to sew some shirts and pajamas for me. I could not believe how much money I needed to secure the material on the black market alone, and I felt ashamed of the time wasted on fittings for the dear old tailor, Mr. Slama. My biggest problem was to secure at least one decent pair of shoes. Having no luck, sheepishly I suggested to my Father the idea of removing the leather from two of our dining room chairs and asking Ruzena's husband, at the homestead, to make two pairs of shoes for me. Dad did not blink an eyelash, and after taking a few trips to the homestead, I did have two beautiful pairs of shoes, one pair black, one pair brown.

As the day of my departure was approaching, I was concerned about the very sentimental mood of my father. Almost every day, as we talked about my stay at Hartford, he was near tears, always elaborating the idea that we never know the number of our days, that I had to accept as a possibility the idea that we would never meet again. I was distressed, I did not know how to handle those conversations. My effort to change the tone of the conversation did not work, in fact, Dad often scolded me for refusing to face reality. This mood was not getting better as we stepped over into October.

Finally, I put the blame on myself, and told Father that the parting was very difficult for me, and that I begged him not to go with me to the airport. I was very much surprised when he agreed that we would say goodbye at home, and that Vera alone would go with me to the airport.

Of course, our parting at home was dreadful. Father offered a beautiful prayer for me, and then he really fell apart as we were embracing in the hall. I was terribly shaken by the scene, and it took me about twenty minutes of our journey to the Ruzyne airport to gain control of myself. It was very fortunate that at the airport so early in the morning, was not only Mirko and his mother, but also all members of "our group." Vera somehow miraculously arranged that coffee and pastries were served to us all. Consequently, the time passed quickly. I visited with everyone, and the moment came to board the plane. After embracing all, Vera and Mirko were the last. Vera ever so typically whispered to me, "Who cares what people think, if you don't like it there, or if you are unhappy, return home at once!" Mirko literally blessed me but, thank God, managed to smile, wishing me well, promising to see me in the USA the following year.

I hurried up the long stairs to the plane and with a great relief sat down next to Jarka Stolar. He was an avid photographer and asked me to switch places with him so that he could sit by the window and take pictures. I could not care less. I explained that I did not sleep any during the night and that I was most anxious to sleep. Tired, yes, exhausted I was, but sleep I could not. I could not enter any conversation and as a sleep pretender I had the freedom to think about the upsetting parting with my father. I am still thinking about it, and after more than five decades I have the strange suspicion that in October 1946 my father had prefect reasons for his tears. He was not saying, "see you next year!" to his son, he was giving him away. He loved "the little one" so much that he wanted to save him even if it meant a broken heart for him. Since in our family there were never any secrets, this time my father had to keep his plot all to himself . . . No, my father was not sentimental, and as a man of faith he was always an incredible optimist. He certainly proved that to us all during the Nazi era. When the Nazis began to hang their victims, as sorrowful as he was he would remark, "They surely must be short of ammunition." His faith that God's truth was marching on, that His purposes could be upset but never ultimately defeated was the daily affirmation of his prayers during those difficult years. Of course, he often reminded us that God did not work according to our calendar. He was a realist. The people who liked to whine were not his favorites. I shall never forget his sermon on Jacob who in his old age, forgetting all the blessings of his days declared "Miserable were the days of my life."

I saw Father terribly broken when his dearest friend, Consul Jiri Sedmik was beheaded by the Nazis. Sedmik was the Mirko of his life, and he never had such a friend again. At the death of Sedmik, however, we all cried with him, we comforted him, and sat by his knees. When I was leaving for the USA it was all different. He could not control his sorrow, and yet it was his idea that I would apply for the scholarship to Hartford. Against all his, almost Calvinistic principles, he put "the best robe on me" although he could not afford it, day by day he was encouraging me, yes, pushing me. I could understand that perhaps he was overcome by sentimentality. After all; I was the last one of the Bednář clan who was "unattached" but what I could not understand, at that time, was his constant reminder that one never knows what might happen next, his swearing me to secrecy and giving me a code in which we could communicate in case something happened. That was not enough for him. Knowing my flighty temper he actually forced me to compose three letters in the given code. Then there was a long list of acquaintances in Great Britain to whom I could turn in a moment of distress, and in the USA it was a list of friends of friends. Another strange imperative was to put down but also to memorize the meaning of salutations in letters. If the letters started with the words, "My dearest son" it meant that everything stated in the letter meant just the opposite. "I do hope that you will make a special effort to be here for my birthday" meant "under no circumstances try to return." I shall never know his reasoning, but knowing me, my tremendous sensitivity but also my outspoken attitude to the Communists, obviously he took an enormous risk. He wanted me to be as far away as possible until the 1948 elections would be over. He was hoping for the best but at the same time he knew that in 1948 the Czechoslovak democracy could be finished for good. He could not imagine me living again under a totalitarian regime, he was determined to give me a chance just as my mother would have wanted it. There was an enormous greatness in his love for me.

*   *   *   *   *

The inconvenience of taking the journey to New York the long way about proved to be a great blessing in disguise, because I really was not ready to enter the world untouched by Nazism, the horrors of wars, and economic uncertainties. It was easier for me to take it in small doses. My sleep pretending after we left the Prague airport shortly turned into a blissful sleep. Suddenly there was time for a slight and delicious refreshment, and soon afterward we landed in the beautiful, prosperous, clean Sweden. The Czechoslovak National Anthem starting with the words "Where is my home?" describes the Czech land as a land of wondrous beauty. Nationalism does dictate lines of this sort. It is true that there is an amazing amount of beauty in my little native land, but it is an incredible shock to leave the Czech paradise only to realize that there is the paradise of God's creation in whatever direction one goes. A two hour flight from Prague, and one lands in the wondrous beauty of Sweden but one could land in the wondrous beauty of the Austrian Alps, or the Bavarian hills. It is a big lie to sing about one nation which is "über alles," for we are a part of God's wondrous creation which knows no boundaries. My nationalism was being destroyed hour by hour, but most certainly not my spiritual identity. Unquestionably in many ways Prague is a mysteriously, uniquely, beautiful city in its mixture of architecture, in its location in a deep river valley, a city in which stones speak of history. A native of Prague has to get away from it to appreciate it and to demythologize some of the national myths. There are for instance dearly revered buildings such as the National Theatre with a magnificent, proud inscription above its majestic stage "THE NATION BUILT THIS FOR ITSELF." Here is the spectacular uniqueness, a persecuted, Germanized nation, with donations from ordinary men and women, building this enormous building in honor of operatic and dramatic arts, every artist wanting to be a part of the dream of having a big Czech theatre. There is something tremendously meaningful in this fact, which I want always to celebrate, but as a building it does not represent Czechness but rather a desire to prove that we too can have an opera house comparable to Vienna, but once we get out of Vienna, the opera houses are just a variation on the given theme of architecture. The Prague National Theatre is a replica but nevertheless its ethos is unique, one has to get away from it to understand it.

Descending to Sweden, the neutral land untouched by war was a unique experience. Of course, personally I could never comprehend how any country could remain neutral to Hitlerism. It was even harder for me to comprehend when I realized the proximity of Sweden to Norway in which so many people suffered under Nazism, and in which Bishop Bergraf by his position gave Christianity such a wonderful stamp. Nevertheless, Sweden offered a bit of human paradise. As soon as we landed, I felt the tenets of Marxism, and almost convinced myself that indeed "man is what he eats!" I could hardly wait to sit down in the elegant cafe in which we were to await the bus which was to take us to Götesborg. All the temptations of the culinary arts seemed gathered in that cafe. Big baskets of fruit, with bananas, oranges, tangerines, and grapes, lined the top of the glass vitrines featuring incredible arrays of pastries. I had not seen tropical fruit for years, and these big baskets were right in front of me. As a primitive man, I just could not resist touching the bananas to be sure that this was not any still life, or imagination, but a part of real life. Yes, these were real bananas, oranges, tangerines. Incredible! Then came the question of price, of translating the pitiful, almost worthless Czechoslovak crowns into dollars, the humiliation of knowing that all the marvelously printed Czechoslovak paper money practically had very little value. Actually, the exchange then was sixty crowns for a dollar, and a cup of coffee at Stockholm was almost three dollars, a stack of Czechoslovak paper money! Yet I could not resist. All the years of the war I was promising myself a most delicious cup of coffee, topped with a mountain of whipped cream. That's what I ordered, sinfully, unashamedly. It was most delicious, yet my stomach was no longer used to rich food, and after this splurge, I felt so ill, that I never drank coffee with cream again.

A bus took us to our next stop, a delightful Motel on the outskirts of Göteborg. Wonderful rooms, plenty of hot water for showers, after breakfast, buses ready to take one to the city. It was all like a dream. Jarka Stolar was a remarkable traveling companion, never dominating one's schedule, just spelling out his sight seeing desires, and suggesting meeting at such and such a places at a given time for lunch or dinner. On my part, contrary to Jarka's determination to see as much as possible every minute, I was yearning to take it easy, to have the second and third cup of black coffee, and to savor the incredibly high standard of living. Then I just walked up and down the main boulevards from shop to shop, looking at window shops as Alice in Wonderland. In the forties, before the birth of shopping malls, the shop window displays were a professional art in the cities of the world, the posters at kiosks were designed by modern masters. This was a true feast for my eyes. For hours I stood in awe in front of florist shops and gift shops, marveling at the magnificent arrangements and their placements, admiring the sense of color and texture. In every shop window there was something to admire. I visited a number of churches, the extraordinary modern buildings housing the symphony and theatre. Our days were wonderful, and every night Jarka and I had a great deal to share.

The boarding of the ocean liner Grispsholm from the Göteborg harbor was an experience for which we were not prepared. Just about everybody had a farewell party. The champagne corks were popping, the crowds were noisy, there were the sounds of firecrackers and later on fireworks. Along with a great many refugees, mostly young people, orphans, especially from Slovakia and Poland who having lost everything, shared a common hope of finding a new beginning in America, we boarded the ship. All of these people were sponsored by different organizations or by some "rich American uncle." None of us was a tourist. We were asked to board the ship first, to settle in our third class cabins, and then we could observe the festivities from our deck. There was no one to wave good bye to us, but for me as the Gripsholm moved out of the harbor and entered the open sea it was a strong experience. As if glued to the railing of the deck I stood there until the last lights of this European harbor looked like Christmas candles in the wind.

The scenario of the ten days on the luxurious ocean liner to a considerable degree represented to me the drama of a purposeless humankind. I realize, of course, that I am really meant for *terra firma*, but I learned to cope with the discomfort of seasickness, and surprisingly enough I did not miss a single meal! Here was the hellish paradox for me: At last you may take it easy. No work is required. If you wish, you may skip breakfast and sleep all morning. Food is no problem. There is more than enough of the most delicious food on this ship. Most wonderful meals will be served to you in our elegant dining rooms. You will be waited on by our trained stewards who are anxious to hear your needs. You will be assigned to tables, and some people will be strangers to you. Many will speak languages you cannot understand, but understand that they are human like you, yearning to eat and drink and be entertained. You will taste some food you have never eaten before. In the morning, for instance there will be a grapefruit, and you will learn from others how to eat it. Then there will be some cereal. What is that? Most civilized people eat that for breakfast, but also there will be rolls and coffee you like. Every day at lunch and dinner you will discover new delicacies, you will be amazed by the divine lightness of the chocolate mousse or the baked Alaska, yes, a cake with ice cream baked in a hot oven!

One thing will surprise you. Your wardrobe of three white shirts is less than minimal. The favorite pastime seems to be getting dressed to eat. If you have money, you have no problem. Your shirts will be laundered and pressed within hours and delivered to your cabin. In between the meals, plenty of activities are planned for your pleasure.

Of course, to fight the slight discomfort of possible seasickness it is highly advisable to walk round and round the ship. It is also a necessary exercise to develop an appetite for the next meal. Otherwise, there is a library and a wonderful lounge in which you may enjoy reading the books you have always wanted to read. Tea and cocktails are served in the lounges in the afternoon. Notice on the bulletin boards the variety of daily entertainment which include concerts, the screening of the first class Hollywood extravaganzas, square dancing to a live Swedish band, lectures, floor shows, fashion shows. There is a fine fully equipped gymnasium, a number of ping-pong tables, and the constant opportunity to enjoy shuffle board. The casino is open from early afternoon until midnight. The management is also aware of the spiritual needs of the passengers. A chaplain is available to the first class passengers, and Divine Worship services are held in the First Class Lounge every morning at 8:30. The Holy communion is celebrated for the first class passengers at eleven o'clock on Sundays (Although this did not apply to us, the third class Christians, I had some difficulty in translating for myself the words "Divine Service"). The Methodists were scheduled to have a worship service for the Second Class travelers at ten on Sunday (but who are the Methodists?). Just a worship service was scheduled for us the third class passengers at eleven o'clock, no details were given. It was all so shocking that our curiosity did not stop us from at least peaking through the big glass doors into the divine service of the first class. Behold the cocktail table was replaced by a high altar, we could smell a bit of incense, the feeling was definitely churchy, but for the world we could not see anything divine. Luckily Jarka and I were not the only curious Christians standing outside the glass doors. Our own Sunday worship experience left a permanent impression on me. After singing many evangelistic hymns with mighty piano interludes, the preacher assured us of our sin and of our need to repent, so that we might receive the gift of grace. We were sitting in a circle and he asked us to verbalize our sins going round the circle. To this day I recall that I did not know the meaning of the word "adultery." I knew it had something to do with adulthood, but adultery seemed to be the favorite, horrid sin which attracted a great interest in that congregation. Jarka and I were sitting there for an hour in absolute terror. What on earth would we say about our sin in English? Thank goodness the man next to us was such a sinner that we ran out of time and we had to close with a benediction. It may sound quite incredible but before coming to the USA I had no concept of denominationalism, the line was drawn between the majority of the Roman Catholics and a few Protestants of different shadings but such bodies as Episcopalians, Baptists, Presbyterians, Methodists, Quakers, Universalists or Congregationalists, and *ad infinitum*, were totally unknown to me.

Among all the activities offered on this dream boat, I spent a great deal of time learning and finally mastering the game of ping-pong. Jarka and I walked miles talking about important observations, finding life on the Gripsholm intolerable, boring, nauseating. People everywhere yearn for time precisely like that on the Gripsholm, not knowing how hellishly devastating life is when it has no other dimension than pleasure, entertainment, eating, drinking and getting dressed. I was thinking about the scientists who experimented with monkeys and gave them all the toys and food they would enjoy. The first two days the monkeys played to exhaustion, the third day they began to use their favorite toys to hit one another! We could not take it much longer, and when the first seagulls appeared over our heads, we welcomed them most joyfully as the proclaimers of the good news that we were approaching the other shore.

As I was walking round the ship, I was thinking a great deal of Mirko, and felt a strange distance from him, realizing that I could not possibly write him about the Gripsholm, its luxuries, its classes, its glitters and almost total absence of art. It would only confirm some of his false assumptions, and I knew that the experiences on the Gripsholm could not be generalized. Who could possibly comprehend the hidden anxieties among all those "happy" people on the ship? At the same time, I felt a growing resentment of the people at "my table" in whose presence I felt an immense spiritual homesickness, feeling with my whole being that my separation from most of the people on the ship was not a matter of my limited ability to communicate in English but that these people indeed spoke a totally different language of life with a horrid accent on everything that money could buy. Although I could not participate in the dinner conversation and perhaps I was guilty of practicing snobbery in reverse, I did understand much of what was said and I was amazed that these people in their thinking and attitudes were actually pushing me to the thinking of the political left.

Of course, Jarka and I were not the only students or escapees on the boat. There were a great many young people, the lonely survivors who were being sponsored either by distant relatives or by church groups. Most of these young men and women lost their families, their homes, everything, and I marveled at their vitality,

their expectations. One of the great entertainments on the Gripsholm was the Swedish square dancing. The Swedish love to
dance, and when they dance a polka aboard an ocean liner even
when the sea is rough, they seem to defy the law of gravity. I never
tired of watching it and the courage of the young people from different nations in joining the dance. That was the best entertainment
worthy of being recorded on a film. These young people did not
mind making perfect fools of themselves, at times they fell, but
they got up laughing. Among these passengers was a beautiful Slo-
vakian girl named Bozenka. We noticed her already in Göteborg.
She carried two bundles, one small and another large, bulky one.
Her beauty was so distinct that one could not help but stare at her.
Her black eyes were sparkling, her shiny dark hair was braided.
Day after day very proudly she wore her brilliantly embroidered
peasant blouses to the ritzy society tables. I could not stop marveling at her magnanimity. Bozenka could care less what the people
said about her, and every night she put on her ancestral, embroidered headpiece with a big bow at the back. I think she was actually pitying the people around her as if she were saying: They don't
know anything about me, they all paid for their trip, I paid nothing,
simply because someone loves me and has taken compassion on
me. Someone believes that I should have a chance in this world! It
was not at all surprising that a handsome, tall steward from our
dining room, named Carl, fell desperately in love with her. Carl
was a student of philosophy at the Stockholm university. During
summers until October, every year, he was earning spending money by working as a steward on ocean liners. Carl was an interesting
man, and we had long discussions on the deck after his duties. It
seemed only natural that I became a personal messenger of his
notes to Bozenka. The funny thing was that Carl tried to express
his devotion to her in Slovak, and I actually dictated those notes.
The romance flourished especially when Bozenka discovered that
her big bundle containing a small plum tree from the garden of her
much loved grandmother would not be allowed to be taken out of
the ship. Bozenka was desolate. The plum tree was the only thing
she cherished. Suddenly Carl became the hero of her life. He promised to take the tree out for her.

     The last days of our voyage the people seemed more friendly than in the previous days. At last this pleasure trip was almost over. Of course most of the passengers knew where they were going, with us the students, the refugees, it was quite different. I was very much excited when I received a cable from Dr. Spinka: "We shall be awaiting you at the pier. My wife will be wearing a yellow suit."

Considering the number of passengers on the ship, and if everyone was awaited by two or three people, there would be a considerable crowd. The crowd at our departure in Göteborg was enormous. How would I ever find a woman wearing a yellow suit?

The approaching arrival in New York was tremendously exciting. Of course, the night before our landing in New York the Captain gave the usual balls, and indeed in all the dining rooms splendid jazz bands played until the morning hours, but those of us who were arriving in New York for the first time decided to spend the second half of the night on the deck, wanting to see the outline of New York and the Statue of Liberty first. It was cloudy and drizzling, and even when I wore a trench coat I felt chilly, but it was worth waiting for the incredible sight of the shimmering lights of New York City in the distance. Soon the mysterious awesome structures and shapes of many lights gained the shape of skyscrapers. Jarka and I stood in silence by the railing recognizing the famous buildings, known to us from postcards, and films. It reminded me of the magic of Christmas Eve, when the Europeans turn on the lights on their Christmas trees for the first time.

After that, the Statue of Liberty was a disappointment due to my own misconceptions. Of course, I saw somewhere a picture of the famous statue but that was long, long ago, and in my mind freedom was as fragile and beautiful as a Dresden figurine, and here was this massive, shapeless colossus, a woman hiding her waistline with folds of her gown. The Gripsholm stood still in the vicinity of the Statue of Liberty for hours, since we were shrouded in a heavy fog. The dining room officially closed right after breakfast when we were suppose to embark, and at two in the afternoon we were still in the same place. The Gripsholm was howling, the Statue of Liberty was then only a massive silhouette, but suddenly there was something tremendously strong in that sight. In the depth of the fog one could hardly see anything, but one was deeply aware of the presence of the Statue of Liberty, strong, massive, unmovable never obliterated by any historical fog. I began to feel that perhaps that was the intent of the artist, and fell in love with that fat lady.

After a sleepless night, a hurried breakfast, and then hours without any nourishment we were slightly wobbly as we walked out of the Gripsholm with our heavy suitcases to the customs.

In one of my suitcases I had an old and very lovely cut glass bowl which I wanted to give to the Spinkas for their great kindness to us. The custom officer removed it from my suitcase and admired it with a deep appreciation, and then he said "That will be five dollars!" I just about broke into tears since, as I remember, I had only twelve dollars. Seeing my reaction, the man put his hand on my shoulder and in perfect Czech said to me, "Go on, you fool, a Czech has a brother in every port. I felt just like you feel, when I came thirty five years ago. Enjoy America!" I was so shocked by this incredible experience that I almost missed the most important miracle, namely noticing the unknown lady in a yellow suit!

The Spinka's welcomed us most graciously. When they heard that we had had nothing to eat since breakfast they took us to some buffet for a quick bite, and then we drove in incredible traffic, seeing the endless ribbons of headlights of cars going in both directions.

As a novice I certainly could not imagine the exhaustion of the Spinka's after their waiting for us in New York almost all day, and then driving in the horrid traffic and drizzly weather, first to drop off Jarka at Yale in New Haven, and then to their home in Hartford. After saying good night and some words of appreciation, I literally crashed on the bed in a beautifully appointed bedroom, but I did not sleep well. In my ignorance I did not know the sounds of American ambulances, police cars and fire engines, and every time one of these woke me up, I was sure that an air raid was at hand and was getting ready to get dressed. Toward the morning all seemed quiet. Then I could sleep forever, but shortly after seven, Mrs. Spinka knocked on the door of my room, saying, "Denny, breakfast is almost ready." I was ready to die . . . I thought that they would surely let me sleep, but being both teachers, totally dedicated to teaching and learning, they were always obedient to the principle. Mrs. Spinka was a delightful witty woman. I had so many practical questions to ask her, but professor Spinka glanced at his watch, and announced that we were expected to meet Dean Van Dyke, and then he would take me to my room, before his lecture. In all my years at Hartford, I do not think Dr. Spinka ever missed giving his carefully prepared lecture. He had a passion for teaching, and expected the students to have passionate interest in learning. Before he left me in my room he said, "In case you get bored after you unpack, you are welcome in any of the classes. And, by the way, we want you to be sure to drop in after supper tonight." Shortly after nine he was gone, and I was left in my room, on the second floor of the main male dormitory: Hosmer Hall. All students were in classes, the building was silent. I looked around my room. It was a sunny, lovely room with two windows facing the big lawn in front of Hosmer Hall. Although it was October 29, the grass was green and free of leaves. All the buildings were built in the style of British universities, and Hartford in the fifties, in its scholarship, ecumenicity, and in world wide sense of community; while maintaining all the niceties of the Western world was far more British than American. My room! I really had to convince myself that it was my room. There was a good rug on the floor. The furniture consisted of an easy chair, a desk, a dresser, a bookcase and a bed which waited to be made. To my astonishment, I realized that every student was expected to bring bed linens, blankets and a bedspread. Nothing of that sort was in all the literature from Hartford and in spite of all my planning the suitcase was full of dirty laundry. As I contemplated what to do, I heard the sound of organ music, and soon wonderful, enthusiastic singing was coming from the open windows of the Chapel across the lawn from Hosmer Hall. I was thrilled, and then strangely petrified at the same time. I could not believe my ears but the first hymn I heard in Hartford was the hymn, "Not Alone For Mighty Empire," a lovely melody but a melody which the Nazis desecrated and used for their national anthem "Deutschland, Deutschland Über Alles," a melody I swore I would never sing again. My heart was beating fast but soon came the singing of a melody which was not familiar to me, a melody capable of quieting one's turbulent spirit, "Dear Lord and

Father of Mankind, Forgive Our Foolish Ways." The poetry of Whittier, who wrote that hymn, was not familiar to me, but it welcomed me to America, and it has always been one of my truly favorite hymns.

PART II

THE TABLE IS PREPARED BEFORE ME

Although my first days in Hartford meant one humiliation after another, and as my mother would say, "I did not represent myself too well," my memories of the Hartford years are bright, touched with the dew of happiness unknown to me before. For the first time in my life I lived in a dormitory. The university was not a place to come and go, but a place to live in a community of men and women from all corners of the world. The brochure which was sent to me to Prague, described Hartford as a "University of Religion," undoubtedly an exaggerated term, but Hartford Theological Seminary, at which I was to study, in those days indeed was only a part of an institution which effectively brought together scholars and students of different disciplines, the men and women preparing for ministry or biblical or theological scholarship, those who were trying to learn how to apply the educational principles to church life, studying at the School of Religious Education, a true pioneer in early childhood development, which more than fifty years ago maintained an exemplary laboratory day school, in which the learned principles were tested in practice. Other members of the Hartford academic community were the Kennedy School of Mission, known especially for its outstanding department of Islamic studies and the School of Social Work, where the scholars studied the ethos of that era. Since the students were not only encouraged, but to a point required, to take some courses in each of these interrelated schools, and all meals were shared together, the students knew each other, and the professors certainly knew the students. At the very first glance, I realized that I was in an unique place of a true international ecumenicity in which denominationalism was set aside, and in which scholars were united by a common purpose. In the thirties there were two students from Prague before me at Hartford. The first one was Jan Dus, who gave us an enchanting translation of Henry van Dyke's *The Other Wise Man* into Czech; the other one was F. M. Dobias who occupied the chair of Systematic Theology before I left Prague. Dobias was dearly loved at Hartford for his charm and was affectionately remembered as, "dear Dobie," consequently I had someone with whom to compete! One of my first visitors, was an aging couple, the former classmates of dear Dobie. They brought me some gifts and all they wanted to know was about Dobie. They were all wrinkles, wobbly and quite pathetic, as they were repeating for me that the happiest days of their lives were spent at Hartford, and they wished that Hartford would give me the same. All I could see were their wrinkles, their unsteady steps, their past tense orientation, and I whispered to myself: May the Lord deliver me! While these people remembered nostalgically the past, I was still hoping for some better things to come, yet I think that most of us who studied at Hartford and participated in that international, interracial community set in the park like setting near the plush West Hartford, will recall Hartford, in spite of its slightly blue nosed snobbishness, as a liberating and formative force.

The first days in Hartford were a hell for me, one disaster after another; a very proof that something good can come out of a total chaos.

*   *   *   *   *

My first glimpse of my future fellow students was as delightful as the sudden outburst of spring flowers. They emerged from their classrooms, laughing or engaged in lively conversation, and in a minute the big lawns were covered with the blossoms of bright yellow, blue, red, orange, pink sweaters and cardigans, covering the white, black, bronze skin of the students. What a difference from the blue, gray suits and ties of my colleagues in Prague!

My immense excitement was interrupted by two sharp knocks on my door, my first visitor arrived, a Swiss student named Maurice, who was obviously instructed to welcome me and to show me around. He insisted on speaking French, assuming that all Europeans were multilingual civilized people, but at every step I was proving to him that I was a very much a *"specie vulgaris."*

Maurice was a rather uninteresting looking man but he had a quick, endearing smile. Without much ado, he perceived my bedding dilemma. He laughed. Quickly he left my room and just as quickly he returned with an armful of pillows, and bedding, immediately proceeding to demonstrate the art of American bed making. There was no blanket, but I could care less. The room was warm and in the worst case I did have a winter coat to toss over me. Maurice also helped me to solve the second problem, the suitcase full of dirty laundry. "Do you have a laundry bag?"

For the world I did not know what a laundry bag could be, and I did not have one. We made our journey three flights down to the laundry room carrying soiled clothing in a pillow case. By that time, the students were coming down for lunch and I was introduced to many on each floor. The introductions by Maurice were formal, "May I present. . . ." And "How do you do," followed with such embellishments as, "I just love Smetana's *Moldau*" or "Prague must be a beautiful city," or, "You must tell us about Lidice."

As I am writing these lines I realize that during the last fifty years the people of the USA really discovered much of the Slavic culture. Was it because the USSR suddenly had to be taken seriously, or was it because more and more, in the euphoria of the newborn United Nations, we were aware of our interdependence and of the emergence of the global village? Undoubtedly it was a combination of many factors, but the people stopped talking about "Böhmishe Mädchen," the Bohemian girls as outstanding and cheap housekeepers, and it became quite chic among the cultured to talk about Bolshoi, or Kirov ballet, and about the splendor of the Russian literature. Mrs. Onassis in connection with the publication of a book on Russian art which she edited, helped to sponsor a spectacular exhibit on Russia in the Metropolitan in New York. Who would ever forget the enchanting staging at the entrance to the Metropolitan: A lovely, hand crafted troika carriage, the door of the back seat a jar and on the maroon velvet upholstery long white kid gloves and a bunch of violets. Thousands, including myself stood in line in front of the Metropolitan to see the Russian masterpieces. At colleges Russian studies became very much "in," the great orchestras began to play, Smetana, Dvorak, Martinu, and

Janacek, and after all the decades, they made it to all major opera houses. Just today before writing these lines I read in the *Washington Post* (January 98), an article, "Czech Dogs Are Better for K-9 Duty." The article points out that the Czech German shepherds are stronger, friendlier than others, they provide the least problems. "These dogs are social and you can pet them. They also hold up better physically, they are capable to endure stress. It's like the difference between a truck and a car. The handlers, however, must address them in Czech. For this reason the Maryland State Police ordered number of these dogs from the Czech Republic." This is really going to the dogs, all we need is to ask the world breeders to change the paradoxical name of Czech German shepherds into Czech shepherds, but this is surely a great, positive development from the fifties when the Czechoslovakians were known especially as good workers described by Marcia Davenport in her *Valley of Decision*, the producers of Pilsner beer, of fine glass and costume jewelry, the people who gave us the "Beer Barrel Polka" in the dark hours of the World War II, the nation of Dr. T.G. Masaryk, who was a son of a serf and became a much loved and admired President of the slightly primitive Czechoslovak people who love to dance and to wear peasant, embroidered costumes. I had some fleeting moments of this perception, and I felt that I was a disappointment in my meticulously tailored double breasted suit, pants with a zipper and not with buttons, or better yet Leder Hosen drawbridge with the rows of buttons and embroidered with the edelweis and poppies! Yes, a good natured woman, shortly after my arrival at Hartford congratulated me on my quick adjustment when at her breakfast table, I helped myself to a banana and peeled it!

This false perception was largely due to foreign, primarily German scholarship which was the source of American research. Such a revolutionary phenomenon as the Czech Reformation with its militant emphasis on social justice, sovereignty of people under the sovereign Lordship of Christ was interpreted as an insignificant footnote to Wyclifism (Losarth and others). Of course, such a brilliant scholar as Ernest Troeltsch in his *The Social Teaching of the Christian Churches*, rightly guessed that Hussitism had a revolutionary effect on Europe, producing a deep yearning to realize an absolute Christian social order as well as a theology which ought to be researched but even Troeltsch, at the end capitulated, and sighed that the Hussite movement—the knowledge of which in German research was totally inadequate, and the Czech sources were not available. How could a persecuted, germanized nation present its own history? It is easy to say that one of the positive contributions of the forties was that a great many eminent Czechoslovak scholars came to America, escaping Nazism, giving us a new, and growing perception of the Czechoslovaks and of the Slavic people in general.

Maurice was gallantly carrying my dirty laundry in a pillow case, and since we met so many students, the three flights to the basement laundry room took us much longer than expected. For some unknown reason Maurice assumed that I was too tired to eat lunch while in reality I was starving. He glanced at his watch and led me to a room with several washing machines. He explained the procedures to me. It was all very simple and clear. "Voila!" he smiled and was gone.

Americans seem to like giving explicit instructions on their gadgets. It is almost like the old recipe for Irish Rabbit Stew which starts with "First, catch a rabbit!" Quite rightly, I was reminded that I needed soap which was left three flights up in my room, and I also assumed that it was a good judgment to bring down a dictionary to consult it carefully before the count down in this adventure. Everything went nicely. I congratulated myself, and while I was checking on the iron and the ironing board, which, thank goodness, looked quite normal, the washing machine made an awful noise and was overflowing with sudsy water, flooding the room! I wanted to die! A Czech peasant among the fabulous American machines! I heard Maurice returning in the company of my immediate floor companions to whom he wanted to introduce me. One Chinese, one Hawaiian, one black, one student with the Czech name of Bartunek who could not speak Czech. In horror Maurice exclaimed "Mon Dieu!" and everyone frantically dispersed in search of mops while Maurice deftly showed off his technical expertise and stopped the machine.

I was embarrassed, but also afraid that my clothing would be in shreds! My next door Hawaiian neighbor, Dick Chun did not make me feel better when he said with a very serious face, "This will cost you at least one hundred dollars!" Seeing my horror, yes, despair, laughingly he gave me a welcome hug. Thus my future colleagues and I met in the laundry room with mops in our hands and much gaiety. After this disaster I was actually surprised that I was trusted enough to be left alone to give my laundry another try. When I returned to my room with all my shirts starched and ironed, I had a sense of enormous triumph, and since I never ironed a shirt or anything else in my life, I could not tire of looking at my shirts hanging in the closet. Everything led me to my bed just for a short snooze, but I slept soundly until I heard whistling and laughing coming from the nearby shower room. Everyone was getting ready for dinner. Dick Chun stopped in for me, and warned me that he would introduce me to the Dean of Women, Mrs. Lowell, who presided over the meals, and that most probably, according to the custom, she would ask me to sit at her head table for the rest of the week. Dick communicated with me partly in German, mostly with hands, and helpfully repeating the English phrases I did not know.

I followed Dick with some trepidation to the Hosmer Hall dining room, I did not know anything about Dean Lowell, and I wanted to run away, I knew I could charm for a minute, but this was more than an exercise from, *What Do You Say After You Say Hello?*

Hosmer Hall dining room, where all the meals were shared was a big reproduction of a British heraldic hall, with a large protruding fireplace in front of which was the head table with Dean Lowell presiding. Unlike at Oxford where we sat on benches, in Hartford we had comfortable chairs and there was the ritual of seating the ladies. In comparison with meals experienced in dining rooms and cafeterias of other institutions, the dinners at Hosmer Hall were stuffy. All tables were covered with white damask, and at times it seemed to me that there were more plates than food on each table for eight. There was a definite orchestrated procedure. First we gathered in the downstairs drawing rooms and as soon as the big, melodic Chinese gong sounded we went up the large staircase, Dean Lowell usually leading the procession. Each student was assigned to sit at different tables for a week, and once in a while each was given the task of presiding at a table which meant not only to serve meals American family style, which was totally unknown to me, but also to introduce any guest to all at the table and then during the announcements to the whole body.

The students who earned extra money by waiting on tables all wore white, starched fitted jackets and looked as though they were from the Ritz Carlton. At the entrance to the dining room stood the chief steward, a Ph.D. student, with a number of degrees in speech, voice, and Shakespearean acting—an eternal student. He rang the bell again and as the hall fell silent, in a most affected manner he announced that this man or woman would give the grace. When we had British visitors, which was often, he was in his element, giving all titles and places of residence. When there was a visiting scholar, he elaborated to the Almighty, and to us all his or her academic pedigree.

Undoubtedly many of us students resented this formality, for many it meant a threat, but it was accepted as a matter of fact, and as a part of training for our future careers. Of course, this was long before our mugs, the paper bag lunches, the jelly bean society or the time when America rejected a well meaning and gentle president who tried to impress us by turning down the thermostats and was speaking to the nation from the White House, clad in a sweater, not at all understanding that people everywhere, no matter what, like a bit of glitz (the Kennedy and the Reagan era certainly proved it!). This was still an era of propriety in which manners were studied and observed, and whether one was preparing for the parish ministry, or the ministry of education, an academic career or mission assignment abroad or becoming a social worker or an agent of change, we all knew that hospitality was counted as a Christian virtue and would be expected from all of us in the future. The homes of the academic community, and the smallest parsonages of that era indeed were centers of hospitality, and the missionaries teaching in faraway schools and medical facilities were astonished by the fact that the people of the former colonial nations were more formal in manners, more British than the British or more French than the French. In the past Goethe and his *epigoni*, and host of others, lovingly recalled table talks. At times I think of Martin Luther King, Jr., a fellow student at Boston University in my Ph.D. years, and his gentle, polished manners, his wonderful ability to take time to meet a person. How much was plotted at the dinner tables with his colleagues! Lin Yutang, I think correctly, argued that politically much more is accomplished at a dinner table than at a conference table. If the church of today after all those sessions on creative uses of conflict would only understand it!

Regardless of our views or perhaps contrary experiences to those of Hartford, table etiquette, stagings of teas and participating in them, were an intentional part of the curriculum in that institution. Dean Lowell was the dean of etiquette, and waged a vigorous war against anyone who would dare to serve dessert without an underliner! How utterly ridiculous, and yet to this day I dare to believe that the Hartfordians of that era, including our former ambassador to the UN, Andrew Young, were easily recognizable because of this training.

At the risk of being accused of lapsing here into a fit of nostalgia in which one is fantasizing about the past which never existed, this detour is intentional, for I feel a definite pain as I recall the Hartford years and the vulgarization of church and society today. Comparisons are inevitable, and I cannot be fooled by the snobbery in reverse, which seems to suggest that the uniform of jeans is "more with it" than the uniform of a three piece suit. I am not denying that I am a bit shaken when I am presiding over a committee on ministry, I introduce myself to a seminary freshman who is applying for the "in care status" and he replies, "Howdy Denny," as if Christian frolicking, the immediate camaraderie, the first name calling were a proof of Christian stature rather than an outcome of common faith, common cause and struggle. Similarly the most brotherly and sisterly invitations to bring a brown bag lunch so that we can turn to the agenda at once and get it over with as soon as possible, leave me cold. Suppose my heart is bleeding, suppose my wife, my children or grandchildren are going through the valley of death and despair, is that not the agenda of a Christian fellowship? Twelve or fourteen Christian brothers and sisters come together and the idea that we have to plaster ourselves with name tags is bewildering to me. The regulars in the pool room of a tavern across the street do not wear name tags but they care for each other! The paper cups in which hot coffee burns one's fingers, or the styrofoam cups, even when we forget the ecological factor, filled with most aromatic coffee or tea never tastes the same as if served from a cup. Since the parsonages have become private bastions in many of which the front doors are literally boarded to visitors, we hardly know our ministers and their families. Yes, time is a precious commodity, but what have we gained by the time which we have deducted from that hospitable fellowship? What have we gained by the time saved in not writing letters, in not acknowledging gifts and expressions of kindness, in ignoring manners and in the words of Emily in Wilder's, *Our Town* in not looking into each other eyes? Yes, thank God, we are far more open than we were fifty years ago, we are far more action oriented and far more sophisticated in seeking change in our society than we used to be but at the same time, perhaps we have been so adamant in condemning the dehumanization of this technological society that we have not noticed the dehumanization of our own, this dehumanization in which we have been desensitized, in which everything is justified by pure desire to be accepted on our own terms. The result is that we are unattractive to those whom we want to attract and that our mainline churches are marked with an immense loneliness which puzzles the psychiatrists especially as they deal with clergy.

The Yale professor of Law, Stephen L. Carter in his recent book, *Civility, Manners, Morals and the Etiquette of Democracy* underlines that civility is not a matter of choice or of individual right. He reminds us that unlike the Europeans, who held that good manners were the property of the upper classes, the Americans believed that everybody could learn etiquette. Yes, in the last century etiquette was taught in public schools using such text books as Irvin Beadle's (1859) volume, *Dime Book of Popular Etiquette* and that even Americans who never read any other book studied manners, knowing that if you want to be somebody in America, you must learn to mind your manners. As he observes the illusion that all desires are rights, he writes, "Respect for rule of conduct has been lost in the deafening and essentially empty-talk of our age. Following a rule of good manners may mean doing something you do not want to do, and the weird rhetoric of our self-indulgent age resists the idea that we have such things as obligations to others. We suffer from what James Q. Wilson has described as the elevation of self-expression over self-control."[9] For Carter, civility, manners, etiquette are the ways we treat one another.

Well, we all have our mugs but the end result is that our

grandsons and granddaughters leave their spoons in their cups or dessert dishes, and we stare at them, and worse yet, the graduates with high honors go for their first job interviews with fear and trembling for the meeting is bound to be followed by a lunch or dinner at a country club, and the potential boss may encourage one to have oysters on the half shell, and the subject of the conversation may be the staging of the last production of *Carmen*. Ministers know the terror of being interviewed by committees of "prestigious" churches, and they come to us old timers with such trivial questions as, What shall I wear?. What silver should I use when? I am always astonished by the admonition of my wife, "Just use logic, common sense, or follow the hostess."

Thanks to my upbringing, I have never felt this terror as I dined in big houses of all kinds of Zaccheuses, who in their isolation and loneliness yearned to atone and to do something good. I have never felt uneasy when by the sheer forces of fate I had to deal with the magnates. They sensed it, accepted me, and I discovered in their hearts a certain readiness to serve the common good, which I did not find elsewhere, and I learned enormously from their hard work, and perception. My Hartford years were always to my advantage, never a stumbling block in dealing with those in power whose help I needed in my ministry. In this sense, Harry Emerson Fosdick fully understood what only now, with the help of social and political scientists do we begin to understand, namely, that the poor cannot help themselves, that empowering them and promoting their needs does not bring about the desired change. Martin Luther King, Jr. largely won a bloodless revolution when in a critical moment he demonstrated his moral stature by saying, "We must not lose faith in our white brothers. Somehow we must believe that the most misguided among them can learn to respect the dignity and worth of all humanity."[10] In those days he gained wide support not only of academia but also of the many powerful, influential whites: the day of march has come. Likewise, our task is to scrutinize the rich and the powerful, to touch their hearts without being judgmental and moralizing, or using the "We don't care what you think" shock therapy. Martin Luther King, Jr. is a case in point in my departure of thought. He never lost an iota of his appeal to his people by adhering to the niceties, impeccable manners of the black elite of his family. His speech was articulate, his manners never offensive to those who felt that they had him in their hands. Study his photographs as he goes to jail, as he leads and confronts: his wide spread, most fashionable collars of white shirts and neat Windsor knots in his ties, the well tailored suits were his trade mark, as he dealt with principalities and powers. He surely did not look like Lenin, and he knew perfectly well what he was doing.

No one can ever underestimate what the Charles Danas or the Rockefellers and the host of their kin, and today the leaders of the corporate world, touched by a few individuals, have accomplished in the realm of medicine, education, art and in terms of human betterment both in the USA and in the underdeveloped countries, while often the leaders of our congress, elected by the probable majority of our respectable congregations often do nothing but stand in the way of any social progress. The present day nauseating efforts of many members of Congress to stop foreign aid is a candid example of the contrast in the thinking of our politicians and the representatives of the corporate world who seem to have a far better understanding of reality and of the admonition of Jesus that in dealing with principalities and powers we have to be as gentle as doves and as sharp as scorpions, than many proclaimers of the Word. Decades ago, Reinhold Niebuhr stated that while the Apostolic Church was addressing a pagan society, today a paganized, vulgarized church is trying to say something to a pagan world which as Kurt Vonnegut would say is as effective as trying to solve an algebra equation by chewing bubble gum (M.I.T. Commencement). Thus at the end of recalling my first day in America, I remember my mother but also Dean Lowell with a certain, diverse sense of gratitude.

When I spotted Dean Lowell for the first time at the entrance to Hosmer Hall. I was stricken with horror. Dick Chun presented me to her, and she chattered sweetly as she led me to her table. She was not any blue blood. Her behavior was studied, rehearsed, affected. She performed her assigned duties but unquestionably she was stately, decorative, elegant, her white hair always perfect. Instead of jewelry that evening she pinned to her navy dress three beautiful maple leaves of different sizes and colors which everyone admired. Her diction was perfect, but I still understood only a few words. Fortunately she was used to the blank, idiotic expressions of foreigners and she overlooked these episodes with magnanimity "Before you know it, you will feel at home among us!"

"May God forbid," I thought. As we were served grapes I marveled at the deftness with which Dean Lowell ate the grapes without seeds and without the skin, but she ate them, while chattering at the same time! That was a bit too much for me. No, she would never be able to say with my mother, "*If we stand for something. we are bound to be criticized and if we are to be criticized then for goodness sake let them criticize us for that which really matters and not because of such stupid things as gloves and conventions in general.*" To this plea I still subscribe, and at times I would like to shout it from the mountain tops!

The scene with the grapes eaten without the skin and the seeds made me giggle inside, and after supper I emerged from Hosmer Hall as out of prison, yearning for a bit of fresh air. I took a leisurely walk through the campus in the wonderful, brisk autumn air to the Spinkas. They were glad to see me and I think I provided a live entertainment for them telling them the experiences of my day. I spoke in Czech since both Dr and Mrs. Spinka had a good command of Czech. He was a native of Czechoslovakia, and Mrs. Spinka was the daughter of Czech emigrant in Cedar Rapids. Ironically her name was the female version of my name: Zdenka. They had no children, and from the first evening in their home, I felt I was filling a certain gap. Typically for them, for a long, long time, until I began to feel more comfortable in speaking English, they remained obedient to the educational principle and always responded to my Czech in English. As soon as Mrs. Spinka heard about my blanket situation, she gave me on permanent loan a big, double size coverlet comforter. It was made of yellow chintz and the sheen material was covered with pink and red roses. "At last I have a victim to whom I may give it!," she laughed. It really was meant for the boudoir of Madam Pompadour, but I could care less, and besides the blanket was so big that it could also serve as a bedspread. That was another problem solved.

When I returned to my room and spread the comforter on

my bed, I almost burst into laughter. Suddenly I noticed from my windows the lights of the city behind the buildings and the trees on campus. It did not take me long to convince myself that Hartford was a big important capital, that behind the trees somewhere downtown were marvelous streets lined with fashionable stores, theaters and cafes. Nothing could stop me. Everybody was studying that night, I alone was as free as a bird. Quietly I sneaked out of my room and walked and walked toward the yellowish lights of down town Hartford. From a distance I could see a sort of modernistic cathedral full of lights, but when I got there I had the shock of my life. It was not any cathedral, it was the Aetna Life Insurance Company building, and there were no cafes, no stores to look at, I walked all that distance for nothing! My feet were killing me and I decided to take a bus going in the opposite direction. I put all my change into the palm of my right hand and as I entered the bus I offered the driver a choice. "Token!" he snapped "are you stupid or what?" A kindly gentleman noticing by beret and my bewilderment dropped in one of his tokens for me. "That's perfectly all right," he said as I tried to thank him, "and where is it that you are going?" "The seminary." "Good. That will be the last stop." Something of this sort would never happen in Prague, I thought, with a deep sense of appreciation. Unfortunately, that good man thought only of one seminary: St. Joseph's Seminary which was just about at the end of the world!

I got to my room terribly late, and completely exhausted I crashed on my bed covered with the crazy comforter. Dick Chun flew in, "Bednář, where have you been? I have been worried!" When I told him about my Aetna experience he could not stop laughing, and shortly he brought a box of chocolate covered macadamia nuts to celebrate. Before he left for his room he said, "Believe me, after this day every day will be better." I believed him, and roses or no roses, the blanket was soft, warm, and luxurious.

This was a long day, but boring it was not. I was lightheaded, happy. Dear Lord, when and how shall I ever describe all of this in my letter home and to Mirko? They are worried about the rationing of coal for winter, and here hot water flows from showers in never ending streams, and food is always on the table. I was grateful, but my cup of guilt was also overflowing for suddenly I realized that in the business of the day I forgot to cable home about my safe arrival, as I promised.

*   *   *   *   *

After Dick Chun helped me with the sending of the cable. I was left with one dollar and thirty seven cents in my wallet. Every night the fellow students were urging me to go with them "to the corner" for a bite to eat, and every night I had to come up with some excuse. Finally, I had to share the situation with Dick. I was promised to be given some spending money upon my arrival but no money came, and I did not know to whom to turn without appearing as a beggar. I guess Dick told Dr. Spinka or the Dean directly, for shortly I received what seemed a generous check with a letter of apology from Dean Tertius Van Dyke, who so much resembled his father, Henry van Dyke. As soon as Tertius Van Dyke discovered that I liked to play tennis, we set a date, and we played tennis often until the end of November. Van Dyke had a nasty, studied serve, and he never gave up his hope for victory until the last ball. A day or two before one scheduled match I found in my mail box a tiny visit card with the words, "Dean and Mrs. Tertius van Dyke. Informal supper at seven o'clock." How should I answer that? This was truly a new world for me. I like to recall the large living room at the van Dykes. In the center of the room was an antique, serpent-like settee. Van Dyke liked to sit on that settee, smoking his pipe, and enjoying a glass of sherry, and I enjoyed listening to him talk about his father, and the life at the beloved school for boys in Washington, Connecticut.

Another solution to my pennilessness was in Dick's exited announcement that there was an opening in the kitchen: You do not have to speak English, you do not need to think, all you do is scrape the garbage from plates before they go to the dishwasher. The salary was 50 cents per hour and a free meal, and besides the offer meant definite freedom from Dean Lowell.

It was a new experience. The Europeans only now are being liberated from the idea that youth should be carefree, and to this day many do not understand that the American teenagers and students work very hard to save for their first cars and some of their privileges. For me the work in the kitchen was formative. I met there some wonderful friends, among them even my future wife, Muriel, but my heart surely ached as I observed the American wastefulness. How could anyone leave a quarter of a delicious chicken on the plate to be thrown into the garbage, I could not comprehend. At the same time so many millions of people in our world were starving!

A big shocker was when I received an invitation for my first speaking engagement at the prestigious Asylum Hill Congregational Church. I was to address the Church School children during their chapel service, and tell them about my experiences and my native land. I prepared diligently, and then I memorized and memorized my text. Unlike the Aylum Hill church of today, which is nationally known for its multiple programs and it's outreach ministry, fifty years ago, Asylum Hill Church was a snooty church of high society. The ushers wore cutaways with big white carnations in their lapels. The offering plates were so overflowing with envelopes and dollar bills, that I was ashamed to add a dime to the pile. After the offertory the children were dismissed to their chapel, and I was incredibly nervous, as I followed them. With the exception of my little niece, Miriam, and her brother George, I had never dealt with children, yes, I played with them, hide and seek, but I never read to them or told them a story. As I saw the gathering of children of all ages, I knew that my "speech" was not for them. The children are so wonderfully honest, the only ones who in the words of Hans Christian Anderson are able to verbalize the merciless truth, "the King is naked!"

As soon as I opened my mouth, those merciless dressed up urchins laughed saying, "You speak funny!"

"So I speak funny?"

"Yes."

"You do too."

"No, we don't."

"I shall teach you some Czech, like 'Dobry den,' which means 'Good morning.'" To my astonishment they repeated the words perfectly and there was nothing funny about them. They were good, and I had to include a tongue twister. A la "She sells sea shells by the sea shore."

Say with me, "Push your finger through the throat" which was not too smart on my part. Phonetically it was "Strych Prst Zkrz Krk." The children thought it was hilarious and could not stop laughing.

"Oh, you sound so funny!"

Thus we shared some of our differences. It surely was not a "religious experience." We concluded with the Lord's prayer, repeating one line in English, one line in Czech.

May the Lord forgive me! Never, never again!

The offering followed and the teacher told the children that it would be donated to poor me. To crown her point after the service, she put all the coins into a bag and gave it to me in appreciation. I felt terribly humiliated, and I was fighting tears all the way back to the seminary. "Look what they did," I cried, when Dick came in, looking at the bag of loose coins on my table, like a bag of Judas. He understood, and yet he declared me a total idiot. "All right, all right," he cried, "they did not give it to you in an envelope with a note. Perhaps they don't know any better, but I sincerely believe that they care. They did not mean to treat you as a beggar, and besides, the point is that within this bag is a possibility to buy something which you really need."

The very next day I went down town and bought a cardigan for myself, as yellow as daffodils, my post adolescent protest against everything drab. Would I ever dare to wear that yellow sweater in Prague? I was planning on it.

*   *   *   *   *

My academic advisor was most friendly but not of much help. He was over impressed by my Prague credentials, and since I had my excellent marks in Greek and Hebrew, which were not prerequisites at Hartford, he considered me a scholar, and allowed me to take an enormous load of courses of my choosing, never taking my limited English into consideration. Consequently, with my kitchen job, and more and more dinner invitations, I was swamped, and the only way of studying was diligent memorization, and dependence on the left over drug named "Ropphein," a drug which I used to take during the Nazi interlude when staying awake and alert was an imperative. I was fortunate that this drug, which kept me awake until the morning hours came with me in a very limited quantity, and eventually I had to adjust to a few hours of sleep, especially during the examination periods. I have no idea why I was so possessed with the desire to accomplish as much as possible in the shortest possible time. I did not desire excellent grades. Mediocre passing grades in English were perfectly fine with me, as long as they led to the dream of my graduating as soon as possible. I took a number of the dullest introductory courses, just to have them behind me, yearning to have as much time as possible for the future courses which interested me.

The daily chapel service was an integral part of the Hartford curriculum with both the faculty and students leading the worship. It was important to me and when I was asked to lead the chapel service for the first time, I was mostly surprised by myself, I was a success in spite of myself. Many members of the faculty and students wrote me notes of appreciation. Perhaps my old pastor, Dr. Krenek whose invitation to become a minister I rejected was right in telling me that I had a talent in preaching, and when I pleaded with him to understand that since early childhood I had suffered with a crippling stage fright, he replied, "Anyone who does not go to the pulpit with fear and trembling is not worthy of the pulpit." I thought of him a great deal, and also of my classmate Libuse, a drama student under the tutelage of an old actress of fame. One day Libuse flew to our table at cafe Slavia in fury "That old dame tells me that I am wonderful, but when I ask for a role, she says that I am not ready yet, because I have not lived! I had it! I want a role now! Zdeněk, if I wait for the O.K. of the old lady, I shall be as old and wrinkled as she is. She says I have a wonderful tragic voice," he fumed, "but no sense of tragedy. According to her I just repeat the lines, and as yet my voice does not tremble! Good Lord, give me a break! How can I know that I am any good unless I try it, unless I know more than the views of the old dame. How else can one know unless one risks it, and at least has a chance to measure the response of an audience? And goodness knows, this is not exactly a period of stars in the Czech theatre!" Something of this impatience was also in my being at that time. I yearned for a role, although I did not know what that role would be, but with my whole being I yearned to be heard, to be among people in some ministry. The Nazi era, and the threatening communism which at that time as yet I was not fully comprehending, filled my heart with an enormous sense of urgency. Christianity as a possible life changing and world changing force filled me with an unavoidable Kierkegaardian "Either Or."

In America in the late forties there was still the false security resulting from having the atomic bomb, of being the number one nation. On the other hand, the pacifists were going through masochistic exercises about Hiroshima, there was mushrooming of world federalism, and moral rearmament. And just as the Communists were effectively summoning especially the young generation to a march and were promising them the heaven and the earth, the churches on both sides of the Atlantic with the exception of a few great metropolitan pulpits, appeared incredibly dull, preaching what Bohnhoeffer identified as cheap grace, making an equation between Christianity and being good and doing good, as if Christianity alone had a monopoly on ethics. Church going in America was fashionable, Sunday was a day of "obligation," and special dress, the Church schools were overflowing, and in the so-called Thanksgiving proclamations the political leaders annually congratulated us, affirming that indeed we ought to be God's favorite people because he had so richly blessed us! It was a total departure from the spirit of the first Thanksgiving proclamation in which Abraham Lincoln called for a day of repentance because, intoxicated by our successes, and in the "deceitfulness of our hearts" we have imagined ourselves as the masters of our destinies. Christianity as the redeeming way of life and history, the idea that God made us capable of responding to him, and that only as we respond to him can we be responsible, the assertion that any hope for the transformation of society without understanding that a human being is a spiritual being, capable of being transformed and to transform, seemed to me hopelessly missing. I could hear Albert Camus, who recalling the years of his work in the French underground movement, registered that undoubtedly in those years the church had something important to say but if it said anything, leaders of the underground movement did not hear it. Years later Albert Einstein verbalized the anguish of my mind of those days when he wrote that Christian churches indeed had something very important, and redemptive to say about the foundations of a responsible society, but unfortunately did not know how to say it. This was the anguish of my twenty two year old mind, I was determined to find some way of communicating the Gospel, its summons, claims and promise so that it would be heard. At the same time, I felt a growing sense of isolation. I could not speak about this passionate concern of mine with Dean Van Dyke, a most loving, compassionate Christian gentleman, yet in the pulpit he was incredibly dull. Dr. Spinka would undoubtedly reflect on the spiritual condition of both the preacher and listener, Dick Chun would listen and then would say, "Let's go out for a hamburger!" and most of my colleagues would not understand my sense of urgency at all.

Although I loved the Hartford Theological Seminary and its community, Hartford as a city was a cultural dump. Well, there was the Bushnell Hall, featuring all kinds of cultural and pseudo cultural events. Some splendid American orchestras passed through, giving concerts in the oversubscribed concert series. For the first time in my life, I lived in a city in which concerts were a privilege for those who could afford them; no discounts for students, no free matinees, no opera, no professional theatre. I did take my date, Muriel, to a performance of *Pagliacci*. It took a lot of saving on my part, and it was a total disaster. Opera á la Hartford in those days meant inviting a coloratura soprano, somebody like Patrice Munsel, and a reasonably good tenor to give her at least some support. The rest, the chorus, etc., were all volunteers. Undoubtedly they had the experience of their lives, singing with Patrice Munsel, but it was quite a different experience for us in the audience! Of course, the names of the stars guaranteed the profit. This was one of the hardest things in adjusting to life in the United States, I was culturally terribly homesick (let us understand that this was long before some possible television treat!) Most of my colleagues surely did not share this cultural homesickness. The Spinkas attended their concert series regularly, but to mention opera or ballet was really a mark of snobbery. There was no use talking about this one particular need of my soul. I felt that even the Spinkas would never understand. The deepest secret of my heart was, that I was saving every penny and whenever an opportunity arrived, whenever I was offered a ride, or whenever I had an opportunity to speak at the John Hus Church in New York, or whenever I could make a legitimate excuse about checking on my passport, I went to New York City, that beloved mistress of mine. Like a hungry wolf I spent hours at the Metropolitan Museum, and then hours standing in line in front of Carnegie Hall or the old Met. Unforgettable, unbelievable, although I felt I had to lie about these cultural excursions, telling everyone that I had a memorable visit with aunt Olga who arrived for a short visit, while in reality there was an incredible performance of *Faust*. These secret excursions to New York City were often weekend trips, and on Sunday mornings in those days it was really difficult to decide which church to attend. It was the era of the princes of the pulpit. In absolute awe I listened to Buttrick, or to Paul Scherer, or to Sockman or McCracken. It was an unforgettable inspiration and experience! Theatre, concert, opera, topped by truly outstanding preachers who were often reflecting on those cultural events from their pulpits.

In those stolen, secret weekends my soul was fed but my cup of guilt was surely overflowing!

The reader can possibly have some difficulty in perceiving that for instance Washington D.C. until the Kennedy era was not a cultural center; great concerts and operas and dramatic performances were imported. One simply cannot overestimate the change the Kennedy Center has made not only in Washington but throughout the USA. Also thanks to that era of cultural enlightenment and to the establishment of the National Endowment of the Arts, America has truly discovered the formerly unknown magic, opera and ballet, and welcomed such stars from out of nowhere as Nureyev, or Barashnikov and a host of others who have literally changed the perception of arts in the USA. Being sensitive to the realm of arts, understanding how much during these fifty years the arts have contributed to our understanding of the Gospel, I have a tremendous difficulty in accepting the fact that to this day, concerts, operas and ballet performances and the arts in general are to a great degree treated as the privilege of those who can afford them. We have certainly made great progress since my secret journeys to New York to enjoy a standing place at Carnegie Hall but it still troubles my heart that culture is very largely the privilege of the affluent. It is a denial of freedom and every so often the rich who take their seats in the opera houses for granted are not even aware of the great injustice as they pass their severe judgment on those who are culturally less refined. I have been troubled also by the shabby treatment of arts and the artists by the churches. With the exception of some organ music and ministry of music, our churches have been barren of the arts. It is safe to say that the most expensive "objects of arts" in our churches are the dishwashers, but if the dishwashers have helped to make it easier to bring lonely people together in the fellowship, perhaps the dishwashers deserve the title of artistic instruments. When we compare, however, the impact of the preaching and of all the theological and "inspirational" works published during the last three decades with the spiritual enrichment of Broadway and off Broadway one cannot overlook the millions of men and women and young people who have been led to deep thoughts and considerations after seeing *Godspell* or *Jesus Christ Superstar* or *Man of La Mancha* or the exquisite production of Les *Miserables*, (balanced by some true gems of Hollywood), we must humbly conclude that the pulpit from which the Gospel with its promise and summons has been preached with passion, was not always in the cathedral setting!

I was very much aware of this during my New York weekends, often comparing the Saturday night performance with Sunday morning worship. At times they complemented each other, at times the dichotomy was horrid, but already then I promised myself to seek the fellowship of the artists and to encourage the ministry of arts in the local church, an endeavor which often has been frustrating but always enriching.

On Tuesday and Thursday evening we had vespers in Hosmer Hall led by the students. Those services with most of us sitting on the floor of the Hosmer Hall drawing room were especially meaningful to me, and thanks to my Quaker friends, for the first time I experienced the power of silence. During those silent moments I often thought of home and of Mirko. Being so far away from him, I realized that I could not even read certain biblical passages without thinking of him, and actually hearing music, I could not read the twenty third Psalm without hearing the comforting assuring, Dvorak's score, I could not say, "Bless the Lord, oh my soul," without hearing Bortniansky's melody and his pregnant pause.

From my early childhood on, I watched reformed preachers mounting their high pulpits and saying, "Hear the Word of God, as I am reading from . . ." Of course, nobody in his right mind assumed that the preacher was actually conveying the message of God, and at times the preachers made it abundantly clear! Yet a reformed preacher before the sermon always offered a prayer for illumination by the Holy Spirit and that the meditation of his or her heart may be acceptable in God's sight, which at times, certainly meant overtaxing the Lord. Karl Barth and Emil Brunner both warned us against making out of the Bible an object of idolatry, and affirmed that the Scriptures communicate the Word of God when the Holy Spirit is upon us, when the Bible, by the power of the Holy Spirit, speaks to us afresh, directly, personally. Most people in the pews, however, do not take it that way, they believe the Word of God is preached whether the Holy Spirit is upon them or not. It is difficult to argue or even to debate with those who have a good knowledge of the Bible and like to refresh our memory and remind us what the Bible says.

At Hartford Theological Seminary a most gentle Old Testament scholar, named Moses Bailey went against all possible superstitions like a bulldozer. After dissecting the Old Testament and identifying the documents J and D and E and on and on, and asserting that the Old Testament was written by different writers at different periods of history, Moses Bailey insisted that we, the students, take some old Bible, and actually tear it apart according to our study of the given documents. Of course, I would not take my Czech Bible apart, but there were plenty of Bibles around just collecting dust. The assigned exercise appeared to me so awful that I wanted to pull down the shades in my windows! After all, the Bible was the book for which my forebears suffered. As I mentioned, in the years of persecution, the only Bible in the village was hidden under the flooring of the living room in the homestead, and my great grandmother, night after night, in the light of a candle, copied the whole Gospel of John to give it as a most precious possession to her daughter on her wedding day. When I finished my job of tearing the Bible apart, I felt the need to go to confession, and yet, at last, I understood the difference between the Word and words. Moses Bailey, at an early age truly liberated me from the blind dictum "the Bible says   . . ." That did not endear me to the fundamentalists but nevertheless only after this exercise was I ready to deal with revelation and reason.

Matthew Spinka was unquestionably the most brilliant lecturer on the campus, and although he occupied the chair of Church history, for some selected students he always offered directed study in some great personality such as Berdyaev, or Commenius or seminars on leading Russian thinkers. He knew Russian, was in the Soviet Union, and the Soviet system was familiar to him. I was fortunate to take with him his celebrated lectures on representative Christian thinkers, and then I spent a year with him studying Berdyaev. It is most ironic, but I had to come to America to learn from Spinka the pathological anthropology of Karl Marx, I had to come to America to discover through Spinka the depth of the Russian soul, the native Russian prophets who were totally put aside by the foreign thinking of Marx. It was not in Prague, but in Hartford, where I dealt with the great concepts of inner freedom, of spiritual aristocracy and of that life which is stronger than death. Although in Prague, premier Gottwald declared that communism was not the only way to socialism, my growing comprehension of Marxism filled me with immense anxiety, and I was moving further, and further away from those at home, while the Russian thinkers, interpreted by Spinka were truly formative for me.

During the question and answer period Matthew Spinka could be dogmatic, impatient and nasty. At that time there were plenty of those who in their wishful thinking perceived that ugly communism died by itself in the horrid years of World War II, and who tried to tell Dr. Spinka that a new kind of communism with which even Christians could coexist was on the scene. Matthew Spinka controlled himself, but I could notice that he was getting red in the face, "I do not know the source of your information," he snapped, "all I know is that at the last Congress of the Communist Party in Moscow, Marx-Leninism was unanimously reaffirmed including the assertion that religion is the opiate of the people. No philosophical or political changes were made. I am a historian preferring to deal with the concrete facts of the past. I cannot join you in some speculation about the future. If the ideology of the Soviet Union has changed, we simply must wait and see."

As a teenager studying T. G. Masaryk, I underlined his words, "To think hurts." I had some serious questions about that statement yet after some lectures of Spinka my heart was heavy, I was ready to cry. My ignorance of Marxism and of the Soviet system were a sheer bliss. My new knowledge led to sleepless nights about Mirko and to so many who were fooled. How could I ever write to Mirko and to so many others who were fooled. How could I ever write to Mirko about Berdyaev and his influence on me, when this Berdyaev spent most of his creative years in Paris as an exile, rejecting communism as superficial, as not radical enough, affirming that a Christian must demand more, that is the reformation, revolution of heart and mind. I could see in my mind thousands of Ivan Karamazovs, defying God and therefore defying decency, humanness, announcing that everything is permitted and I visualized thousands of Father Zossimas' mysteriously bowing in front of these Ivans, bowing deeply, perceiving the immense suffering which all Ivans are bound to endure. I had nightmares about Roskolnikovs, the masters of their destinies, waiting and waiting for some Sonia to crack their stubborn hearts, and at times, I thought I heard Mirko crying, "Zdeněk, dear Zdeněk, why have you allowed America to take you away from me? Why so soon?"

It was not America, it was the consideration of the truth. Will you ever understand that? When I removed the hammer and sickle pin from your shirt, the last day of the Prague Revolution, I acted instinctively, ignorantly as a bourgois fool, now it is different, I know now what that hammer and sickle stand for, and I truly hate those who led you to the membership of the Communist Party . . . Dear, dear God, it hurts to think. Why does every truth unite and divide? We have loved each other as true brothers, the only way that love can be restored is the hope of meeting under the cross of Christ.

When we are far away from our families and friends, we want them to be free from worrying about us, and we do our utmost to cover our true feelings and hurts with metaphors, hints and expressions of wishful thinking. For a long time my correspondence with the members of my family and with Mirko suffered with these hide and seek exercises. It is terribly hard to put on a piece of paper, writing to someone you love, that you are terribly lonesome, or ill, worried, especially when you know that the recipient's life is not easy. It is equally hard to write about being happy, happy beyond deserving to those who struggle to keep their heads above the water, it is like kissing one's child in front of an orphan. The airmail letters took at least seven days to reach their destination, and in a era of anxiety, no one could imagine how much could take place in seven days. Caught in this situation, I had to get used to the idea of receiving some important family news after the fact.

My father wrote regularly, long typewritten letters, and often registered his disappointment that I could not submit to a similar discipline. Of course, the first letters contained the description of my brother's wedding, and the confusion which ruled in the household around the event. Since my new and much loved sister-in-law, Cecilia, was an orphan, the wedding was organized in our household, although the wedding reception dinner according to the given customs was held in some hotel. I was touched by Father's lines, "My dear boy, we surely missed you during all the festivities, but before the wedding there was complete chaos without you. Everyone was exclaiming, 'If Zdeněk were here he would know! Where is this or that? What to do about this?' Suddenly all of us realized that ever since the death of your mother you have been literally in charge of this household, and we have not even noticed it. You must forgive me and forgive us all!" Another news was: "We are getting used to the socialist way of living." It was fortunate that my father subscribed to daily papers from Prague for me, and, therefore, I was well informed about the developments in the Czechoslovak Republic as the papers were coming at the same speed as the letters. Indeed, the postwar shortage of housing, especially in the cities, was critical, and the communist paper "Rude Pravo" pointed at the example of the Soviet Union in which every citizen was entitled only to the given square footage of living space, while in Prague the members of the old bourgeoisie lived in palaces. Obviously, my brother Blahoslav, could not find an apartment, and the accommodations for him and his wife were discussed and accepted before I left, but somehow in the business of my last months at home, I did not register that considerable changes were planned, that my father's study and the adjoining reception room would become the private quarters of the young couple. My father had a filing system which I have inherited, only he knew what was where, and hated anyone to touch his things. I could not imagine the moving of his library and his headquarters to another section of the apartment. Father was not complaining, and sent me sketches of the new arrangements, praised my brother for his great technical skills, and was delighted that his wife gladly took over the management of the house. In the long run it was a good arrangement but for me it was the first news of the progressive disappearance of my home, I was no longer able to orient myself in it.

Father in his letters usually summarized the family news, touched on his work at the university, at his schedule, at his writing and plans for the first assembly of the World Council of Churches in Amsterdam in 1948 which he planned to attend. His involvement in the international ecumenism only deepened his anguish over the petty antagonism of Christian denominations in Czechoslovakia. Precisely because the nation needed to hear some uniting voice he was led to take the initiative in getting the leaders of the Christian communities to one table. I saw Father's picture in the papers as he was conferring with cardinal Josef Beran at the archbishop's palace. It was a historic meeting. For the first time since the fifteenth century the leaders of the Catholic and Protestant communions gathered to reason together about what the Christians, in spite of all their diversity, could do together for peace in the post war world in which insurmountable hostilities were rising in the climate of the atomic age. It was typical for Dad. He threw himself into the task of planning an all Christian gathering early in 1948 with all his heart and mind. Cardinal Beran shared his enthusiasm, and those two became good friends. Considering that from the first meeting between the cardinal and Father, the representatives were meeting regularly, working on a theological statement, decades before the First Vatican Council, it is historically significant. Father was excited, and wrote pages about this undertaking, it was his deepest yearning that above all politicized, party oriented voices, the churches would come up, ready to say in unison that unity in the nation and in the world may be restored only if we are governed by something higher than ourselves and our self interests, that the only possible way to peace among individuals and nations is in taking the road revealed by God in Jesus Christ.

Of course, Father concluded every letter with at least a dozen questions, a few reminders to remember this one and that one on their birthdays and, finally with the prayerful admonition not to lose my soul in "business." Father was genuinely happy for me, and responded to every letter almost immediately. Only in between the lines was I able to assess the practical situation. Such remarks as, "The ordered coal finally arrived and with careful planning we should be all right. It is also a blessing that we do not need to use the cellar as a shelter, and that we could get a big supply of potatoes from Vir. Ruzena is raising a pig for us. That should be a great help for all members of the family at Christmas. The shortage of fats seems always acute."

The correspondence with Mirko was far more difficult. He studied brilliantly, was happily engaged to his Olga, was applying for a scholarship in the USA and was mentally planning trips which we would take together. I marveled at his tremendous faithfulness in friendship. When my sister Nadia was moving, I knew he would be there helping her. It was a matter of course for him to be there in my stead. In the same way he was helping at our house at the time of my brother's wedding, and he was meeting regularly with my oldest sister Vera. I was distressed, however, at his increasing complaining about frequent migraine headaches and moments of total disorientation, "When everybody in the tram or bus thinks that I am dead drunk."

His political thinking was somehow pushed aside. In one most poignant letter he verbalized his fear of the future or better said of the reality and his sense of calling. His studies were coming to a conclusion and his ordination to ministry was facing him. He was a Prague boy through and through. He was never out of Prague except in Vir visiting us at the homestead. His life celebrated the city and its freedom. He was the only child. His father was severely handicapped, but kept on working in a printer's shop, his mother gave herself fully to the household. Both parents lived for Mirko, and their every sacrifice for him was a joy for them, yet

Mirko was not a spoiled brat. They all knew that the time was approaching for Mirko to establish himself as an independent man, who was planning to get married. "Zdeněk, my dear boy, you have no idea of my anguish. Day by day I observe my parents. All these years I have been the child of their sacrifice, it is time to take my turn and to provide for them, to take care of them, and I do not know how. If you saw my mother getting up at five to stand in long lines in freezing weather to get a bit of butter, some meat or potatoes, and coming home chilled through, bringing practically nothing, your heart would ache. Dad is more and more handicapped, and gets furious when the kitchen is cold and when he is reminded that the supply of coal is limited. I felt ashamed to tell them that I feel miserable, I do not want to add any anxiety to them, and I am not good in role playing . . . Of course, I would not like anything better than to be called as an assistant minister to some large church in Prague or its vicinity which would also give me a chance to continue in my organ study, and I certainly could earn some money playing at funerals and weddings. But Prague is Prague. You have no idea how petrified I am of being a minister in some hick town of Moravia! The trouble is that many city churches no longer offer an apartment for assistant ministers. I would not mind to combining the job of an assistant minister and sexton if the housing were provided. Olga and I cannot possibly get married and move in with our folks. We are crowded in the two rooms as it is, and she would have a terrific commute to her teaching . . . Not long ago I preached three times in a row in the little village of Olesnice, not too far from Vir. One room in the parsonage and the kitchen are furnished and I stayed there on those weekends. The people always left so much food for me that I lived like a king and always brought true treasures to my folk's kitchen. I am sure you know that parsonage because you mentioned visiting one of the previous pastors. The stucco parsonage on the square of Olesnice is a stately house, it has three floors and at least ten rooms. At the back of the parsonage is a pretty garden, and a tiny orchard. The last time I was there the plum trees were covered and I brought home several bushels. Mother went crazy making dumplings, and trying to find jars to preserve them for the winter, over and over saying, 'A gift of God! A gift of God!' I was walking through the empty parsonage one night, thinking of you, how you would help me to furnish it, dreaming: this could be for my parents. They could have a whole floor for themselves. There is plenty of wood, heat is no problem, just to keep the stoves going; Dad could putter about the house, he could raise chickens, Mother could have a garden. Olga and I could live downstairs. You know that Mother and Father would not be idle, they would be servants of any church. Of course the organ in the church is awful, but the people are friendly, I do not doubt that they would call me. . . Do you see how I am actually dictating the Lord Almighty the terms of my call."

I shiver at the thought of answering the question, "Are you persuaded that God has called you to minister in this church? In all honesty, I would choke, for I am fully aware that our stomachs, the care of my parents are foremost in my mind, and I have no answers for some very difficult questions. Do pray for my soul."

Mirko, dissatisfied with some of my letters, wrote the wonderful suggestion of having a common denominator in reading the same books. He suggested Paul's letter to the Romans, and Chekhov's, *Fathers and Sons*,—an idea which appealed to me a great deal. Mirko knowing me, wasted no time and elaborated the schedule of reading. Some most wonderful correspondence followed. There were some lapses, but we always caught up. Mirko grew more and more reflective although his beautiful handwriting seemed to be getting smaller and smaller. It was a very sad day for me when I could hardly read his handwriting, when he could not control his shaking hand and with obvious pain wrote, "For the time being I cannot read or write. Love you."

*   *   *   *   *

The Spinkas informed me of the invitation of Prof. and Mrs. Hromadka to visit them in Princeton, and they suggested taking Jarka Stolar along so that I would have some company. It was our first get together since we dropped Jarka off at Yale, and we had a great deal to share. The trip itself was wonderful. We stopped at Hyde Park at the grave of Roosevelt and at some other points of interest. The Spinkas and the Hromadkas were very dear friends. For many years the Hromadkas vacationed together with the Spinkas at their cottage at Echo Lake in Maine. The Spinkas liked to recall the frolics of the Hromadka's daughters, and never removed their chiseled sign on the door to their bedroom, "If you are kicked out stay out." Thus the arrival at Princeton was an occasion of much hugging and kissing.

The Hromadka's faculty home was spacious and well furnished. It was a home. One felt that the occupants had lived there for a great many years.

Jarka and I shared a well appointed bedroom, and enjoyed the long walks through the Princeton campus, talking about our experiences. Jarka, like me, had only positive experiences and loved Yale. He went on and on, describing his opportunities in biblical research, and the generous encouragement of some of the great American biblical scholars. On top of it all, Jarka gained the friendship of the well known American Church historian Ronald Bainton, a man of remarkable wit and humor, whose friendship Jarka truly cherished all his life. There was no doubt that Jarka, with his education at Yale and his outstanding scholarship, was meant for a brilliant career in the department of New Testament in Prague. Of course, he was very much committed to his girl Vera in Prague, whom he planned to marry. He was hoping to finish his doctorate at Yale, not a minor ambition, and then to return to Prague. Knowing that Hromadka was the future light of our school in Prague, this visit at Hromadkas was important for him. We laughed a great deal, because Jarka was petrified by Mrs. Hromadka, and asked me many questions about the protocol before the dinner. He certainly also wanted to ask Dr. Hromadka about his opinion concerning Jarka's career, and about the possible other courses he ought to take. We rehearsed the conversation with many laughs during our walks. Of course, we did not skip the political development at home in our conversations. He did not mind asking about Mirko and I did not mind telling him that he was a member of the Communist party. We shared a great deal, and both of us agreed how profoundly America, in a very short time, delivered us from political naïveté, but at the same time, we affirmed our hopes for the possible development of Czechoslovakia as an independent state. After all, there were so many remarkable representatives of democratic thinking in leadership positions in Czechoslovakia.

They would not be in those positions if they felt the struggle was lost.

Mrs. Hromadka staged a glittering American dinner. Candles and flowers adorned the dinner table and Professor Hromadka served skillfully, American style. We could not help but admire the beauty, and the graciousness of that home. Both Dr. and Mrs. Hromadka recalled their arrival in Princeton with just a few suitcases, and the enormous generosity with which the American people of the Princeton community helped to furnish the big house. "Indeed, it's very true, as de Tocqueville observed, America is great because it is good," Hromadka interjected, and Mrs. Hromadka then added her litany of regrets about leaving America. "I am not exactly ready to reenter the society in which men kiss the hands of the ladies!", she said. On the other hand she was excited about being reunited with her parents and family. She laughed describing how cleverly her parents Dr. and Mrs. Lukl saved all the furnishings from the hands of the Nazis, and how they are trying to secure for them the very same apartment which they had occupied before coming to America. "It's big, but I certainly want that kitchen changed before we return!" Mrs. Hromadka remarked. "And what will you do with all the furnishings of this house?" asked Mrs. Spinka. "Well it was given to us and since the Czechoslovak government pays the moving expenses we will take all that we can. The girls one day can use it."

There was profound silence at the table until Dr. Spinka changed the subject.

I kicked Jarka under the table since there was a slight pause, and an ideal opportunity for Jarka to spell out his questions. Jarka did magnificently, and Dr. Hromadka answered enthusiastically. He commented on the age of the present New Testament professor, and on the great need to strengthen the New Testament department in Prague. He encouraged Jarka to finish his doctorate at Yale, if at all possible, and promised him any assistance possible in starting his career in Prague. I was glad for Jarka to have this encouragement but at the same time I was a bit embarrassed. After all, my father was the dean with tenure until 1949, and Hromadka at that moment certainly spoke as a self appointed leader of theological education.

The dinner otherwise included a combination of sadness and determination on the part of the Hromadkas which I witnessed again in his final speech in Chicago at the assembly of Czech-American protestants, shortly before the Hromadka's returned home. Both Dr. and Mrs. Hromadka were extremely happy at Princeton. Hromadka was dearly loved at that university, his brilliant career in the USA was well secured; they enjoyed the American life style. Dr. Hromadka verbalized his enormous feeling of indebtedness to the people of the United States, and especially at Princeton and Chicago, and shared with us his desire to write a major work on the spirit of America as soon as time would permit it. Thus the departure of the Hromadkas to Prague had a certain aura of sacrifice. He repeated over and over again how the political leaders of Czechoslovakia urged him to return, how desperately his presence was needed. He laughed as he elaborated his conversation with the leader of the Communist party, Klement Gottwald. He was very much impressed by his extraordinary perception of both the domestic and international situation, and felt that Gottwald was genuinely sincere in urging him to return. Hromadka considered it an utmost compliment but also a proof of historic changes in the soviet thinking, when a communist leader, trained in Moscow was inviting a Protestant theologian as an unofficial advisor to a troubled nation at a crossroad of history. As far as I remember the name of President Benes was not mentioned at that time, but it was certainly assumed that Benes was among the political leaders urging Hromadka's return, and there is no doubt that during the war years, and also in the immediate post war period, Hromadka diligently sought Benes' favor and consistently praised him for his political insight.

After the dinner Jarka and I offered to do the dishes, an offer which Mrs. Hromadka gladly accepted, and we were happy to do that for her. She was a wonderful hostess, and cherished the time to visit with Mrs. Spinka. As Mrs. Hromadka led us to the kitchen to show us what goes where we noticed a framed photograph of a man with bushy hair above the kitchen table. "Who is that?" "You don't know him?", she asked, half believing, "He is one of our gods, Henry Wallace, a wonderful man who truly represents the other America, the true America, a man to whom my husband dedicated his book."

We still looked at the photograph blankly, ashamed of our ignorance. In retrospect it occurs to me that at that moment we were not as stupid as we thought we were, for the political stardom of Henry Wallace certainly fizzled like a Chinese firecracker, and today hardly anybody knows who this former secretary of Agriculture and at one time Roosevelt's Vice President was, but this was rather typical for Hromadka, to reserve so much admiration for a man who appealed to him but who did not pass the marks. Although I read Hromadka's book, *The Doom and the Resurrection* and heard him speak many, many times, not once did he attempt to explain why that book was dedicated to Wallace.

The visit to Hromadka's at Princeton is extremely clear in my memory, and I have been returning to it often especially at times when not only his pronouncements but also his behavior were misleading and truly unforgivable.

I searched and searched through the memoirs of the leading political personalities of that era and J. L. Hromadka is not even mentioned in them, and if he is mentioned he is dismissed as a traitor. Such is the case of the memoirs of Chancellor Smutny who served President Benes until his death and primarily of the four volumes by Prokop Drtina, *Czechoslovakia—My Fate*. We are indebted to Vaclav Havel for smuggling the manuscript of this historically important work abroad and gladly suffering Communist prison for this deed. Prokop Drtina, who was Minister of Justice in post war Czechoslovakia, literally spent his life in the service of Dr. Benes. President Benes certainly did not have much respect for Dr. Hromadka in his last years, and it is hard to imagine Benes urging Hromadka to serve in the capacity of a spiritual advisor. Perhaps the key, and I think tragic words, for our understanding of Hromadka's role in the Communist era are in his appreciation of Klement Gottwald's invitation. While Dr. Hromadka considered it a great compliment, Gottwald was performing a trick which worked like magic for the Communists in the first stages of their conquests. Systematically they were seeking the support of highly admired men and women of liberal democratic views who would give the communist pursuits an appearance of respectability. They did not mind having as premier Zdeněk Fierlinger, known to the nation as a follower of T. G. Masaryk, although they knew, they had him in their hands, similarly they kept two Roman Catholic priests in their government although they abhorred their religious views, and they did absolutely everything to retain Jan Masaryk as a foreign minister, because he was perfect for misleading the world, which went on saying, "If Masaryk works with them, there must be a chance, there must be something good in them." In this sense J. L. Hromadka was a perfect choice. He had a tremendous following among the protestants in Czechoslovakia and he was highly respected among the influential academicians in the USA and Great Britain. Although he was known for his liberal views, for his great opposition to Franco, he was also known for his devoted interpretation of T. G. Masaryk, and the great chapters of Czechoslovak history. He was a perfect catch and he performed his tasks magnificently.

When we parted the following day, I still felt a great admiration for Professor Hromadka, for his humor, tremendous intellect and ability to think on his feet, yet I was glad that I would graduate from Hartford and that I would not need to deal with him. No, I could never label Hromadka as a salon socialist. He was capable of taking risks, he could be extremely compassionate, he was tremendously able to open our eyes to suffering humanity but on the home front, his father-in-law, Dr. Lukl, arranged affluence and privileges, Hromadka's listeners did not even dream about. That was hard for me to swallow, but thinking that our family would never need to deal with Hromadka again, it did not bother me.

*　*　*　*　*

As I approached the anniversary of my arrival in the USA in October 1947, I was ready to say to myself, "How time flies!" With the help of the philosopher Karl Löwith from the University of Marburg, I understood, however, that time was static. Time itself does not fly, does not heal anything, change anything, it does not even mature wine. Breathlessly, however, I realized, that a frantic non-stop year was behind me, yet strangely enough I was hoping for more! I was ecstatic when I was given a full scholarship for another year, and happily I traveled to New York equipped

with all the documents about the scholarship, to ask the Czechoslovak Consulate, located on Time Square, to extend my visa. To my
surprise, my visa was extended only until March when I was to
come and to apply for another extension. That did not bother me, it
promised another trip to New York!

Behind me was a frantic academic year, but at last, all the
introductory courses were behind me, and I was able to deal with
such unknowns as Jonathan Edwards and the Russian Prophets as
Soloviev. At last, I was able to manage in English. I had a number
of speaking engagements, my work in the kitchen and my new job
in the mission church of Warburton Chapel in the slums of Hartford provided an income on which I could manage and even send
some packages of food home. The people at the Warburton Chapel
were mostly of Italian origin, and they appreciated my reading the
Scriptures in Italian. Otherwise they generously tolerated my
preaching in English, and every Sunday night we cooked supper
together and enjoyed good fellowship. We also had a small Church
School and annually produced magnificent Christmas pageants.
Our organist and piano player was a night club entertainer named
Victoria, who insisted on smoking cigarettes from a long silver cigarette holder as she was rehearsing with the children. Once in a
while she burst into an uncontrollable flow of tears, and when I
comforted her and asked what's the matter, she would answer,
"Nothing, I just feel so ashamed of my rotten life, I just wish to be
one of these children again!" There was something of Dostoevsky's Sonia in her, and at Christmas time she really led us to spiritual heights in which the last were the first. I must add that at times
I gratefully recalled Vrana from the depression years for the preparation for this particular ministry! Behind me was also a memorable summer in the state of Vermont, where I went from church to
church, from village to village for almost three months. I stayed in
each church about a week preaching on Sunday and conducting vacation school during the week. At times I spent a week in some
camp, which I considered the punishment of God for I had to get
acquainted with the evil of American May flies and mosquitoes. I
returned to the campus from Vermont with a second hand typewriter, and cherished gifts of a small radio and one wonderful wool
blanket made in Chester, Vermont. I had my extended family

among my Hartford friends, and I too felt with de Tocqueville that America was great because it was good. I was profoundly touched by the kindness of men and women who touched my life that year. Perhaps Frank Sinatra somewhere at a distance was rehearsing his hit, "It was a very good year."

At the same time my anguish about the development at home deepened. The USA offered a saving help by inviting Czechoslovakia to participate in the Marshall Plan, economic help which was desperately needed. It was a tremendous blow when so to speak at the last minute Stalin informed the Czechoslovak government that its participation in the Marshall Plan would have to be interpreted as a hostile act against the Soviet Union. Poor Jan Masaryk had to travel to Moscow to get whipped by Stalin and his cohorts. From Moscow he traveled to the session of the United Nations and then to Washington where his deepest worries were confirmed: in case of any Soviet aggression in Czechoslovakia, the USA would do nothing. Ironically, the churches in Czechoslovakia said absolutely nothing about the horrid dictate of the Soviet Union not to participate in the Marshall Plan, yet the leaders of the democratic parties in Czechoslovakia fought gallantly for the survival of democracy.

It was a wonderful surprise for me that on my return from Vermont, I was given new headquarters, a suite for scholars on the second floor of Hosmer Hall consisting of a living room-study, and small bedroom. It was my dream to finish my studies at Hartford, then to extend my visa for some travels and to meet Dad in Amsterdam at the first Assembly of the World Council of Churches on the way home.

At last Hartford was ready for its fall semester, and the first dinner was held at Hosmer Hall. There were a great many new students, and we were told more women scholars than men. The women had to walk from their Mackenzie Hall dormitory along the long lawns to Hosmer Hall. It was a sort of ritual for men to look from the windows and see the procession. When Mrs. Lowell was not in sight, there was always someone "vulgar" enough to whistle, and then we all tried to hide behind the curtains. Among the new students, walking toward Hosmer Hall was also a very petite, and chic young lady, named Muriel Stowe Eddy. I was determined to meet her.

WATCHING FROM A DISTANCE

The Communists learned a great deal from the Nazis, they even noticed what the Nazis did not notice, namely, that as long as families and friends are allowed to share joys and sorrows they represent a formidable strength. With passion they concentrated on the destruction of the family institution, on the destruction of any fellowship in which men and women felt some loyalty to each other. It was a superior dictum to turn brother against brother, fathers and mothers against their sons and daughters, to create horrid suspicions so that in the formerly loving families no one trusted anyone else. Grandmothers and grandfathers who possessed memories of what it meant to be human were quickly isolated or labeled as senile, slightly insane tellers of fairy tales. The main emphasis was on separating person from person, destroying their instinctive desire to share joys and sorrows, to be present to each other, and to create an unbearable vacuum, loneliness which the party would be able to fill with its own agenda. Even if we did not have the New Testament doctrine of the church, the directives of the communist party for the persecution of the church would tell us a great deal about what we are meant to be, a fellowship in which through our loving presence we are enabling each other to be the children of light, Christ's witnesses.

Although the doctrine of the Virgin Mary is not a part of my heritage, every Lent I am profoundly moved by listening to one of the versions of the *Stabat mater*, especially Dvorak's stirring work with its truly magnificent "Amen, Amen."

Dorothy Sayers used to remind us that there was something unique and tremendously daring in the women who silently stood under the cross of Jesus in the company of the disciple John. It was unheard of in that society that women would ever witness such a horrid barbarity as a crucifixion. In one of her radio plays she allowed her dramatic imagination to say that one of the soldiers around the cross remembered Mary Magdalene from her former days, overlooked the rules and let these strange women and their friend stay. In any case, we do know that sufferers, even people in semi coma are comforted by the presence of those they love, that joys are doubly dear in the presence of family and friends, that in the awareness that we are loved and trusted our courage is restored. We cannot imagine the impact of the words spoken by Jesus from the cross first to Mary, and then to John.

"Woman, behold your son!"

"Behold, your Mother!"

The rest of the companions of Jesus were not as gallant and daring as these women and John, and quite ironically, therefore their suffering increased, because they placed themselves in the helpless isolation of a certain distance. "And Peter watched from a distance." Early in my life, I had to learn to understand that it is not true that we are always the creators of the situations in which we find ourselves, that we are not always running away from the crosses of those whom we love, that at times, precisely when we yearn to share the pain of those whom God has given us, we are not allowed to do so, and our horrible cross is in watching their suffering from a distance and not being able to do anything. In February 1948, the unbelievable took place. Under the skillful management of the Soviet Ambassador Valerin Zorin, and the Czechoslovak Communist leaders, a fully orchestrated coup d'état was accomplished. The prelude was a government crisis, followed by strikes. The masses were given the signal. The street took over calling for the blood of the enemies of the people, the foreign inspired reactionaries, demanding socialist rule. "The People's Militia," men dressed in new black leather jackets moved into action, while "the people's police" hunted for the enemies, and filled the prisons and the former Nazi concentration camps. Prokop Drtina, the Minister of Justice, who spent his life in the service of President Benes and of the Czechoslovak democracy jumped out of the window of his villa as he saw his torturers coming. It was a suicide that failed, and was followed by seventeen years of imprisonment which included the ill famed "psychiatric treatment" used in soviet prisons.

The front page of the New York Times showed the photos

of the immense mobs in Wenceslaus Square, the familiar villa of
Drtina, the tortured face of President Benes as he congratulated the
Communist leader, Klement Gottwald on achieving his triumph.
There was nothing for me to do but to think of my family. Our
friend, the Czechoslovak Ambassador, Ivan Papanek, gave an im-
passioned   speech in behalf of Czechoslovak democracy at a special session of the Security Council of the U.N. As expected the
representatives of the Western powers, including Eisenhower, expressed their shock and astonishment at the development in Central
Europe, and exactly as expected, the representatives of the Soviet
Union and their emerging satellites invoked the charter of the U.N.
which they so cleverly had constructed and now piously adhered
to, refusing to interfere "into internal affairs of a sovereign nation."
Although, I was not surprised, the attitude of the Western Powers
was hard for me to take. The people of the Western super powers I
think will never understand how it feels to be a part of a small, unjustly afflicted nation with which the superpowers play as if with a
deck of cards. It takes years, decades and for many the understanding never comes, that the tragic fate of the small nations depends
on the political scenario of the day; if it is an election year, the lovers of democracy and of civil rights look left and right extremely
cautiously, to be sure not to offend some potentially big givers, and
their vested interests. It is a joke at which the Soviets laughed and
which they exploited. Why did the Soviets always stage a major
crisis during the USA election year?

Suddenly a cable arrived from my father, "My dear Zdeněk
- We miss you here in these great revolutionary days. We urge you
to make a public statement against our enemies in the USA. Make
immediate preparations for your return home and your work here.
Lovingly, Dad." I stared at the cable dumbfounded. The salutations, considering the cost of a cable seemed to me incredibly stiff.
Suddenly it occurred to me, the old agreement that in a crisis situation the salutation, "My dear Zdeněk," meant that the exact opposite of the content of the letter or cable was the true message. Con-
fused, I decided to do nothing, and to assume a wait and see
attitude. Then checking on my passport, I realized that I did not
have much "wait and see" time left. In a few days, on March 8, the
Czechoslovak development again was the topic of the first page

coverage of the world papers: Jan Masaryk Found Dead. A Suicide or a Murder?

According to the Czechoslovak Communist sources Jan Masaryk jumped out of the window of his private apartment in the Foreign Office in Czernin Palace, being driven to despair by the hate mail of his Western friends. There is no doubt that ever since his return from Washington, realizing the hopelessness of the struggle for the survival of the Czechoslovak democracy, Masaryk was depressed. Behind him was also the most humiliating "visit" with Stalin. Then the USA offered Czechoslovakia far reaching economic help through the Marshall Plan, help which at that moment of most acute economic crisis meant a possible reversal of a totally hopeless situation.

Stalin informed the Czechoslovak government that the acceptance of economic help from the USA and the participation in the offered Marshall Plan could be interpreted by him in no other way than as a hostile step against the Soviet Union. The Communist ministers, of course, including the Premier, were stricken with panic and dispatched Masaryk to Moscow to apologize to the great Stalin. When Masaryk arrived in Moscow in the company of several Communist leaders who were to supervise him, Stalin was less than gracious, and elaborated what it meant to belong to the great family of Soviet nations. The gregarious, witty Masaryk, as his close friends knew him also often suffered with seasons of great melancholy. The Communists knowing this depressive nature of the most popular member of the government exploited it to the fullest to give their interpretation of Masaryk's suicide a definite credibility. On the other hand, the theory that Masaryk was pushed out of the window and was murdered cannot be dismissed especially when we realize that all servants, butlers and telephone operators were systematically eliminated by the Communists. Early in the nineties, the USA Ambassador Shirley Black was telling me that when Marcia Davenport, the gifted writer, engaged to Masaryk, requested to see for herself the familiar apartment of Masaryk, she was shocked. The Ambassador prepared her for the fact that the Communists spent millions for the reconstruction of the cavernous Czernin Palace. The two entered the apartment. Marcia Davenport could not believe her eyes. The old corridors through which the butlers used to bring suppers to the Minister's apartment were eliminated. The fateful window was beyond recognition. The communists did absolutely their utmost to dispel the theory of Masaryk's being murdered by their thugs. We shall probably never know the truth. There is no doubt, however, that Masaryk whether a victim of suicide or a victim of a Communist defenestration, through his death demonstrated his protest against the Soviet supremacy.

Masaryk's death affected me deeply. Over and over again I remembered his visits in Vir, his laughter and incredible wit. Somebody smuggled out Father's long letter about his visit with Masaryk's sister Alice. They prayed together, and at the end of the visit Alice led Father to Jan Masaryk's casket. According to Father, he looked incredibly peaceful, and there was no scratch on his face. The only thing which Father considered rather strange was a small bouquet of snow drops placed above Masaryk's left ear.

In the excitement of these days in which it was difficult to concentrate on studies I received a registered letter summoning me to appear at the Czechoslovak Consulate in New York. Many people were advising me not to go especially when Father sensing a great danger for me, asked his friend Dr. Visser't Hooft from the World Council of Churches, stationed in Geneva, to cable me the following message: Urgent message from your Father, "Do not return to Prague, you are charged with military treason, and are expected to be arrested upon arrival." What to do now?

The seminary faculty immediately came with assistance and offered a full scholarship for the following year. The President of the seminary wrote a long letter to the Czechoslovak Consulate explaining the importance of my finishing my studies at Hartford.

Arriving at the Consulate I was surprised by the immense portrait of Stalin at the entrance, surrounded by small portraits of Communist leaders on each side. The portrait of President Benes appeared as an appendix. "Yes", said the clerk, opening a sliding glass window above her desk. I explained my situation to her, and presented the letters from Hartford. She read the letters not registering any expression.

"Your passport, please."

It was the last time I saw my passport. The clerk left the

room for a few minutes and then returned with the verdict: "The Czechoslovak Socialist Republic demands your immediate return to Prague. Your refusal would have far reaching consequences in the future not only for you but also for the members of your family. Your standing and your safety in the United States are no longer of any concern of the Czechoslovak Socialist Republic. Good day!"

I stepped out into a busy street unable to control my tears. For a while I stood in front of a large window of a fashionable store featuring women's cruise wear, sobbing. People stared at me wanting to ask, What's the matter? Did you lose anything? Can I be of some help?—but nobody asked.

What's the matter? I asked myself. Nothing really. As millions and millions in this world, I just lost my country, my home, my family, my right to be. No one seems to understand how frightening it is to walk the streets of New York City without any identification. For the first time I realized how comforting it is to have a passport, a document of one's belonging to a larger entity. To have a passport means that the government of your nation is standing behind you, ready to protect you and your interests. Suddenly I was reduced to a number among the countless homeless beings in the post war world.

While I was returning by train to Hartford, my father was recovering from his ordeal of declaring me emotionally unbalanced, an obvious victim of the American reactionaries. He had nothing to do with me. My property was confiscated. Since that moment officially Father never wrote to me but I marveled at the number of messages from him coming from different embassies, and from people who were passing through Prague.

As soon as I arrived at the Hartford railroad station I phoned Muriel Eddy who at that time was becoming very special to me. I knew that she was anxious about my appointment at the Czechoslovak Consulate, and I asked her to wait for me at Mackenzie Hall, the big hall in the women's dormitory, compartmentalized by a great many comfortable seating arrangements. As strange as it seems, I was not at all yearning for some comfort or sympathy, but I felt driven by the desire to be an honorable man. I knew that Muriel's parents were not exactly happy about her going with a foreigner to a concert. It seemed to me totally unfair to date a very lady-like girl, having nothing, being nothing. I felt the need to verbalize my innermost feeling: "Forget me! I am nothing, I have nothing, I have no future, at this point I am a charity case. I have nothing to offer to you but a promise to be a burden to you!" Muriel had a sandwich ready for me, and I ate it with gusto since I had had no lunch or supper. She listened to me very carefully. Sentimentality was foreign to her. Her quietness that night bothered me. I guess I expected her to disagree with me. All she said was that I desperately needed some rest, that after some good sleep I would think more clearly—that was a very "Eddy" advice for any affliction. She remarked that she could understand the feelings which I verbalized but that she could not possibly imagine the magnitude of my tragedy. No American could. Then she straightened up her long neck and announced that no one could possibly dictate her own behavior. She would not budge.

No refugee accepts his or her exile as permanent, and months and years are spent in the expectations of the collapse of the oppressor, and night after night one goes to bed dreaming about returning home. I was extremely fortunate in surviving the years of the Nazi oppression and in having the perplexing knowledge that although God's truth is marching on, the oppressor's falsehood may be triumphant for years. Gentle hearts tremble. How can a loving, just God permit Stalin to triumph? Of course unlike Nazism's blind nationalism and the dream of the rule of the super race, Communism at its best was to be seen as a corrective social movement. I could not forget Hromadka describing the Communist excesses during the Soviet revolution as the rod of God's anger. I was not blind to the tremendous injustice inflicted on the poor and disinherited by the upper classes of society. The years of economic depression and the memories of bread lines while others lived in affluence were not forgotten by me. I had no desire for such a social system to return. At times I thought of the society of my grandfather and grandmother, my mother's parents. They surely loved their children, and they loved us, their grandchildren. Grandfather did not abhor anything as much as idleness, as a Calvinist he often complained about Christians wasting God's time. He was extremely generous to us, yet already in the first stages of my exile I often wondered. Did our loving grandparents really love the world in which we, their grandchildren, were destined to live? All right, the Communists confiscated my property for which Grandfather worked so hard. Would it not be more prudent if he had given us less in inheritance and if he had invested more in the future of social justice? These thoughts were very much in my mind while at the same time I revolted against the superficiality of the Marx-Leninist "solution." Indeed, one of the first serious decisions I made as a refugee was to earn my Master's Degree in studying the religious views of Ludwig Feuerbach and Karl Marx. I simply had to learn to comprehend Marxism as a religious movement first. Fortunately, Professor Karl Löwith from the University of Marburg was willing to be my mentor. It was one research which I have never regretted.

As all those who suffer sorrow, disappointment and defeat, the refugees also yearn for some support group. In every capital there are groups of refugees. The Russian nobility held a court in Paris and New York, the Czechoslovaks have their clubs in Boston, New York, mass meetings in Chicago, in Toronto or Detroit. After February 1948 Czechoslovak refugee clubs and organizations were mushrooming across this land. Of course, I was invited to join quite a few of them, and soon I realized that they were not for me. There were some marvelous people, the women prepared the most spectacular Czech pastries, yet I was like a fish out of water. The subject of the conversation most of the time was who was guilty of our lot. There was always a discussion on who lost what. There was always an exercise in daydreaming, that is, what would be what and who would be who, when the Communists were finished. I certainly wanted to participate in any effort to help the families of the persecuted at home, and to help the escapee families to get established in the USA. From the early fifties I was a regular speech writer for Radio Free Europe under the pseudonym Josef Sadilek, and at that time I often bit my lips as we were encouraged to elaborate the material privileges of the people of the United States. In the early stages of the Eisenhower era, there was a wide spread assumption that the Soviet Empire would collapse because of the economic superiority of the people of the West. Personally I had some difficulty believing that utmost materialists could undermine utmost materialists. The political leaders loved to speak in those days of godless communism which turned churches into museums and entertainment halls but who were totally blind to our own godlessness, for instance to the beloved New England in which we were closing one church after another because people refused to support the ministry, and in the best case, they just maintained the buildings to have them available for funerals and weddings. Many of us also resented the idea that the Czechoslovak people of democratic persuasion would be risking imprisonment by listening to Radio Free Europe broadcasts, which at that time specialized in elaborating that the USA was bound to be victorious in the war of ideas, because it had more flushing toilets, more cars and dishwashers than any other nation. Materialism of that era was appalling to me, and it hurt that so many Czechoslovaks who succeeded in escaping were basically materialists, and could not comprehend that the conflict with the Soviet union was a conflict of ideas, of spiritual, religious doctrines, I felt a stranger among people who spoke the same language. As a refugee I had two choices, either to join those who cried about their lot and hoped for the return of the good old days, or to endeavor to establish an extended family in the framework of a Christian community. In that effort I have been richly blessed with brothers and sisters, aunts and uncles, grandmothers and grandfathers of great affection and stature.

The last message from home saddened me, the homestead at Vir was plundered. It was now considered the property of the enemies of the people, and to this day some furnishings of my mother and of my grandparents are scattered throughout the village. I was especially sorry to hear that the beautiful, pale green tile stove in the dining room was smashed. Interestingly enough the vote of the "National Committee" to confiscate the property was far from being unanimous. To the surprise of all, the chairman of the committee, the leader of the local Communist hierarchy showed very definite softness of heart and was totally against touching the Bednář property. Only the members of my family realized that he was the very man who was caught in our orchard stealing apples and wood in the years of depression. He reminded his comrades that Mrs. Bednář had socialist feelings in her heart before some of them had been born. It was then the vote of the committee to let a local po-

liceman and his family use the downstairs of the homestead, and
let the old professor and his family use the rest as they see fit. Of
course everyone at home was delighted, although in this case, it
was a good move on the part of the Communists. The policeman
who did not pay any rent was making more and more demands for
repairs and changes in the house, and of course Father had to pay
heavy taxes on the property. It was a known Communist trick.
When the owner could not afford to pay the taxes or for the necessary repairs he was *de facto* forced to "donate" his property to the
state. In our case, however, the policeman was so successful that
soon he was able to move to a very fine villa. The homestead was
left empty, the leaks in the roof multiplying winter by winter but it
was a blessing.

The papers from Prague daily informed me about the happenings in my homeland, but most depressing were the three
church papers which my father subscribed for me. In all three professor J. L. Hromadka emerged as an undisputed leader of Czechoslovak protestants and enthusiastic supporter of the communist
leadership. According to Hromadka while the West was building
its policies on romantic guesses the people in the Soviet block
were building their future on a scientific certainty. In every speech,
in every article Hromadka was dismissing the Western democracies with a sweeping word "decadent." What was most devastating
for me was to read Hromadka's article highly critical of Jan Masaryk. We could all remember how Hromadka and the Lukl family
literally crawled in front of Masaryk's family, how Hromadka
posed himself as Jan Masaryk's devoted friend. Two weeks after
Jan's death, Hromadka felt duty bound to interpret Masaryk's suicide as a result of a deeply rooted weakness in Masaryk's character. In that moment professor Hromadka joined the cheapest scoundrels and cannot be excused or forgiven.

After the news about the homestead there was a painful
long period of silence. I buried myself in my studies of Marx, and
comforted my heart by the hope that Father would be attending the
opening session of the first Assembly of the World Council of
Churches in Amsterdam at the end of August, and that during that
week we would be able to communicate freely. At the same time
Ambassador Papanek and many influential friends were urging me

not to waste a minute in applying for the status of a Displaced Person. Dr. Papanek rightly guessed that I lived in an illusion. Indeed as long as I lived on the campus of Hartford I felt secure, I had nothing to worry about, but once I was out of Hartford, a situation which I could not imagine, without some legal document—I was unemployable, yes I was *persona non grata*. It never occurred to me that an application for a piece of paper could be so time consuming and nerve wracking. One had to have not only dozens of recommendations from, if at all possible, influential people, but also ultimate sponsors who would guarantee one's job, housing, and health insurance payments. Poor Muriel Stowe Eddy was furiously taking my dictation and then writing dozens of letters in the basement of Mackenzie Hall. Once, utterly exhausted she looked at me and said, "This is all so idiotic! Suppose you don't get the Displaced Person status, what could they possibly do to you?"

"According to the law the people who are here illegally are deported."

"Where?"

"I guess to their native country."

She started to type furiously. I hated to do this to her. She deserved something better, she was just beginning to overcome the big failure of her life, and here I was, an invitation to a sure failure to come. Muriel was a brilliant student. When she graduated from the University of Connecticut as a Danforth Fellow she was already under the influence of Ruth Seabury, a prolific writer, social activist and educator, a woman who never needed to fight for her rights, who commanded a tremendous authority and respect. It was Ruth Seabury who introduced Muriel Eddy to the Danforths who gladly endowed the Christian Student Association and its work at the University of Alabama with Muriel to be in charge. It is a great pity that the correspondence between Muriel and Ruth Seabury was lost.

Upon her graduation Muriel against the will of her parents traveled to the University of Alabama to assume her new post. Of course, it never occurred to her that she would not be allowed to have any dealing with the black students, and on her very first day on the campus she was seeking conversation with the black and white students alike. The rumor spread. She was immediately summoned by the Dean and put on the carpet. This must never happen again! The members of the Ku Klux Klan took over from that point and all night long they knocked on her window, terrorizing her, describing for her the lynching which was ahead of her. Obviously a considerable group of haters gathered by her first floor window. Late at night the dean entered her room, finding her totally exhausted. He declared her a *persona non grata*, waited for her to pack her belongings and then drove her to the railroad station to take a train home. Of course, she arrived in her gossipy, conservative home town as a total flop, fired even before she had started. Many said, "It serves her right, the nigger lover!" The horror of the mob, knocking on her window, threatening her with lynching never left her. Every so often she woke up in the middle of the night screaming with terror. She ran away to the realm of the business world in Darien. She worked for several years, and at last she had enough money to pay the tuition at Hartford, believing that a change in attitude required a change in early childhood education. She believed in education with the passion of an evangelist. Her story, her horror of being lynched because of treating the blacks as human beings, her understanding that in this world the poor were being punished for being poor, the old were being punished for being old, and the ill were punished for being ill, made me think; does not this world deserve the horror of Communism? At the same time I was aware of the superficiality of Communism as a corrective movement. I also realized more and more deeply that Muriel deserved much more than me as a basis of future happiness, I wanted to disappear from her life.

*   *   *   *   *

It was a great thrill for me to notice on the front page of the New York Times a large photograph taken at the opening session of the World Council of Churches in Amsterdam. In the photo portraying the procession passing by the Dutch queen Juliana it was easy to notice my father, wearing an ermine hood and a heavy gold chain over his academic gown. Next to him was Dr. Krenek, who was then the head of our churches. Behind them was professor Hromadka. Until the last minute Father did not know whether or not the Communist authorities would allow him to travel abroad. Of course he was hoping, knowing that it would be terribly embarrassing and compromising for Hromadka if he were the only one allowed to travel to Amsterdam. Father asked me to write letters ahead of time and mail them to his trusted Dutch friends so that he would have some news from me upon his arrival. Behind me was a memorable summer in Vermont where I had so many friends from the previous year. I served two tiny churches of Belvedere and Waterville in the picturesque, mountain setting of Vermont's highest peak of Mt. Mansfield. I preached on Sundays, and in each church I conducted a month long vacation Bible School, and organized a youth group. I knew that Father was very worried about my standing in the USA and I was thrilled to tell him that with the help of senator Warren Austin who then served as the United States Ambassador to the UN I was granted political asylum as a displaced person. I met the Austins the previous summer at the First Congregational Church in Burlington, and the great help of Ambassador Austin was interpreted by me as a touch of God's everlasting arms, nothing could make my father happier than the knowledge that I was in the USA safe.

Soon Father's letters began arriving. He was incredibly happy in Amsterdam and in meeting old friends. Although he was exhausted by the day long sessions, every night he wrote me a long letter. A great many friends urged him to stay behind but he explained that he could not do that because the whole family would suffer incredible persecution. He hinted, however, that he would come legally, if invited to deliver some lectures, and provided his expenses were paid.

Professor Hromadka and the former Secretary of State, Foster Dulles delivered major addresses, and Hromadka was favorably received. Dr. Krenek as the head of our delegation, however did not agree with Hromadka's political views, and announced that Hromadka did not represent the thinking of the Czechoslovak protestants and that he spoke for himself. Obviously that did not bother Hromadka one bit. Hromadka spoke brilliantly as he raised his doubt that the decadent West, which failed to organize the world justly after 1918 was capable of dealing with the enormous issues of the second half of the twentieth century. Hromadka was always at his best in raising rhetorical questions: Are the Christians of the West representing a new way of thinking or are they simply just endeavoring to restore the prewar society? Hromadka unquestionably saw far greater vitality in the political East than in the political West. He rightly elaborated the enormous sacrifices of the Soviet Union in terms of human life for the defeat of Nazi Germany and its unwillingness to play second fiddle in the post war rearrangement of the world. Although Hromadka was in the Soviet Union for only a week, he did not mind reminding his audience that the Soviets diligently cultivated family life and that the sexual morality of the Soviet young people was much cleaner than in his own country and in Western democracies. A critical observer of Hromadka could register here that already at Amsterdam, Hromadka used different yardsticks for measuring the morality of the East and the West. Although the address by Foster Dulles was far less prophetic, passionate and theologically stimulating than Hromadka's, reading it after fifty years, the well researched speech stands as a political document of that era written from the perspective of a Christian layman.

Before leaving for Prague, Father sent me a dear letter and typically for him, all the money he had left. As his plane was preparing to land at Prague's Ruzyne airport, he noticed that all the flags were at half mast: President Benes died at his county home at Sezimovo Usti. For Father it was terribly sad news, marking the end of decades of friendship. Dr. Benes who spent two world wars in exile working for Czechoslovak independence died as a trapped man; after many strokes his heart literally broken. Although he had short seasons of reasonably good health, the Communists knew that he was a seriously ill man already when he was leaving his exile in London through Moscow to Prague to assume his presidency. The Communists knew how dearly he was loved by the Czechoslovak people, they knew also that his acute arteriosclerosis which was often marked by indecisive behavior was easily manipulated by them. By the time of his death, many of his most loyal colleagues such as Dr. Drtina suffered incredible hardship in the ill famed Pankrac prison, never understanding why Benes did not resign in protest against the Communist coup. I do not think that Benes understood himself. On that fateful February night of the

Communist Coup he told Gottwald, "You talk to me as Hitler, and let me tell you the Soviet Union and the people like you will end as Hitler. . . ." Then Benes collapsed, and Gottwald went on the balcony to tell the blood thirsty crowd that President Benes in his greatness accepted the will of the people. "Long live great Marshall Stalin! Long live the Czechoslovak Communist Party! Long live Leninism! Long live Edward Benes!"

That night Dr. and Mrs. Benes left the Prague castle for their country home never to return to the presidential residence. He returned to Prague only to attend the funeral of Jan Masaryk, a totally broken man.

The whole family gathered that night at a special dinner, hungry to hear Father's news from abroad, about meeting friends they knew, about his visit with Foster Dulles. It was obvious that the Soviets were in a blind military build up, and that the Western powers were more and more concerned about the possibility of an atomic war in which there would be no winners. Of course, the family gathering was overshadowed by the grief over Benes' death. The Communists were taken aback by the overwhelming grief of the nation. Benes was the last symbol of democracy. The people in the streets wept openly. In every store window there was a portrait of Benes surrounded by flowers. The Communists planned to stage a spectacular funeral but this was far more than they ever expected, consequently they quickly staged a far reaching propaganda offensive; the Western agents and reactionaries tried to turn the funeral of the beloved President Benes into a provocation against the Soviet Union. For security reasons many foreigners were discouraged from attending the funeral. On the other hand it was announced that the members of the Soviet Politburo, and all the heads of the Soviet satellite nations would attend the funeral, which was to start in the Pantheon of the national Museum at the top of Wenceslaus Square, followed by a procession through Prague, and finally to the burial in the garden of the president's estate at Sezimovo Usti.

The day after returning form Amsterdam, Father stayed at home, fighting great weariness, and trying to sort the volumes of his Amsterdam notes. His work was interrupted by the unexpected visit of chancellor Jaromir Smutny who came to notify him that it was the wish of President Benes, who was a nonprofessing Roman Catholic, that Father would officiate together with Cardinal Beran at the grave side ceremony. The chancellor delivered a hand written note of Mrs. Benes about her wishes.

Father, very much aware of the sensitive issues of church etiquette immediately called Cardinal Beran and informed him about the president's wishes. Beran, in his typical way answered, "Friend, dear friend, there better not be any question about your participating in the burial service. Give me a call after you decide what you want to say, and let's go to Usti together. Plan on it! We shall pick you up at your house, and then, at least, we shall have a chance to talk on the way to Usti."

As a church historian Father was deeply aware of his participating in a historic moment. For the first time since the martyrdom of John Hus at the beginning of the fifteenth century, a Roman Catholic prelate and a representative of a Protestant theological school, an ordained reformed clergyman would not only stand together but they would also pray together and read the Gospel together, alas at the grave of democracy. The friendship with Beran meant a great deal to him. Through a diplomat, a friend of the Benes family, Father sent me a copy of his remarks, of his prayers, and of three wonderful photographs showing Cardinal Beran and Father standing at Benes' grave, the resplendent Soviet generals, members of the polilburo and of the Czechoslovak government behind them. Between the typewritten and handwritten texts, it was obvious that the story of Lazarus was very much on Father's mind as he was preparing for the funeral. The risen Lazarus suddenly became the object of hatred of the enemies of Jesus. Lazarus had to be eliminated as the evidence of Christ's power and put back into the grave. The enemies of Christ are always afraid of Life with a capital L. The notes brought back to my mind my reflection on Lazarus in one of my last days in the Nazi labor camp. If there ever was a gathering of most mighty men and women who were afraid of real living, it was the group behind Beran and Father. Their hands were stained by the blood of martyrs, one could not imagine how many people had died because of them, nor could one imagine how profoundly these people feared each other, and the idea that the truth would be one day revealed.

According to the quickly written note, as soon as the Cardinal and Dad came to the grave ready to speak, the air force came to pay the last respects, flying at such low altitude that no human voice could be heard. Mrs. Benes lifted her arm and motioned to the two bewildered clergymen to wait until quietness was restored.

After the service the members of the government and the Soviet guests left. The Cardinal and Father with other close friends of the family stayed for supper and until late in the evening.

For years I kept the copy of Father's notes of his prayer and remarks spoken at Benes' grave along with the glossies showing him together with Cardinal Beran as cherished possessions of historical value. Many years later when my wife and I were spending several months in the beloved village of Les Avants, Switzerland, we decided to take a short trip to Rome, and to give these precious documents from Benes' funeral to the archives of the Vatican. The timing was just right. It was shortly after Beran's death in Rome, while the people in the whole world still remembered Beran's passionate speech before the Vatican Council on human liberties, a speech which certainly must be counted among the great Roman Catholic classics of this century.

In the beautifully furnished salons of the Secretariat for Christian Unity two nuncios gave me a wonderful reception, yes, I would say "tea and sympathy." As I verbalized my admiration for Cardinal Beran, holding the documents of his friendship with my father in a slim briefcase in my hand, I was presented a handsome, brand new presentation edition of the just published biography of Beran. It was a Czech edition, and I was told the editions in other languages would shortly follow. In Czech the volume was entitled "Veliká Mse" (A Great Mass). Before thanking the nuncios, I glanced through the volume. I was particularly interested in the photographs taken at the funeral of President Benes. In every photograph the image of my father was eliminated. Benes, in the text was portrayed as a faithful Roman Catholic. The name of my father was not even mentioned in the book. I glanced at the photographs and the text. There was no use making any presentation of my documents. Slightly short of breath I thanked the brothers of faith for their kind reception and walked away. I was hoping so much that the spirit of the Middle Ages was gone, but here it stared at me, history being adjusted to the given dogma. I walked and walked until I stopped and deposited my treasure into a trash can at the bottom of the Spanish steps.

*　*　*　*　*

The economic and military collapse of the Soviet Union did not take place but rather Moscow was marked on the map of the world as a center of military might. The Eisenhower administration began to talk about peaceful coexistence, conflict with the Soviet Union was to be avoided at whatever cost, the theologians started to write volumes on Marxist Christian dialogue. Professor Hromadka and those who shared his views began feverishly developing the international Christian Peace Conference which, as we now know, was largely funded by the Soviet Union and was considered one of the most successful weapons of its Secret Police. While it was not difficult for anyone to find out that the ministers in any country of the Soviet block were the least paid workers in the Communist society and endured incredible hardship, the delegates to the meetings of the Christian Peace Conference, including the delegates from the churches in the United States were housed in the most luxurious hotels and enjoyed their ego trips. For his collaboration with the Soviets and his leadership in the so called Christian Peace movement professor Hromadka was given Lenin's Peace Price which he received in the halls of the Kremlin precisely when the civilized world mourned the brutal treatment of the Soviet Nobel Prize literati Boris Pasternak, and Alexander Sholzenitzyn. The refugees from Soviet countries slowly were getting used to the idea that they would spend the rest of their lives in exile and that perhaps they would never see their families and their homelands again. Their diaries were marked not by months or years but rather by memories of the Soviet inhumanity, by the sad stories of collaborators and by incredible documents of humanity written in the realm of Caesar.

The Bednář family saga began to develop against the backdrop of the new world order dictated by Moscow. Shortly after the coup, my oldest sister Vera, who was already a highly respected scientist was asked along with her colleagues to join the Communist party. Everybody was surprised when she flatly refused stating that she was first of all a Christian believing in a Christian social order. From all of us, Vera was always the most brilliant, possessing a fine balance of a keen mind and kind heart. We often laughed at her. Courage was not her outstanding characteristic. Even as children, when we played hide and seek in the dusk of the orchard, she was fun to frighten, yet during the Communist era she was the most courageous and manifested an enormous inner strength. Shortly after she refused to join the party she was transferred to Jablonec, a provincial town in the former Sudetenland, set in picturesque mountains. One Sunday afternoon she went for a walk through the woodland. Suddenly, she was surrounded by police, and charged with an attempt to escape to the West. She was arrested and sent to prison. This was terribly hard on Father because the police never bothered to notify him of Vera's arrest and she simply disappeared. After her return from prison, she was at last able to marry Lord Pieter, who miraculously met a friend from his youth, now a prominent man in the Soviet hierarchy, who secured a job for him and reasonable safety. It was an extremely happy, totally unorthodox marriage of bucolic quality. Father found in Pieter a new ally and friend.

Vera's troubles did not end with her return from prison. One day as she worked at her microscope, a cleaning woman came to her and informed her that there would be a very special St. Nicholas party, but that the intellectuals were not invited. The woman thought it was extremely funny and laughed heartily. As she started to sweep again she kept on chanting, "Intellectuals out! Intellectuals out!" Then again she burst into uncontrollable laughter and suddenly her false teeth fell out, and dropped into her mop bucket. Of course, Vera could not control her laughter, this was a scene straight from *comedy absurd.*. . . She was charged with antisocial behavior and insensitivity to the working people. Recalling this incident Vera always remarked that she was never aware of her class until she began living in the Communist society.

* * * * *

Father was to finish his tenure as a dean of the faculty at the end of 1949. It was quite obvious that Hromadka would succeed him, and Hromadka did not waste any time. The Communist Secretariat for Church Affairs was ready to unveil its plan for a total reorganization of the supervision of the religious life in Czechoslovakia. The churches according to the plan would lose all their autonomy, the clergy would be paid by the state, which also would pay all the necessary repairs on church buildings. The theological training of the clergy was to be restructured, and although the budget for the administration of the faculty was drastically cut, the government insisted on the appointment of two professors of "social sciences." These men were already selected. They were totally unknown in the theological circles, and there was no doubt that they were members of the party. On top of it all, the school was to bear the name of Commenius, while the so called Czechoslovak Church for some unclear political reasons would maintain a separate theological school. All the members of the faculty and of course its dean were expected to swear loyalty to the State and its new laws on the relationship of the churches to a notorious communist in charge of the State office for Ecclesiastical Affairs.

Although Father was functioning as the Dean at that time, he was not consulted on any changes or any plans, while Dr. Hromadka was not only fully informed but included in formulating the expected changes. How else can we understand the fact, that all of a sudden, he made an urgent appointment with my father, the acting Dean, and elaborated for him that the theological education of the future ministers was at stake as long as my father was not only the dean but also a member of the faculty! With the skill which only Hromadka possessed, he elaborated to my father "purely as a brother in faith" the far reaching consequences of his presence on the faculty for the future of theological education. "Face it, as a Professor of Law, you are finished, your books are no longer valid, there is a new law every day, there is no other law than the State" Hromadka was at his very best, "You have no idea how hard this is for me, but I must put the future of the church above the friendship and affection I hold for you. I give you my word of honor. You have nothing to lose, You have my word of honor that you will be getting a good pension, that you will be given a chance to do your research. On my honor, I promise you your comfort and security." Then came the clincher, "Of course, it is totally up to you, but if you decline my offer, you must take the full responsibility for the future of the church!"

In his letter describing this scene, Father wrote, "I made the biggest mistake of my life in taking the loving advise of brother Hromadka, and resigning as a dean and professor. The resignation was never made public and although Hromadka gave me a word of honor, he never kept it. There were times when my pension never came. I wrote him about it and begged him. He never answered. I ran out of the supply of typewriter ribbons and paper, and I begged him to help me. I had an offer from the University of Basel for the publication of a new work, and I had no heat, no paper, no ribbon. Hromadka never, never answered."

It is easy to point a finger of judgment at the Nazis, it is not as easy to write these lines and to register here that a theologian of stature still revered in my homeland, and ironically in many places of high learning, literally tortured my father in his advancing years. Yet, I must say, that Hromadka, at least politically, was trying to be far more noble than he was to my uncle Dr. Adolf Novotny, a full time professor in Christian Education and Practics. He never even bothered to talk with Novotny, although the family of his wife, and the family of Novotny's were interwoven in the leadership of the prestigious Vinohrady church. Dr. Novotny under the signature of Hromadka was simply fired. It may be registered here, that Novotny's sons, Jan Novotny, a distinguished artist and caricaturist of political personalities escaped to Switzerland, and Dr. Pavel Novotny, a most distinguished cardiologist on the faculty of Charles University escaped to England. The Novotnys were reduced to a life of poverty. Aunt Martha, a highly educated woman, and exactly as Mrs. Hromadka, a daughter of a wealthy, distinguished doctor had no other choice but to work as a domestic for the new Communist elite. Ironically the Novotnys and the Hromadkas lived in the same neighborhood. It was the joke of the family: Martha Novotny dressed in a Persian lamb coat, a bucket in her hand, going to work. Mrs. Hromadka walking toward her on the same street, and quickly crossing the street to avoid meeting Mrs. Novotny. The only good thing about this tragic situation was that uncle Adolf and Father met several times a week for a cup of coffee and theological discussion. Father added another dimension to his dismissal as a theological professor; my brother's wife, Cecilia, by then a mother of two vivacious boys, Paul and Mark, was failing in her health. Father, who as far as I am concerned never enjoyed fatherhood, suddenly found a new role as a grandfather. I cannot say that he was successful, but nevertheless he planned every day for some excursion for the boys, be it a trip to a zoo or to a museum or to a theater performance, giving Cecilia at least some time to rest. Although nobody knew about it, Cecilia was dying of cancer of the lungs. She was hospitalized several times but always wrote extremely cheerful letters. The fact is that my brother Blahoslav did not have the heart to tell her the diagnosis, and since he did not tell her, he could not tell anyone else, even anyone in the family. It was a gallant, gallant performance of love on his part, but at the same time, one cannot imagine the magnitude of loving support of which my brother deprived himself. Undoubtedly there were times when he felt alone, abandoned, but he adhered to his role, and spent every moment he could call his own with the boys and his wife. When she had a good day, plenty of laughter was coming out of their rooms. I felt I lost a true sister when Cecilia died and not being able to be with my family and to be of some help and comfort was extremely hard to bear.

*   *   *   *   *

On this side of the Atlantic Jarka Stolar was our main concern. Almost every weekend he came to Hartford to share with the Spinkas and me his anguish. He was finishing his PhD at Yale, receiving praise after praise. Although once in a while Jarka entertained the thought of staying in the USA, the Spinkas and I believed that his mind was really made up and that there was no use of debating about it. He was assured, as we all remembered that with a PhD. from Yale his career was secured in Prague, and although some wonderful offers of academic opportunities in the USA were coming to him, he always felt duty bound by the commitment to his native church and its future. Although there was no doubt that Jarka was extremely sincere, his rationale for serving his church seemed to us only a backdrop for a decision already reached. He just wanted us to encourage him, to tell him that his decision was right, something which we refused to do. We parted very sadly. It took us several years before we knew the full tragedy of this dear friend. Shortly after his return to Prague, he married Vera and confidently went to visit Dr. Hromadka, the new dean, to refresh the Princeton conversation with him, and to discuss with him his recent letters. Hromadka did not remember anything, and although he was unquestionably the leader of the faculty, he felt that any job would have to be first approved by the whole faculty before his nomination were suggested to the State Office for Ecclesiastical Affairs. He invited Jarka to meet with the whole faculty three days later.

During those three days all members of the faculty were informed about Jarka's desire to pursue an academic career, and the members of the faculty unanimously agreed that Jarka lacked the most essential training in Marx Leninism. Hromadka also elaborated to the members of the faculty that at that particular time, a doctorate from Yale could be detrimental to all. It was then unanimously voted that the faculty would not recognize a PhD from Yale but that, of course, Jarka had a good opportunity to earn his doctorate in Prague. It was one of Hromadka's shabbiest moments. For the first time a doctorate from Yale was not recognized by another university. When the news reached Yale, a great many Yale scholars led by professor Ronald Bainton sent a cable of protest to Hromadka—a cable which Hromadka never acknowledged. The tragedy was not less painful to Jarka by the fact that his brother-in-law, Josef Smolik who himself held a Masters degree from Union Seminary in New York was a voting member of the faculty.

Jarka took a small church in Prague, and while his wife was the chief bread winner, to the surprise of all, Jarka started to work toward his PhD. all over again. The fortitude of that man was incredible. Then his wife was reported as unfit for teaching in public school because her husband was a minister, and for a considerable time, Vera, Jarka and their children were in a desperate financial situation. At last, according to Jarka with the help of "plenty of vitamin F" (influential friends), Vera was reinstated as a teacher.

Jarka did earn his doctorate, but Hromadka again did not keep his promise, and Jarka was never considered for an academic career. At the very end of his life, he was asked to serve on a commission in charge of the preparation of a new translation of the New Testament, which was at last a recognition of his outstanding scholarship.

The last time we saw him was shortly after the death of his wife, Vera, who always believed in him and gave herself for him. He came for lunch at my sister's—a broken man of poor health, wearing a worn out black suit and black tie. We brought him a package in a slim, narrow box.

"This looks like a tie," he guessed.

"You need one! You look as if you worked for an undertaker!"

"Oh no," he protested, "this is the only black tie I have. I shall not wear another tie in my life."

He opened the package and smiled broadly. "A Yale tie! All these years I have been sorry that I did not buy one before coming home. A Yale tie! I don't know if I shall ever have the courage to wear it, but I am so glad to have it. The happiest days of my life were spent at Yale!"

Only about six months later we heard about his death.

*   *   *   *   *

In his last letter Mirko Harych seemed resigned. He did not mind writing me at my own address although he knew that I was the enemy of the people. He was like the same old Mirko, this time fully describing his attending a party meeting, shortly after the death of Jan Masaryk. He held his party membership card in his hands. "Comrades, I have trusted you, and I have served the party in genuine hope that it would bring about a better society for our people. You have all lied to me, and I have been so stupid that I have believed the big lie, that Communism and Christianity could coexist. Now I see my folly. Dostoevsky explained this most fully when he said that once we eliminate God from our thinking 'everything is permitted.' You are making it absolutely clear, as you persecute innocent Christian people in cold blood, you are not ashamed of any crime—Everything is permitted if it is approved by the party. I am ashamed of ever trusting scoundrels like you. Here is the party ticket! I do not know where to hide in my shame!"

"That's your problem," answered the chairman, "and undoubtedly your leaving will be for the good of all."

At the time Mirko was very ill, and it was a gallant, gallant act on his part. His hand writing suddenly was quite legible. He wrote about the scene at great length, and of his long reflection about the despair of Judas, who in the dark hours of Good Friday was actually the only one who cast the vote for Jesus, admitting that he had betrayed innocent blood, throwing the thirty silver pieces on the cold floor of the temple only to hear the cynical response, "That's your problem."

"I can't help it," wrote Mirko, "but in my misery, I try to comfort myself by thinking that Judas, undoubtedly a Zealot, who obviously did not share the nonviolent principles of Jesus, but nevertheless gave up everything and followed him, loved him, wanted him to act. He betrayed him and was driven to absolute despair. Such a man as Origen speculated that this Judas wanted to be in the realm of death before Jesus, that he wanted to be there first and await him and beg him for forgiveness. As you can see, in my horrid feeling of guilt, I do not mind thinking even of Origen, yearning to be forgiven more than anything else!"

After reading lines like these I wanted to run across the ocean, to embrace Mirko, to renew the covenant which we sealed so many years before.

After many surgeries Mirko died a cruel death of cancerous tumor on the brain. His every scream stabbed the heart of his parents. At his request my father prayed with him asking the Lord for the gift of deliverance. It was a matter of course that Father officiated at Mirko's funeral.

I never asked about Mirko's last moments or about his funeral, and nobody ever told me about them, but Mirko has never stopped being a part of me.

* * * * *

At the end of his life my father lived with my younger sister Bohunka and her family. As he was failing and fewer and fewer friends were coming to visit him, I was told that news from me was the only source of joy for him, and I tried to supply him only with news which was good. As I finished my studies of Marx, I was surprised by joy, masked by layers of anxiety. I did not want to admit it to myself, but it was obvious that I could not be an eternal student and stay at Hartford forever. One day Tertius Van Dyke called me to his office, and told me that he had a special opportunity for me. A prominent Boston industrialist Harry Kendall needed a young man like me to change the young people in his native town of Walpole in three easy steps. Before I knew it, I had in my hands the train and bus schedules, and was told that Harry Kendall and the committee would expect me at such and such time in a couple of days.

I traveled by train to Boston which was love at first sight. From Boston I went by bus for about forty minutes to a typical suburban town of the fifties, from my point of view a punishment of God. Only the thought that Walpole was in the near proximity of Boston kept me from turning around and going back to Hartford! In the center of that typically New England town was the village green with a white gazebo in the center. On one side of the manicured green was a mansion size parsonage, and next to it a huge funeral home!

Harry Kendall was a towering figure, he did not need to introduce himself. The people around him, including the minister literally crawled, and raised questions with the preamble, "with your permission."

The meeting was held in a rather large parlor of the United Church. After the introductions, Harry Kendall who was obviously a good friend of Tertius van Dyke looked at me with the eyes of a man considering buying a new truck.

"Young man," he said, "are you a Bohemian?"

"Sort of."

"Good! Bohemians have always been the best workers in my mills. You are hired." Only after that introduction did he ask the members of the committee to ask any questions.

Soon it was obvious to me that Harry Kendall not only was ready to subsidize the youth ministry in Walpole, but that he was also planning to donate a tract of land in the vicinity of the church to develop for recreational purposes of the young people under the auspices of the church. The members of the committee got involved in a lengthy discussion on how the land could be cleared and on who could do what. Suddenly, Harry Kendall turned to me.

"What do you think?"

"This is all new to me but personally I think that the young people have to develop a sense of ownership, they are the ones to clear the land, and not just come to play."

"Do you realize the responsibility?" asked someone.

"We do not have any insurance for that," said somebody else. Then somebody asked me about my training, my interests.

"Are you planning to get married?"

"It could be arranged," I answered.

"Put it in the minutes," remarked Harry Kendall. "Mr. Bednář plans to get married."

The question of my ordination followed.

Later on in the afternoon, to the surprise of all, Harry Kendall excused everyone and offered to take me for a ride in his convertible. We drove through his woodland until we landed in a charming cottage. Harry Kendall served sherry and crackers. We talked about many important things as if we had known each other for years. Of course, I accepted the job. Arriving at Hartford I stopped to see Muriel and told her that our engagement would be announced in the Boston papers, and laughingly we set the date of our wedding for January 28. Muriel's parents did not think that it was too funny but agreed "to make the best of it."

I hope very much that my letters to my father in which I tried to cheer him up and portray these events in most hilarious ways got lost, because I stretched the truth a bit, especially about my ordination to the Christian Ministry which was far from hilarious.

The problem which I was totally unwilling to admit was that all the years in Hartford I lived in a complete detachment from the institutional church. I did not need it, I did not miss it. On Sundays I preached at Warburton chapel, a mission church supported by Center church in Hartford. On Sunday night I had my youth group in the same church. I spent summers in Vermont in Congregational churches, that is where the job was offered, and all of a sudden I needed the blessing of the institutional church. The first question was in which denomination I ought to seek my ordination. Since my church at home was Presbyterian in polity I decided to be ordained in the Presbyterian church so that I would be acceptable at home in case of my return.

I made an appointment with the minister of a very large Presbyterian church in the vicinity of Bushnell Hall, asking him to advise me. Of course, it never occurred to me that I was actually asking for a great favor; I accepted a call to serve the United Church in Walpole which was a part of the Congregational church and I was seeking to be ordained by the Presbyterian church! The reception by the minister was extremely cool. The first question was,

"Why did you ever study at Hartford Theological Seminary and not at Princeton?"

"Because Princeton did not offer any scholarship."

It took me a while to realize that I had no comprehension of American denominationalism. At last, I cooled down, and explained that I was seeking ordination in the Presbyterian church because I was still hoping to return home and some day serve a church in Czechoslovakia, and that our churches not necessarily in theology but in polity were Presbyterian. Then the minister slowly and precisely elaborated for me what was expected from me. First of all, I was to prepare a paper of theological significance which I would present at the Ecclesiastical council. An examination of the paper and also of matters of Presbyterian polity would follow. I was allowed to invite faculty members and friends to the Ecclesiastical Council. They would be allowed to ask questions but they would not be allowed to participate in the final vote. The Ecclesiastical council consisted usually of about thirty members and the candidate was expected to provide supper for them following the examination. Usually the service of ordination was held the same day in the evening. It is a large service to which you will want to invite your friends and colleagues. The service is followed by a reception for which you are responsible. You are also responsible for paying the the organist, and the custodian, and it would be also nice to have some flowers on the altar and the reception table. My heart trembled since I was almost broke, and I asked the minister to give me a reasonable estimate. He paused for a minute, and then said, "If you cut corners about two hundred fifty dollars should be enough."

I was totally crushed, crying, damning the Presbyterians for being unreasonable, rushing to tell the news to Dean Van Dyke. He was speechless and shortly excused himself obviously to place a call to the Presbyterian minister, wanting to verify the information. Tertius Van Dyke returned to the study red in the face but assuring me that there was nothing to worry about, that the seminary family would take care of things. Before I knew it half of the faculty wives were working on a buffet supper for the members of the Ecclesiastical Council, the students were baking cookies and making sandwiches for the reception, and Dean Lowell was in her element planning the flower arrangements and the whole affair. It does not need to be underlined that this development did not deepen ecumenical relations, in fact when I arrived to present my paper before the Ecclesiastical Council, I was greeted by several members of the Hartford faculty, by my new boss and Harry Kendall from Walpole. Otherwise the atmosphere was chilly. Shortly before the meeting was called to order I introduced Muriel to my boss Mr. Bozarth and to Harry Kendall. To my horror Mr. Bozarth took Muriel's left hand into his, saying, "May I see your diamond?" There was not any. Observing the situation Harry Kendall turned to us and said, "By now I hope you know, that some ministers are wonderful guys but they have absolutely no manners."

My paper was chiseled in terms of the reformation tradition and the tenants of neorthodoxy. My professor read it and gave me a straight A for it. I delivered it well, and I was not worried about it. When it came to the examination I had the shock of my life, and I was getting deeper and deeper into trouble. It was a rather conservative gathering, and it seemed that from the very beginning the venerable fathers and mothers, mostly fathers, were concerned about the condition of my soul since I was unable to define hell as a place. How could I ever preach eternal salvation, how could I preach salvation with passion if I did not know its opposite? I invoked Paul and Calvin, I quoted (not too wisely Dostoevsky!) and before I knew it, the members of the council were slugging each other. I never dared to ask about the actual vote, but I knew that I passed that ordination examination purely by the grace of God. It meant a lot to me when Dr. Spinka came to me afterwards and said, "I hope you will not allow this to bother you."

At the evening service Dr. Spinka preached; poor Tertius Van Dyke tried to offer the prayer of ordination. He hardly put his hand on my shoulder when he broke into tears. He tried to gain the control of himself by switching into the Lord's Prayer, and we were all helping him to finish.

Although I made my ordination promises with all my heart, I already knew in that moment that I could never serve the conservative Presbyterian churches of New England.

Our seminary friends and the wives of the Hartford faculty were all magnificent. We thanked them all, and embraced many. Muriel and I wanted to be sure that the sinks were immaculate, we even double-checked on all bathrooms before paying the custodian. "We walked home quietly, Muriel knew how profoundly I was hurt, and that I could never describe the fiasco of my ordination to my father. Then we burst into laughter, saying to each other "After this, even a most disastrous wedding is bound to be spectacular!"

With the exception of the description of my ordination, I never lied to my father. For him the beginning of my ministry was the fulfillment of his dreams, and an answer to his prayers. I just could not describe for him the pitiful reality, but I exaggerated all which spelled out for me the words "Una Sancta"—the seminarians of different religious orientations, the faculty wives all working together to make one little guy happy, the members of the faculty and the strange ministers laying their hands upon my head and praying for me, and then all the funny details of the day. My sisters wrote that Father read my exaggerated letters with descriptions of all the funny details with pleasure over and over again, sharing them with friends, his cup of joy overflowing. Although at that time I gave him only half truth, I thanked God for being able to give it to him, for Father in his own, wonderful way led me to the full joy of ministry.

*   *   *   *   *

My sister's apartment at the beginning of July was terribly hot. Father could hardly breath and just waited and waited for the time when he would be able to return to his beloved homestead in Vir. The nights at the homestead were magical, cool. The windows were wide open, one could hear the sound of the flowing river Svratka, the moon illuminated the gray dew on the apple trees in the orchard, one gladly reached for a quilted blanket. "When shall we go to Vir, when shall we go to Vir?" Father asked over and over again. His seventy-ninth birthday was at hand and his birthday was always celebrated at the homestead with mothers special raspberry filled cake. The doctor came, and considered Father's condition critical. As soon as the doctor left, father summoned the family to his bedside, and crying, he begged them, "Do not allow me to die in Prague, do not allow them to use my funeral for their evil purposes, please, please, I beg you take me home!"

Even as he walked through the valley of death he had no illusions, he knew that in Prague, Hromadka would have to stage a faculty funeral. The ambulance was called and, in spite of all misgivings, took him home.

He revived when he was put into his own bed, as the windows were opened and he could hear the humming of Svratka. He happily rested. That evening Vera offered him a piece of his beloved birthday cake, and he ate a piece of it with gusto. That night he died.

As his father and grandfather before him, for years my father paid an old woman to ring the bell in a small bell tower whenever someone in the village died. The Communists eliminated that custom, but when Father died somebody saw to it that the bell rang and the men and women busy harvesting wheat, as in the past, stopped for a minute and bowed their heads.

My family arranged the funeral in the church about four kilometers from Vir, in the Rovecne church in which Father was baptized and confirmed. Then the burial was to take place in the cemetery in Vir. I was the only member of the family missing. All members of the family gathered at the homestead. It was to be a small funeral on Wednesday afternoon. Dr. Václav Kejř, a very dear friend of our father and our family, who was then the head of the Church of Czech Brethren agreed to make all the arrangements for the funeral at the church and then at Vir.

Long before the funeral the sleepy village of Vir was alive

A surprise procession of ministers leading the crowds for the burial of Zdenék's father in a tiny cemetery at Vir. The first on the right is Dr. Václav Kejř, graduate of Duke, and the distinguished leader of the Church of Czech Brethren.

with traffic. As my family arrived at the church, the sanctuary was packed. Dozens of ministers, most of them dad's former students came on foot, by bicycle and by bus, and put on their vestments, ready to walk behind the casket to the final resting place. It was an incredible, spontaneous, unrehearsed demonstration of affection and respect. The photograph showing the many ministers walking through the potato field to the Vir burying ground certainly belongs to the great documents of that era, it shows who is who. Dr. Hromadka never came and to my knowledge never wrote to our family. Undoubtedly the members of my family were deeply touched by this outpouring of respect for our father, but at the same time, I am sure, they were worried. Of course, they made preparations for refreshments for the family and friends after the funeral, not a minor task considering the shortage of food, but here was a crowd, and the tradition of post funeral fellowship was unchanging, unchangeable. I can imagine my sisters saying to themselves: well, we have done the best we could, it's not the food, it's the fellowship which is most important—but at the same time, it did not take much imagination to understand that many people came from afar and were hungry.

Among the many weeping, sad looking people was Vlada Stastny, the old Postmaster, the son of the old innkeeper, smiling broadly, embracing everyone, tears of joy in his eyes, saying to everyone, "Something of the Holy Scriptures had been fulfilled here. It's a miracle. The old inn is open today, and there is more food than anyone can imagine! Just come in! It's the Lord's doing!"

Of course the people of the village had known Vlada for his exaggeration, but this was the Lord's doing—even the Communists from early in the morning were bringing the best pastries. There was not just enough for everyone, there was enough to send a small package of pastries to the families of clergy.

Of course, I was not there, I missed being there, but looking at the photographs I know that father would be happy to see his friends, and that indeed something of the Communist stone was turned into bread of hospitality. Something of the Holy Scriptures was fulfilled, the impossible became possible, and many were able to lift up their hearts.

BECAUSE OF YOU I AM GLAD

When I finished writing the previous pages it was late at night. The thermometer mounted outside the window of my study, illuminated by an almost full moon registered fifteen below zero. Our dachshund Loui, ever so comfortably situated in an easy chair by my desk, poked his head out of layers of blankets and gave me an anxious look: You cannot possibly mean it that you are sleepy, that you are on your way to bed, that you will take me out. I can't stand the thought of it! This is the time for you to listen to the silence and not to move an inch!

No, I was not sleepy. By the right side of my desk was a big wicker laundry basket full of my father's letters which I was planning to read again before destroying them. On my desk there were several musty smelling notebooks, which I discovered among Father's letters, for they were the documents of that era. Indeed, in the Communist society problems were not allowed, and problems were considered the favorite pastime of the capitalistic society. Psychology, psychiatry were disciplines not needed in the Soviet block. At the same time while the people of the Soviet block specialized in denying problems, in the late fifties and sixties, on this side of the Atlantic we specialized in producing problems and in learning to deal with them. The search for the Father dominated the literature of that period. Just a glance at the scribbling in my journals brought back to my mind issues of that era: the deterioration of family, desperate yearning for belonging to community, the rebellion of sons and daughters against their parents and their values, the despair of fathers and mothers, the feeling of being rejected by their sons and daughters ruled the schedule for every counselor, minister or psychiatrist. "Look," cried the parents, "ever since they were little no sacrifice was great enough for them. We sent them to the best schools, we established big trust funds for them so they could be free to go to Harvard or Princeton or Yale, or any prestigious school of their choice. Now they refuse, saying that they do not want to perpetuate the society which we had produced. The fathers and mothers cried, "we do not know our sons and daughters, we do not understand their reasoning," and far more emphatic was the cry of the children, "We do not know our parents, their goals. Of course Mother is always caught in the middle! All right what is the biggest goal of my father without the obvious desire to strike it rich? And why do I have to subscribe to the same way of thinking! Why?"

I was thinking about my father, about the way he thought, lived, loved and about the way he died. When I received a cable informing me of his death I was at home alone. My family was in New Hampshire, and I felt terribly alone, but only now do I realize that when my father died, my sense of having a home was finished. There was no longer a place where I could come unannounced in the middle of the night as one of our own, nowhere in this world was a room which I could claim as my room in the same way as when I was a boy. The demigods of our safety and child-like trust who kept the home together were dead, and much of our safety and trust was gone from our hearts. I knew that this was coming when Mother died, but at the time I was so grateful for her smile, yes in all her pain she smiled, knowing that all of us, her children were miraculously well and alive. I greeted her death as a friend, delivering her from seeing Nazism being replaced by a tyranny beyond all her imagination. Father, on the other hand, had to drink the cup of incredible spiritual suffering in full. Yes, after Mother died we tried to keep our home with the appearance of some normalcy, but it was with difficulty, we were all role playing. By that time all of us were either married or planning to get married, Father and I were left alone in that old establishment. It was at his urging that I left, and when he died, my home as I remembered it, was gone. All that I had left was my name, a piece of paper stating that I was a displaced person, protected by the government of the United States.

Since I spent most of my life in exile but also because I am the youngest in the family of five children, many would say that I knew my father the least. To be exact, I knew my father in the traditional sense only for twenty plus years when we lived under the same roof, and were a part of the same family. We surely did not know the term "quality time." We knew and believed that our parents always gave us all the time they had, they helped us to understand that by the sense of their calling, they belonged to others. They never complained about it. They brought us up believing that there was no higher calling of honor and trust than ministry and that by tolerating some of their parental negligence, we were making a very important contribution to their ministry. We were a team. Once in a while when I talk with my oldest sister, I am sorry that I did not know my father when he was still young and playful, I was born when he was forty two, when he already served a very large church, and shortly afterward the University. We must also remember that Hitler and his followers confiscated seven years of our lives, that is a block of time they can never give back to me. Considering all the other complications, that cut our living together to only about ten years. Before we get our hankerchieves ready to wipe away the tears of self pity, I want to register here that perhaps I knew my father better than my brother or my sisters. I certainly knew my father far better than the sons and daughters who for years formed the majority of my counselees, most of whom were troubled by the mystery of their fathers, one after another saying, "I don't know my father, I have no idea what is really important to him, I don't know what makes him happy, I don't understand him and he surely does not understand me."

The leaders of the corporate society taught me that good politics does not allow communication by letters especially when controversial matters are involved, that it is also advisable to be guarded in our phone conversations, that in dealing about important issues which matter to us, nothing can take the place of an honest face to face conversation. Unfortunately, my father and I could not afford this luxury, but there are very few sons and daughters who would have literally hundreds and hundreds of letters in which their fathers made themselves known, registering their hurts, hopes and dreams, above all, out of love freely describing the biggest failures and presenting them as a warning.

*   *   *   *   *

"My father never cared," Joanna cried, "he never cared enough to inflict any discipline on me. Good God, night after night as the streets were getting dark, I heard the monstrous voices of the fathers of my friends, calling them to stop playing and to come home at once. The kids bargained, pleading just for a bit more time. They cursed their unreasonable fathers, and congratulated me on having "a neat" father. Every evening it was the same, the fathers with a godlike authority called the kids home, I was the only lucky one; nobody ever called me. I smiled while I cried inside. My father, goodness knows where he was, never cared to call me home." After several afternoons of dealing with variations of Joannas, I was not exactly a sweet husband when my wife dragged me to see a splendid performance of T.S. Elliot's *The Cocktail Party* in which the problems of each day were translated into poetry.

> . . . contended with the morning that separates and with
> the evening that brings together, for casual talk before
> the fire. Two people who know they do not understand
> each other, breeding children whom they do not under-
> stand and who will never understand them . . .[11]

I never understood why we applaud our tragedies. Why do we applaud after the last scene of Hamlet when the whole stage is full of dead bodies, but at least Hamlet uncovers for us the source of rottenness, the contemporary playwrights seem to be afraid of speaking plainly. Although I was grouchy when we went to see *The Cocktail Party* for the first time, the notebooks found among Father's letters, documents that T.S. Elliot and Christopher Fry were very important to me at that time. On one page in my notebook Colby's desperate cry in Elliot's *The Confidential Clerk* is printed in capital letters "I WANT TO KNOW WHOSE SON I AM!" Colby is obsessed by the search for his father, and when he finally finds out that his father was a disappointed musician, who died during Colby's infancy—the revelation helps Colby to affirm his sense of vocation. At last he knows something of his father, and says,

> Whose life I could in some way perpetuate
> By being a person he would have liked to be,
> and by doing the things he had wanted to do.

Now I know who was my father
I must follow my father,
so that I may come to know him . . .
I want to be an organist.[12]

The horror of trying to escape one's loneliness and finding a sense of community at the cocktail party, making a lot of noise, spending the evening in chit-chat which we call conversation, and then returning to the old cave of loneliness from which we tried to escape, that seems to be only a theological prelude, in *The Confidential Clerk*. The community, the sense of vocation depends on our knowing the common denominator, God the Father.

To this day I cannot read Colby's lines aloud, "Now I know who was my father, I must follow my father so that I may come to know him . . ." without some trembling of my heart, without an almost Faustian desire to have more time to perpetuate my father's life, by being a person he would have liked to be, and by doing the things he had wanted to do.

Well, Father, before the stars get pale we better talk about the then and now. If discipline is a mark of love and caring, you really did not need to go to extremes, the definition of right and wrong seemed to be written all over the house. I have never known the yearning of Colby, "I must know my father!" We never had any questions about your principles and priorities in our house. Also unlike Colby, I never pursued the ministry because of you. I had my own sense of calling, but you and mother from our early childhood certainly gave us a sense of responsibility for our heritage, for our names; to perpetuate that which was good and noble, from your point of view, seemed to be a task which came with our name. During the years of my ministry I thought of you often, you have become dearer, and I admire you much more than I would otherwise.

All through the years of your ministry your evangelistic zeal was never dormant and you established several new churches. I understand that you were one of the first ministers to have a fine typewriter. What a pity that you do not live now, you would never tire of playing with computers! You never had a car. In your young days you went to preach in the surrounding villages by a fine carriage. In Prague you used trams, and very often when you preached out of town you took an early train. Just the physical exhaustion I cannot imagine, yet I really do not remember you ever complaining about ministry. You complained about individuals who complicated your life and work, but you loved your ministry and together with our mother you made us feel that your work was important to God, and to the people who needed you, therefore whatever we did to make your life easier was also our contribution to the ministry at large.

In my years of retirement all of a sudden some of the younger ministers started to come to see me, to open their hearts and I became a counselor in quotes. I often talked about you and mother, and your love of your vocation, because you have been a source of inspiration to me, but my young friends answered one after another. "My marriage, my family living could not take that kind of commitment." Therefore I must admit that my remembering you and adhering to the principles which you gave us deepens the chasm between my colleagues and myself. I shall blame it on you, I am very lonely. You would be furious but all of a sudden we have an enormous problem in the perception of ministry in distinguishing ministry as a calling and as a profession, in fact some seminaries are helping the students to prepare a professional profile, and when ministers accept a call to a new church, they often speak to us excitedly, saying to us that the terms of call represent "a pretty good package." The contemporary church has almost completely accepted the terminology of the corporate world, it makes us more relevant. I just wish the word downsizing were not as prevalent! Dad, do you see what you did? To this day, just the thought of you, makes me lonely in the "beloved community" fashioned in the spirit at the end of this century!!

As a Dean you exercised strict discipline, and your expectations were extremely high. There was no dialogue with you about principles. We resented that, I am sure some really hated you but you felt an almost holy obligation to give the students the very best education and to give our churches ministers who were prepared for their task. During the sixties which had such a profound influence on the USA, the racial injustice and political reality called for action. The main object of study was strategy, and then something of the excellence in theological education was lost. I recall my mentor in Social Ethics at Boston University, Dean Walter Muelder. He certainly was a social activist but he was also a brilliant scholar unwilling to give us excellent grades for demonstrating in front of the State House. Once he was telling me that at times he was embarrassed by the poor quality of the ordination papers, and what bothered him most was that the churches, that is the institutions which financially supported the seminaries, were totally passive in verbalizing their expectations from theological schools. Dean Muelder was sadly telling me that whenever at faculty meetings he called for higher academic excellence, his was a lonely voice. We are slowly recovering from that but our mediocrity shows especially in your departments: in homiletics, in our understanding the late reformation piety, its educational principles, its renewal of koinonia, its refusal to tolerate the conflict between private and public ethics. You taught us to reserve the priority time for the preparation of the sermon, the weekly Bible Study group and the weekly training session with the church school teachers. I thought you were magnificent in telling us that we must not teach children something which they would have to unlearn in the future. You recognized a story as an art form and mercilessly criticized those who felt duty bound to end with a moralization. You flunked them one by one. Well, you would be amazed by what we have to endure in our churches in the late nineties. We have so few children coming to our churches nowadays that it is good to see some of the little ones coming forward, sitting down in front of the minister; it melts our hearts! You would be the first one to admit that to come up with a good story every Sunday is an impossible expectation, therefore we listen to all kinds of nonsenses. The only good thing is that the children like the minister, they touch his robe, and know that he is human, that he is their friend, you would flip, however, when you would hear the people saying to the minister that this or that cute story was the best part of the services!

As a teacher of homiletics, father, you were extremely strict. A few times I sneaked into your class and I trembled, but I realized that you never expected less from the students than you expected from yourself. I saw how diligently you prepared your sermon. Your parents, your grandparents were all the people of the Book. Your first emphasis was to help the people of the church to be biblically knowledgeable. You always preferred to preach in the country, because in the country you were talking to the people of the Book, and you also felt that the people came to church spiritually prepared, rested, while in the cities the people often come to churches exhausted, sleepy and then they blame the preachers for being dull.

How many times, after coming home late at night from a Saturday night dance, we got this sermonette at breakfast! Fortunately, we, the young sinners had a wonderful secret, and the assurance of unconditional grace from the only saint we knew. You hated to admit it, but Mother's opinion meant a great deal to you. After a sermon it was only natural for you to ask "What did you think?" or "How did it go?" Once in a while, especially when we had Saturday night guests, Mother was tired. It was not an easy task to get all of us five to church on time in a respectable shape. It is only natural that on those Sundays Mother snoozed but then on the way home she was stricken with panic, she swore us to secrecy and asked us "What on earth did dad preach about? I slept all through it! Just tell me at least something you remember!" Those were always memorable Sundays for us because Mother was not an exceptional actress, and the more she tried to say that you developed the main thought rather well, the more we giggled.

Recently I read some of your sermons. You give your text a careful exegesis, you explain why the text appeals to you as significant for us. You ask some very probing questions. As a farmer and lover of nature you use illustrations that are simple, once in a while you react to the happening of the week or to a new book, you repeat those questions, you repeat the promises of the Gospel and our possibility and give thanks for them. Undoubtedly we would dissect your sermon as old fashioned, but we would have to admit that you presented the Gospel, that you applied it to our present situation, that you asked some very pertinent personal questions with which we had to deal, and you concluded with the promise of the Gospel.

Of course today preaching is more complicated because precisely when ecumenicity reached its lowest level since the days of the founding of the World Council of Churches, we have found the common denominator in using the lectionary as the basis for preaching. I know that you would growl, I never preach from the lectionary and I do not mind enduring the dirty looks of my colleagues. It is not so easy to endure listening to it. Recently, on Epiphany, there were four lessons and not a single one had anything to do with epiphany. I was wondering what the poor preacher would do with that. I was rested. I was attentive, yes I was yearning to hear the Word, and the more I tried to listen the more my mind was traveling to the ghastly tradition at the North Bennington Congregational Church in Vermont. According to the By-Laws which seemed unchangeable, at every Annual meeting of that church, the Clerk read the roll call, and every member was to respond with a Bible verse. When your name started with A or B it was easy, one could always answer with a verse from the twenty third Psalm but if you name started with W or Z, like Ziedlick it was quite pathetic and we ended with such a verse as "Jesus wept." The use of the lectionary has a similar impact on me, and Sunday after Sunday we go home empty, not stimulated to think, and it hurts to see students bored stiff. Again, as I think of you, I feel spiritually homesick, lonely but knowing from you that we are able to rise above mediocrity. I thank you for pointing out to me the giants of the spirit, people like Commenius who are still waiting to be discovered by us. There is so much for which I am grateful to you, for your theology of hope which you shared generously and bravely with so many desolate ones. During the Nazi era, when the son of our butcher was tortured to death as a horrid Bolshevik, you did not hesitate a minute and late at night you went with the old Bolshevik and gave his son a Christian burial. When Mirko died everybody knew about his parting with the Communists, you never hesitated for a minute, it was only natural for you to thank God for Mirko and to minister to his family. When President Benes died, and his wife moved to an apartment on Hradcanske Namesti you not only visited her every week but also at her request, brought her a sermon which you discussed, and which later she shared with her friends. This was you at your best, and at times I worry. Is this heritage safe in my hands? You worked hard all your life only to see the Communists with their bulldozers going over everything that has been holy to you, and yet you have never given up your hope, always affirming that God alone will have the last say, that God alone will write the epilogue to our best efforts and to the outcome of history.

In your fashion you would laugh, perhaps because as Lincoln put it, it hurts too much to cry. But while the pamphlets of our denominations celebrate our wonderful diversity, today in a local bookstore I made the following list of new scholarly works in the realm of religion:

> *The Empty Church*
> *Reclaiming the Church*
> *The Crisis in the Church: Spiritual Malaise.*
> *Fiscal Woes*

At times, my dear father, I take courage by imagining you in the company of Reinhold Niebuhr, John Bennet, Henry van Dusen, Karl Barth and John Bailey. We are on the porch of our farm house. It's still winter but truck after truck goes up the hill. The stench of the manure is obnoxious. All of us but you wrinkle our noses. Smiling you take a deep breath and say, "They spread manure everywhere. Manure seems to be their specialty. Such a stench cannot mean anything but a promise of a new harvest, of a new renaissance."

Because of you I am always glad, because of you I know that underneath all the churchy garbage and manure is a promise of a new renaissance.

THE CZECH DON QUIXOTE

It was at the glittering dinner given by our former ambassador to Paris, Dr. Osusky, in honor of Sir Alfred Zimmern that I heard the guest of honor using the words, "That Czech Don Quixote," for the first time. Since that day the metaphor has been widely used to portray Dr. J. L. Hromadka and the naïveté with which he embraced the Communist movement. It is a metaphor which may possibly describe some of his wishful thinking but which does not fit his ultimate tragedy. Indeed I would not be at all surprised, that as Hromadka was leaving the USA, he played with the idea of transforming, humanizing the Communist movement. That is why he was ever so excited by the positive attitude of Klement Gottwald, and why he was so enthusiastic about the short rule of the American born Alexander Dubček who coined the phrase "socialism with a human face." Dubček was not any gentle little lamb, he was trained in Moscow during the Stalinist era, his hands were not clean, but he was astute, he understood that the game of elimination could not go on forever, and I think he was politically perceptive in assuming that Communism with some liberties had a chance of success in Central Europe.

If Dr. Hromadka returned from the USA, in hopes that Communism would be eventually transformed and humanized, he certainly had plenty of company—mostly men and women who had only very superficial knowledge of Marx-Leninism, and absolutely no knowledge of Moscow's control of all Communist parties—the gentle souls yearning for righteousness and justice. After all, the majority of the members of the Czech and Slovak Communist party had no idea of the Soviet involvement in the leadership of their party! If Hromadka believed in some possible transformation or democratization of communism, to my knowledge he never verbalized it, but rather from the very beginning he pleaded with his vast audiences to stop day dreaming and to start taking the Soviet Union seriously as a power which would formulate the future of the world. After the Communist coup Hromadka wrote that the February crisis, which shook the very foundations of the nation, had to be taken as a part of an inevitable world revolutionary process. Amazingly enough, at this time, Dr. Hromadka who spoke so passionately in behalf of the prisoners in Franco's Spain, who rejected Hitlerism because of its inhumanity manifested in concentration camps, had absolutely nothing to say about the suffering of those who were dragged away by Communist agents during the nights following the coup.

The Communists and the leaders of the Soviet block rewarded Hromadka rather nicely for his collaboration, granting him not only the Lenin Peace Prize but also the privileges accorded to a few. He certainly did not have any concept of living in the poverty of the ministers or of professors whom he asked to resign. The foreigners whom the Hromadkas entertained all reported that the table was overflowing with delicacies and that according to the Hromadkas food in Prague was plentiful. On the other hand, the metaphor, "That Czech Don Quixote," has a very tragic twist. In Hromadka's case, at the end, the Soviet Dulcinea does not thank him for changing her, for giving her a new name, for believing in her when everyone else despised her. No, this Dulcinea, at the end, laughs at the well meaning professor, she spits at him in disdain and tells him that if he ever thought of changing her he wasted his time. She enjoys being a slut and wants to remain a slut. She laughs hysterically as the professor cries, she laughs, "I can't believe it, how stupid a brilliant professor can be! For once I won, I have used you, and because of me you have betrayed many perhaps not knowing it. Go now, get lost, and before you die say your prayers at the graves of ideals and principles and men and women you betrayed!"

If such is the case of, "that Czech Don Quixote," and we cannot use just the beginning of the metaphor but we have to deal also with the end dictated by Cervantes, then we have a first rate Czech tragedy waiting not for some protestant Pope to canonize Hromadka but waiting, waiting for some new Pirandello to notice not six but just one Czech character in search of an author!

Dr. Matthew Spinka was extremely courageous but also honest in publishing his short and precise critique of Dr. Hromadka with the introduction by Reinhold Niebuhur. The book is entitled *Church in Communist Society*. As I previously mentioned the Spinkas and Hromadkas were devoted friends. Matthew Spinka really suffered when Hromadka did not answer any of his letters, some of which were hand delivered. It was totally ununderstandable because Spinka was more than careful not to mention any political issues. Even if we overlook the fact that Spinka was a close friend, we cannot overlook the fact that Matthew Spinka had an honorary degree from Prague, and that just at that time he was honored for his volumes in which he introduced John Hus and Commenius to America. As a dean Hromadka owed Spinka at least an official letter. Foreigners visited Hromadka frequently, and they also traveled abroad often. There was no excuse for Hromadka's silence. Niebuhr was also Hromadka's friend, he appreciated his last visit, but he also could not understand Hromadka's behavior and thinking, in fact it was Niebuhr who encouraged Matthew Spinka to write the study on Hromadka.

Spinka never stopped being Hromadka's friend, the publication of the book was painful to him, but to him the principle of truth always had to come first. He tolerated Hromadka's statements until they were misleading and contrary to the truth. Interestingly enough to this day the existence of this book has not been acknowledged in the Czech church press. One would think that by now, one of the professors would translate this small treatise and help not only the students but also the people of the Czech churches to level with Hromadka's thinking and unquestionable collaboration with the communists, but so far no one has dared.

Professor Spinka summarizes his critique of Hromadka by underlining that whether or not Hromadka was a member of the communist party he adopted the basic, the essential principle of the Marxist philosophy, i.e. that the communist order of society must inevitably, irresistibly and unfailingly secure victory over the old order. "Hromadka presumably still repudiates the principal tenet of the Marxist 'dialectical material'," writes Spinka, "but if he does not accept 'dialectical materialism,' why does he hold to its conclusions?"[13]

"Ethics has no place in naturalistic determinism. Even Marx held it as a self-evident axiom that there could not be antithesis unless there had been first a thesis; hence, there cannot be a proletarian class without capitalists. Lenin, of course disregarded this axiomatic Marxist principle, and declared to his astonished Bolshevik fellow leaders that in Russia (which certainly had no highly developed capitalism in 1917) the capitalistic stage of development must be omitted and Russia must jump from feudalism directly into communism. But Marx proved right against Lenin. To this day the Soviet Union does not have the communist economy or the communist order of society, whether political or social. What does prevail there is state capitalism. For in Russia there is only one capitalist, the state, which employs the entire nation in its enterprises, but without the check of competition or the workers' right to strike. And even so the economy cannot operate without slave labor. As for the political form prevailing there, it is the most rigid of totalitarianism, a dictatorship not of the proletariat but by a small clique of men, or by one man alone, and over the proletariat, even over the Communist party itself. In the social organization, far from the classless society, the small and highly privileged class exploits the vast masses of the workers."[14] Contrary to Hromadka who repeatedly affirmed his seeing the hope for just a free social order, Spinka affirms "this vicious system is not Christ's revolution, not even Marx's revolution but a travesty of all social justice. Communism does not represent the beginning of a new order of social justice, but the last stage of the old secularist era which, by destroying faith in God, has also denied faith in man."[15]

Since Hromadka wrote a great deal about the hope of resurrection, Spinka categorically states that no Christian can believe in the resurrection of Christianity when at the same time he actively cooperates with the forces of doom.

Professor Hromadka to this day is often seen as a great theological prophet. Considering that Matthew Spinka wrote the book on Hromadka in 1954, we can easily recognize where the prophetic assertion of the biblical truth rests. "Evil always destroys itself. It would not be a moral universe if such were not the case . . . Communism will collapse as the result of its own inner weakness and falsity. We believe that only good is permanent, and that evil will destroy itself. The collapse of Communism may be accelerated, even without war, if the democratic nations of the world are united and on guard against further Communist aggression. If by a spiritual revolution they get rid of social evils which infect their own body politic, and if they aid the oppressed people everywhere, both inside and outside the Iron Curtain—to secure for themselves a better life. The supreme task of the Church in this common objective is, as it has ever been in the past, to preach the gospel in the confidence that God's power will thereby transform men dominated by their own perverse will into His own obedient children. Our aim is to produce responsible persons filled with the love and spirit of Christ, who will transform society in accordance with the mind of Christ. The fault that the Kingdom tarries is not that of Christianity but of Christians. And the way to transform the evil world into one imbued with the spirit of Christ is not merely by changing the environmental forces economic or political—but by changing men."[16]

Professor Hromadka organized and for years was the spokesman of the so called Christian Peace Conference which was generously funded by the Communists. The pronouncements of this body which were read in churches in many parts or the world as can now be documented from the publications of the work of the Czechoslovak Secret Police were first approved by its offices. Dr. Josef Smolik, the Dean of the Commenius of Faculty of Charles University, speaking in his deep voice put it bluntly, "Well Communism collapsed, and so we must say that the World Christian Peace Conference has collapsed." Indeed the Christian Peace Conference has not met for the last ten years. I think it is a pity. We have been misled by professor Hromadka and others. Our churches *de facto* in their zest for peace actually spent some money to send delegates to support this Communist front forum for the sake of keeping the dialogue open. I do not see anything constructive in remaining silent, but I see a tremendous opportunity for the restoration of our credibility by saying, "we have been mistaken" and by reaffirming the timeless and uniting words of professor Spinka.

Shortly before Christmas 1949, I was surprised to receive a note from professor Hromadka. He thanked me for a special note which I wrote him to congratulate him on his birthday. Then he wrote, "Once in a while I hear all about you from your father. We wish that you may spend the coming holidays in the new under-

standing of the Christmas Gospel. Do return home so that you may
be embraced by us and be among your own. With all good wishes
J. L. Hromadka and family." I could not comprehend the note. It
was written shortly after Dr. Hromadka asked Father to resign,
when it was generally known that I was declared "the enemy of the
people," and when he undoubtedly knew that I had a job and was
planning to get married within a few weeks. How could he know
all these circumstances and yet urge me to return?

Many, many years later when I studied at Oxford, we met a
very interesting man, a former student of Hromadka at Princeton.
He spoke of the Hromadkas with great admiration and affection.
Since my wife was planning to go to Prague I offered that she
would take his letter along. Of course I did not know their address
by heart but I knew my sister would see to it that the letter would
be delivered. I added a personal note for Mrs. Hromadka, mentioning our mutual acquaintance and recalling with much gratitude
Hromadka's hospitality to me in Princeton. To my great amazement shortly after the "Velvet revolution" I received a letter from
Mrs. Hromadka. She thanked me for my note, recalled some of our
mutual friends and then she asked, "What would my husband think
of the tremendous changes in the world?" The question mark
seemed definitely out of proportion but here was something very
typical for Mrs. Hromadka and for all Hromadka followers in the
Czech Republic. They do not seem to understand that it does not
make any difference what Dr. Hromadka would think but that the
world would like to know what we think of Hromadka's political
and theological perception.

Up to this point Hromadka is counted among the saints in
the Czech Republic. Every year the Church of Czech Bethren together with the theological faculty of Charles University publishes
the so called "Evangelical Calendar." It really is a book of about
two hundred fifty pages providing short inspirational readings. The
calendar is extremely popular especially in the country and the
people enjoy having a book which they can read at random. My
last edition is for the calendar year 1997 and it contains many interesting articles and stories. At the beginning of the volume is a
calendar clearly marking great holidays, and birth, and death anni-
versaries. The twenty sixth of December is marked as follows, "26

December—Thursday, St. Stephen, martyr; J. L. Hromadka (1969)."[17]

Late in 1989 the Christian Peace Conference published a Festschrift commemorating the one hundredth anniversary of Hromadka's birth. The volume has an unfortunate title *He Who Believes, Always Looks Forward.* since quite obviously we do not know which direction is forward. Hromadka himself wrote an interesting essay on the subject published in a collection, *Theologie a Cirkev* (Theology and the Church), in which he portrays the decision of the Prodigal son to return home as a step forward. The book prepared by Dr. Milan Opocensky gives us a good summary from Hromadka's writing from 1918 on including a very interesting letter written by Dr. Hromadka to the leadership of the Czechoslovak Communist Party starting with the salutation "Esteemed Comrades!" The introduction was written by Bishop Karoly who states that Hromadka's anniversary reminds us that the fear of socialism was ungrounded. Dr. Opocensky concludes his description of Hromadka's life journey with the assertion that Hromadka unmistakably must be counted among the spiritual giants of the Czech Nation, next to John Hus, Commenius etc.!

The most embarrassing fact about this volume is that it was published in Hromadka's firm conviction that communism represents the new world order, but it appeared in the bookstore a few days after Václav Havel stepped into the Prague castle calling the citizens not only to love the truth but to live in truth!

Somebody thought of saving the total fiasco of this book by hurriedly enclosing in each volume a mimeographed copy of Hromadka's brilliantly written letter of protest to the Soviet Ambassador following the invasion of Czechoslovak territory by the Soviet forces to stop Alexander Dubček in his effort to create "socialism with a human face."

The publishers of the book really owe Hromadka an apology for sneaking this document into the volume in such an underhanded way but obviously the printing of the protest was not permitted.

Quite obviously neither the Soviet Ambassador nor any of the Czechoslovak Communist leaders felt that it was important to answer Hromadka. Their silence was the painful Dulcinea's laughter at "the Czech Don Quixote."

Perhaps it is only proper to quote one of Hromadka's favorite sayings, "Let us not be disillusioned, when we have built on an illusion."

A CITIZEN OF THE UNITED STATES OF AMERICA

After almost three extremely happy years at the United Church in Walpole, we moved to assume my first pastorate in North Bennington, Vermont. As soon as the Walpole people heard that we would be moving to a big parsonage somebody organized a search of attic treasures, and the Church gave us a set of lovely living room furniture as a farewell gift. At the same time the women of North Bennington were also trying to find some furniture for us. At the end we had more than enough to furnish the ten room house without offending anyone, not a minor achievement, in the realm of diplomacy.

The North Bennington community was a remarkable combination of workers, cabinet makers and upholsterers who for generations worked for Cushman Colonial Furniture Mills, then there was the old time elite, living in huge houses: the Wellings, the Whites, the Townsends, the Wellingtons, the Cushmans and the whole dynasty of the former governor McColough; then the students and the numerous members of the faculty of the Bennington College, known as the "fountain of secularism!" Since Bennington College was one of the most expensive colleges in the USA it maintained a truly outstanding faculty, some living in our neighborhood. The famous pianist Lionel Nowak, the playwright Shirley Jackson, the renown cellist George Finkel, the late novelist and biographer Bradford Smith among them. Bennington College did not have the monopoly on liberalism, once you crossed the railroad tracks and walked toward Arlington, you passed by the house of Dorothy Canfield Fisher, and then the rambling house of Norman Rockwell after that one got lost both philosophically and geographically. Many of these neighbors became our good friends and were helpful to us in our ministry.

The Bennington College, was located on a hill outside the village. Its entrance, which is the former Jennings' estate is most misleading. No other buildings on the campus match the splendor of the Jennings Tudor building, in fact the dormitories, the class-room buildings, laboratories and offices are built as a pseudo colo-nial village with a lovely view of Mt. Anthony and the Bennington hills. North Bennington itself was an ugly village. Next to our brick church which is now a historical monument, there were other brick buildings of distinction. Across the street from the parsonage was a big building housing the local bank. One good thing about living across the street from the bank was that two clerks knew everything about the ailing furnace at the parsonage, and we could call them for assistance whenever a boiler crisis occurred, which was often. The most monumental brick building was our railroad station. Yes, once late at night and once during the day a sleek Washington-New York-Montreal train made a stop here, and every child from first grade on knew that for high school graduation the class would go either to Montreal or to New York or to Washing-ton. The presence of this kind of railroad station was not of minor significance for me. By the time we moved to North Bennington, I had met most of my class requirements for my Ph.D and I was able to arrange a schedule of tutorials with my major professors, name-ly the historian Edwin Booth and Dean Walter Muelder. It was agreed that I would travel to Boston University once or if neces-sary twice a month going to Boston by train with a huge suitcase full of books, unloading the books at the library, spending several hours with each professor, going to the library and filling the suit-case with a new load of books and hurrying to the railroad station. Once in a while, to my great joy, I missed the train, and had four hours in the city.

The last of the four brick buildings in North Bennington was a most attractive Town library, which was not my favorite be-cause it was unquestionably the domain of a town witch. North Bennington was a town of readers, and the people of the North Bennington Congregational church took great pride in the fact that for ten years in succession they read more books than any other church in Vermont. That was in the days when the United Church of Christ took the literacy of its constituency seriously, and every year published a list of books which a designated committee con-sidered important. The so called qualified reader had to read at least two books in each category: Biblical scholarship, Church History, theology, Ethical issues, Biographies, fiction. The people of North Bennington church were proud of their record, and were determined to encourage each other in reading books of significance. The North Bennington Church certainly was one of the most literate, if not the most literate church, I ever served.

Jeanette Scofield was the social, moral, and educational conscience of the community beside being the librarian of the Town Library. She looked so awful that meeting her for the first time, one took two quick steps back saying, "Nobody will ever believe it but I have met a real witch!" She was tall and skinny. Long grayish hair framed her wrinkled face. A sizable wart emeblished her prominent nose but she did not have the voice of a witch. Her voice was weak and raspy so that one had to come close to her to hear what she was saying, and that presented another problem. Jeanette had such bad breath that when one encountered her for the first time, one immediately made at least two steps back. As is often the case Jeanette wore clothing which emphasized all her ugly features, long coats and dresses, in winter she wore a gray knitted sock hat, and wherever she went she carried a huge canvass bag in her hand. In the classical days of Saturday Evening Post she appeared on one of its covers, a sin for which Norman Rockwell was never forgiven. Jeanette just waited for the moment of revenge. As a librarian she knew everyone and everything, she served on every committee and most unfortunately she was also a member of my church. Of course she was quick to tell me that she had taught the third grade Sunday School class for twenty years. She was absolutely delighted when she heard that we were offering a training session for teachers. "Something like this has been needed for years!" she sighed, and then she dissected my predecessor. Of course, after teaching the same grade for twenty years she would hardly need training, but she planned to come to encourage others, to see what we had to offer and what was new in the field. She did remind us that in her youth she taught at Riverside Church in New York. "The main thing is to help the children to memorize. That will stay with them all their lives," she repeated. After this introduction we knew that Jeanette Scofield was our cross to bear.

Before the meeting which was held in the parsonage, I noticed that my wife was removing a nude statue from our bookcase, a wedding gift from my sister. I was furious. We agreed on a strategy: Jeanette must leave the meeting very appreciated but she must not be allowed to take over. In this respect we largely succeeded, in fact Jeanette had such a good time that she suggested having a meeting of this kind every week!

I have never thought that being nice to a witch could be so totally exhausting! When everybody left we assessed the situation, and Muriel reminded me that I had to visit the library as soon as possible. I growled but Muriel went on. Three times during that evening Jeanette told her that she understood how busy I was but that as yet I was not at the Library and that it was giving the community a wrong message.

My first visit to the Library took several hours. I was given a guided tour with the description of all Jeanette's achievements. At the same time the people were coming in and out. She was ever so sweet to everyone, introduced me, and as soon as the people left, she covered her mouth as if they were still in hearing distance and whispered to me most outrageous gossip. I made the horrid mistake of being shocked, Jeanette considered it an applause, and gossip was her speciality. Indeed Jeanette had formidable knowledge of books, it almost seemed that she knew every book in sight. When someone came in asking for a book she would say, "You don't want that, that is trash," and then turning around she would pick a book of her choice and say, "This is a book for a person like you."

After spending considerable time in the library, I explained to Jeanette that I was interested in André Gide and that I just finished reading his beautiful *Pastoral Symphony*. "He is a Communist, did you know that?" she interrupted. "Yes, he was a Communist and he wrote a rather remarkable book about his disappointment in the Soviet Union. It is called: *God that Failed..*" Obviously she did not know that book because she did not say anything, but when I asked to borrow Gide's novel,'*The Immoralist* she almost fainted.

"I am shocked," she repeated, "really shocked that a minister would ask for a book of that kind."

"Have you ever read it?"

"Of course not, I would not allow a book of that kind in this library! For that kind of trash you must go to the college library. That is their speciality!"

I came home without a book but knowing that I gained an enemy.

For months I tried my best to atone, I quoted only Tennyson and Browning. we smiled at each other at the door of the church after the worship services, but I really did not dare to enter the Library again. Everybody in the church, however, noticed a change. For the first time ever, Jeanette changed her seat. She moved to the second pew right in front of the pulpit. Also she attempted to write every sermon. I tried to ignore her, telling myself that this woman would not dictate my behavior, that she was just a pathetic lonely woman, and that everybody knows her. What could this miserable woman do to me except make my life miserable? I kept saying this to myself until one morning Mrs. Cushman, whom we loved and admired, called me and asked me to stop by. She took me upstairs to her study and told me that two FBI agents came to ask her about my political views. They asked her a great many questions including "Did it ever occur to you that Mr. Bednář could be a Communist agent?" Mrs. Cushman was furious. She was concerned that the FBI agents asked only political questions about me. She offered help, "This is a period of American history I am not exactly proud of. When I think of the fact that a little senator from Wisconsin is accusing that gallant general Marshall of being soft on the Communists and our President does not say anything to defend him, that turns my stomach. Of course, eventually they will defend General Marshall but they always have to call a meeting! Well, I just felt that I had to tell you about my visitors and we simply must find out what this is all about. By the way, Denny, are you by any chance applying for citizenship? If you are, then an investigation of this sort is to be expected."

"No, I am not applying for anything."

"Well, don't worry about this, with your permission, I shall try to find out about this."

I walked home puzzled. Until Mrs. Cushman mentioned the case of General Marshall, the dirty work of the Committee on Un-American Activities, headed by Senator Joseph McCarthy, did not even cross my mind. I thought that perhaps all the documents needed for my status as a Displaced Person were not in order or something like that, but the more I thought about it, the more troubled I was.

In a few days I found out that I was in good company which, however, did not help me one bit. The same FBI agent went about the village, seeking information about Norman Rockwell, Lionel Nowak, Shirley Jackson and several members of the Bennington College faculty whose names I cannot remember. When we put our heads together, it became quite obvious to us that Jeanette Scofield was the informer. The accusations were all the same but I was the only one among the accused who had no passport and who was a native of Prague, now a Communist capital!

I felt morally beaten, spiritually sick. How could this ever happen in America, sweet land of liberty! What was so upsetting for me was not that one demagogue named Joseph McCarthy over night became a celebrity by charging innocent people of treason, but the most nauseating fact was that our press gave McCarthy enormous coverage, and the scandal hungry Americans wanted more and more. McCarthy at that time was affirming that our State Department was permeated with socialists and communists. His numbers were changing from day to day. It occurred to me that the precious freedom of the press in America also meant the freedom to make as much money as possible. Every scandal is exaggerated because people strangely enough love to read scandal pages. It was interesting for me that nobody ever questioned the political past of the German scientists who helped us to develop the hydrogen bomb! Of course, I did not doubt for a moment that the Soviets had numerous agents in the USA but McCarthy's technique which represented a total denial of the freedom of speech and of the American sense of justice was like a gift of God to the Soviet propagandists. At last the Soviets could accuse the USA of hypocrisy, of persecuting people who differed from McCarthy's views. General Eisenhower in his volume, *Mandate For Change* writes about his hurting for Professor Robert Oppenheimer, one of the truly great American scientists who was loudly being accused of being a Communist sympathizer, only because as a matter of conscience Oppenheimer opposed the production of the hydrogen bomb, a view which interestingly enough Eisenhower shared. Eisenhower in his book elaborates that no one was safe from the danger of McCarthy's axe. Indeed people like Jeanette Scofield were settling old hostilities comforting their hurting egos by the knowledge that at last they were being taken seriously. Shortly before his death, Dr. Oppenheimer was presented a presidential decoration by president John F. Kennedy. It was a nice gesture but no medal could ever pay this remarkable man for being persecuted and insulted on false account. Yes, thank God, the time came when McCarthy was finally repudiated by sixty seven out of eighty nine Senators who voted that Mr. McCarthy was an unbecoming member of the United States Senate. It must be registered here that it took the courageous leadership of one man, the Republican Senator Ralph Flanders of Vermont to introduce the resolution and to stop McCarthyism.

Only twice during my life in America did my heart trembled for the soul of this nation. Once during the McCarthy rule of terror, and the second time during the Watergate crisis, when president Nixon, finding himself in an impossible situation, was determined to do everything to stop the power of the press and delegated the leadership of the total war against the press to Charles Colson. Some of our broadcasting studios started dismissing people known for their anti-Nixon views and many of us will never forget the sight of Colson shouting, "The corporation's money, will bring the press to its knees!" That was a sad, crucial moment for American liberties.

It was during the McCarthy era that I started seriously thinking about American citizenship. Of course a great many well meaning friends urged me constantly to take at least the first steps toward securing United States citizenship. For them it simply meant to make me more marketable. They meant well, as one of them put it "Good Lord, you don't seem to realize that it is much easier to get into Vermont than to get out of Vermont! Just think of it. Soon you will have a doctorate and then a little piece of paper stating that you are a refugee. Who could possibly be interested in you?"

Personally I was not in any hurry, I paid my taxes, I tried to be active as a responsible citizen, I hungrily studied American his-

tory, and devoured volumes on Lincoln and Jefferson, my true political saints. On the Fourth of July I think I could preach a more
passionate sermon on the meaning of liberty as interpreted in the
most precious documents of this Republic than most of my colleagues, but on Memorial Day to this day, I feel uneasy. In my
mind I see the haunting sight of the fields of white crosses. I was
liberated, all the years of Hitlerism I did nothing and just waited
and waited to be liberated. For this reason I feel uncomfortable at
Memorial day observances and usually I am out of town but very
much aware of the cost of liberty.

McCarthyism, however, brought to my mind the value of a
vote. It took only the one voice of Senator Ralph Flanders to make
the Senators think, a few votes make the decisive difference.

I desired a vote in this democracy, and I felt deeply that I
did not want to be a citizen of any other nation.

It was a hot July day when I had to interrupt my New
Hampshire vacation and travel to Boston to be sworn in as a citizen
of the USA. At first I was examined and then the solemn proceeding gained the elements of a farce. A spinsterish woman, who
seemed totally bored by her job, asked me to rise and swear to
speak the truth and nothing but the truth. The solemn questions followed. "Reverend, have you ever committed adultery? Have you
ever been a member of the Communist party?" It was fortunate
that my wife was not present because we would never have been
able to control our laughter. After this farce we were ushered to a
large hall, several hundred of us, and the local judge gave a lecture
on the meaning of liberty. What a pity that the lecture could not be
given by one of the refugees who gave up absolutely everything to
live in freedom while the judge repeated the same old chestnut of a
speech and certainly for good pay.

After we swore all our loyalty to the USA we were congratulated, and the representative of the Daughters of the American
Revolution came with token gifts, according to them a small flag
of the USA, but it was big enough to cover a table, and there were
other nationalistic trinkets. I understand that to this day the cere-
monies follow the same format, and if that is the case, it is a great
pity, for this could be a very moving ceremony of welcome, and of
affirmation of human commonality so marvelously verbalized by

the founding fathers. As far as I remember this was a ceremony affirming the pursuit of happiness (the very doctrine with which those who stood at the cradle of this republic had the greatest difficulty), the celebration of our opportunities and not at all an invitation to participate in building a republic. All that I heard at that occasion was foreign to the spirit of Abraham Lincoln and Thomas Jefferson but since everything else was just a matter of formality it did not bother me. I hurried to catch the train to Potter Place, New Hampshire. The train arrived on time, I was happy, knowing that I would have time to go swimming before supper. At the railroad station was my wife and the two children staging a minor demonstration, waving American flags. Jimmy, the younger of the two children was the first one to reveal the secret, "Tonight we shall have a big American picnic, steak, corn and all!"

Little did I know that in the sixties my American citizenship, my loyalty to the principle of liberty and justice for all would be as severely tested as it was. In the USA the issue of the separation of Church and State is not debated, in fact we show a definite sense of superiority to the countries in which churches are supported by the State. My father always hoped for the day when the separation of Church and State would become a reality in the Czech lands. The opportunity certainly is now and yet no one even dares to talk about it, for the fact is that the churches are supported by very old pensioners like my oldest sister. At the same time the members of the young generation are not church goers, and most of them being total materialists have no concept of stewardship. It will take twenty, thirty years of education before the churches in Central Europe will be able to take care of themselves. At the same time the doctrine of the separation of Church and State in the USA most often is not what we read into it. Indeed the State cannot dictate to the local church, the denomination cannot speak for the congregations which consider themselves autonomous yet, there is one hitch which in our boasting about the separation of Church and State we like to overlook. Every local church depends on the resources it can raise, and there is no doubt that the most generous givers have the greatest power in the local congregation.

In the sixties, for instance, in many churches the rich organized themselves in the effort to "starve the minister out." They refused to pledge and rather enjoyed watching how the liberals would manage by themselves. To my knowledge the sociological study of the factor of the sixties which later on led to the continuous decline of the mainline churches as yet was not published but, as many pastors of that era, I observed that as a public figure, I had to be prepared to bear the consequences of my social stand in the institution I served. My personal vote was not just a personal affair. The church I served as a pastor would be either supported or punished for my stand, for saying yea or nay, for raising my hand or not raising my hand.

In the sixties the issue of bussing black children who desired better education in our schools became a big issue in Massachusetts towns. I was the pastor of the town's largest church, which had a rich history, an extremely attractive colonial sanctuary, and a most popular program for teenagers and an outstanding ministry of music for all ages. That was also the church where all the successful and proper people worshipped.

After much discussion the question of allowing qualified black students to attend our schools so that they may be better prepared for higher education had to come to a vote. The School Board called a special meeting in the huge gymnasium of our school. The room was packed. Our daughter, Marie, who was then in the seventh grade and who was always interested in the issues of justice, begged us to take her along to the meeting so that she could observe it. The local dentist presided at this meeting with enormous skill. At last he called for a vote. "All in favor raise your hand." As my wife and I raised our hands and it was quite obvious that we were in the majority suddenly several of our parishioners from the upper crust started to spit at us and call us names and threaten us and our church. At that point our Marie, who always was able to control her emotions burst into horrendous tears, saying, "How could Christians do this?" Her Sunday school teacher, a wonderful woman took her aside, and later on a few of us met in her home. It was a horrendous evening.

Recently I was invited back to that town and I was greatly honored. One of the speakers mentioned those times when we debated the issue of the bussing of the black students, and mentioned that out of the few black students bussed to that town several became outstanding doctors and two or three became known scientists. Of course we were glad to hear it, we were also glad to know that these black students did not bring criminal elements to the community as it was predicted. I could not help but recall the horrid night when the members of one family and their friends were spitting at us. By the power of fate most of them were no longer living. They were not the only ones who hated us that night, there were many others but they did not have the courage to spit on us, they were hiding behind niceties. What bothered me during our return visit was that not a single person who hurt us and who was indicted by history had the courage to come to us and say, "I am sorry, I was mistaken, I did not use the right judgment." The examples of this sort only remind us how far we have to go in our citizenship, how often we salute the flag and deny everything for which the flag stands, having no idea of our folly.

There is a photograph which is very dear to me, and which constantly reminds me of what the United States citizenship means. When our son James was recalled from Africa and ironically was sworn in as the Director of the Agency for International Affairs in Prague (AID), it seemed to me a fulfillment of a dream. The photograph shows my oldest sister Vera holding the Bible, Jim's right hand is raised, his other hand rests on the Bible as he makes his promise to serve his country and to uphold the Constitution of the USA. Everything in that photograph seems just right. My sister, that gallant survivor of Communism is solemn but serenely happy. There was no reservation on the part of our government that she, a foreigner, would be a part of the ceremony. In a way, as a true student of the Bible she represents in the photograph nationalism as perceived by the architects of this republic. Our most precious national documents were given to us by men rooted in the Bible, and today the people who are biblically illiterate simply cannot even comprehend what American citizenship requires. What does it mean; one nation under God? How can we wish liberty and justice for others unless in biblical awareness we simply wish for others what we wish for ourselves?

PRACTICE MAKES PERFECT

After years of not seeing each other, it was unbelievably exciting to welcome my sister Bohunka at the airport. In spite of years of Communism she looked extremely chic, was happily smiling, but her cheek appeared to be swollen. As we embraced I noticed also that she lisped. As she greeted my wife and spoke with her in English, her lisping seemed to me even more pronounced. Only when we were in the car on our way home did she tell us a secret: She was bringing for Muriel my mother's diamond ring which was taped inside her mouth so carefully that she was unable to remove it during the flight. We stopped as soon as we found a rest area and Muriel assisted Bohunka in what was quite a painful operation. Whoever did the job knew what he was doing but my poor sister! Whenever I look at that ring on the finger of my wife I think of that incredible scene. Of course, this exercise in international intrigue took place after years of practice, and I want to point out that even after years of exile, the refugees never seem to give up the idea of seeing their families and relatives. It is quite incredible that after forty years of Communism, I am as close to my family as ever, and it is even more incredible that the children of our children developed genuine family ties.

Our first family reunion took an enormous amount of planing and plotting. The success of the whole plan depended on smuggling American dollars to Prague. After many ideas failed it was agreed that my wife and children would visit my family in Prague and would bring in the money. Then some acquaintances of my sister would take the money out to Jugoslavia and prepay our stay on a small island near Rijeka, in the village of Nerezine. For Muriel that was extremely difficult because she really does not know how to lie, and we had many practice sessions. There were days when we were tempted to give up the whole plan but finally we went. We had a couple of days in Brussels and from there we drove in a Volkswagen through Germany to Vienna where we spent several memorable days. I was sad and tense when Muriel and the children boarded a plane named, Franz Schubert, and headed for Prague while I had to stay behind. The week in Vienna seemed to me endless, and it was a real family celebration when Muriel and the children returned, happily reporting that the mission was accomplished. They came laden with gifts from members of the family, and in love with Prague and the homestead. The very next day we had to pack the Volkswagen and start our journey to Jugoslavia. At the same time, my sisters and my sister's son, Honza, about eighteen years old, boarded a third class train to Belgrade. At the Belgrade station they were to look in the main railroad lobby for a gentleman dressed in a trench coat. He was to have a copy of the New York Times in one hand, and a camera was to hang on his shoulder. My sisters were to greet him with a given phrase. Personally I had some great misgivings about entrusting all the funds to this unknown man, but after some moments of hesitation, the man with a copy of the New York Times in one hand and camera hanging on his shoulder appeared on the scene. The plot worked out without a hitch and my sisters and Honza continued on their journey.

We arrived in the port of Rijeka with a slight delay, and the boat which was to take us to our island could not take one more car. There was not much time for any debate. We locked the car and boarded the ship since the family was to meet us at the port.

We really could not believe our eyes when we greeted one another knowing that the complicated plot had worked out. There could not be a better or more lovely hiding place than the fishing village of Nerezine. The sea was calm and bright blue, the beaches dotted with palm trees, and soon the children discovered the fragrant lovely blossoms of almond trees. Our host, who was already prepaid for our stay, was most kind. She prepared most of the delicious meals on the grill, and her husband took us several times on his fishing boat. Every day was full of new experiences, and when the day came for us to part, we could not say good bye, we knew that we would meet again. Indeed we met several times in Switzerland, and when our children studied in Europe, they celebrated

Christmas and holidays with the family in Prague, and two times my sisters came to the USA as our guests for a month. The only one who was deprived of these trips and reunions was my sister Nadia because of her ill health. She suffered with diabetes since she was in her twenties. Ironically she survived her husband. As her health was deteriorating I was determined to do everything to obtain a visa to Czechoslovakia even if it was only for two days. I heard that the Communists at that time felt politically pretty secure but economically desperate, so desperate that they allowed some Czechs and Slovaks who emigrated to return for a visit as long as they prepaid everything in dollars. Even if these visitors were planning to stay with their relatives, they had to pay for each day in dollars as much as if they were staying in a luxurious hotel. I felt encouraged. I applied for a visa only to be rejected. When I inquired at the Czechoslovak Embassy in Washington for the reason for my rejection especially when others were allowed to visit Czechoslovakia the man on the phone said, "You are listed as an enemy of the people, and you are a minister. What can you expect?"

We did not have much time to lose. I was planning to study at Oxford that summer, and we were hoping to make the trip to Czechoslovakia immediately after the semester was over. When our Jimmy, who was then a freshman in the foreign service heard of our dilemma he remarked that our trouble was in having connections only among politicians. "The Soviets do not care what the politicians think, the only ones whom they take seriously at this point are the top notch people in business. You must think of someone who is a big cheese in the business world." Without much strain we thought of one, and after phoning him he promised to help me. Later on, his advice was to leave for my studies in Oxford and not to be at all discouraged by all the refusals of the Czechoslovak Embassy in Vienna until late afternoon before our departure. We were to leave for the Czechoslovak Republic on Saturday and hoping for the best, we reserved a rental car.

Vienna has been one of our favorite cities, although its heart is the Hofburg palace, the seat of the Hapsburgs who for centuries treated the Czechs and Slovaks as slaves and the Czech and Slovak Protestants as derelicts. My wife and I always made a special effort to visit the delightful Schönbrunn, and the Belvedere with its lovely gardens, and as we walked through all the parks, I often remembered aloud and my wife patiently listened. My grandfather Novotny was known as "his royal counselor for architecture." He designed one of the bridges across Vltava in Prague, he supervised many projects of the Empire and he was responsible to the Emperor. Of course, we know that he was a man of the Book, in his free time he learned Greek and Hebrew, and prepared the publication of the first Czech Biblical Dictionary. Grandfather Novotny was the only Protestant in his department. In his journal he tells us that once in May, shortly after the holiday of Corpus Christi, Count Kolowrat called grandfather to his office and scolded him for not being anywhere in sight at St. Stephen's Cathedral on Corpus Christi. "If His Imperial Majesty was present, it was expected of all of his servants!"

"Your excellency" answered Grandfather Novotny, "I am of protestant persuasion, I am a serious student of the Holy Scriptures. I feel that it would be hypocritical of me to attend the Corpus Christi service just to be seen. My attendance at worship services in any church has nothing to do with architecture, or the work I perform for his majesty."

"That is your opinion. I inform you that you are demoted. You are no longer Royal counselor." Grandfather was upset, and immediately made an appointment with the Emperor. The audience was at the Hofburg Palace. After the welcome niceties, Grandfather explained to the Emperor the reason for his audience. His work, his architecture, the quality of the work he performed for the empire had nothing to do with his personal religion or better said the perception of biblical truth. The Emperor rose from his desk, crossed the large room to the window. Standing by the window the Emperor looked at Vienna's busy streets.

"Go on." he said.

"I feel it is extremely unfair to be demoted not for the failure in my field which is architecture, but for the failure to attend a service which is against my conscience."

"Agreed. Go on," the Emperor replied, not looking left or right, motionlessly observing the traffic of fiacres from the window.

"Anything else?"

"Yes, your Majesty. When can my standing be restored?"

"Make an appointment in two weeks."

My grandfather described that scene which took place only shortly before the collapse of the Empire. "The Emperor did not move from his window. He did not want to meet my eyes. I was astonished when he said, 'Agreed' . . . the rest appears in my mind as if the Emperor, looking aimlessly out of the window of his study, were saying 'Have some compassion, the Emperor is not what you think he is!' To my amazement, I was never demoted, and therefore I never had another appointment with the Emperor again."

Our next stop was the parliament building where my father as a student earned his "spending" money as a stenographer. The University where he studied was only a few blocks from the Parliament. We walked the long streets which were familiar to my father and grandfather, astonished by the ironies of our own lives.

Next day was Friday. My wife planned to have her hair done, and then do some shopping. I had no other choice but to plan to spend the day in the vicinity of the Czechoslovak Embassy located in the former imperial stables. When I stopped by in the morning, I was told that my application for reconsideration was rejected. When I stopped two hours later, I was told I had to have a new set of photographs for the new consideration. A photographer was located at a street about ten blocks away but the embassy was closing for the weekend at four.

I felt desperate and took a taxi to the photographer, and I think the taxi driver gave me a few rides around the Ring to make his trip worthwhile. The photographer was just ready to close for the weekend, and it took much begging to persuade him to take a picture of me.

I flew to the embassy at half past three, and all the officers looked at me as at the punishment of God, being ready to close the shop. The clerks spoke in an offensive vulgar Czech "Can't you read or what? Your visa was rejected, is that clear?"

"Yes, it's clear, but I have submitted a new application for a visa, and I understand that the approval is to come from Washington this afternoon."

"Sir, as I said, we are getting ready to close the embassy for the weekend. Come Monday morning."

"No, I am staying until four o'clock." I answered and sat down on a bench.

"As you wish, you American swine."

About ten minutes before four, another officer appeared at the window and said, "What did you say your name is?"

"Bednář."

"There is a cable from Washington, your visa is granted."

In a few minutes I was out of the embassy holding the all important document in my hand. Only after our return to the USA did we learn that our second application for a visa called for a major plot. The Ambassador and his colleagues were invited to a country club for a few drinks, and as soon as they left the embassy, the cable was sent to Vienna. Our supper celebration was justified, it was a minor miracle that I had a chance to visit my sister, share some moments with my family and friends, and to be in my native country again after so many years.

Our rented car was parked in front of the rental office on one of the major streets of the city. We could not believe our eyes. The car was a bright red Ford! In the office as soon as we paid and signed the lease, they were not interested in answering any questions. For every question we were given a map or a brochure. After we loaded our red car, we sat in it and helplessly looked around. In the glove compartment there was no manual, and our technical abilities are minimal. At last we figured out how to open the windows and the doors, and located the windshield wipers and the lights. Suddenly Muriel exclaimed that according to the map the street on which we were parked, was a one way street for several hours each day, and that meant we had to drive round the city to get to the neatly marked road leading to the Czechoslovak border. I was petrified that we would cause some international sensation yet before leaving Vienna, but by the grace of the Lord, within an hour we were approaching the Czechoslovak custom station. A very friendly Slovak officer studied my passport. Another office rummaged through our suitcases, and then one of them stepped forward and said, "Open the hood please!"

Muriel and I look all over the dashboard in an effort to find some button with the sign "hood" but no luck. We shrugged our shoulders and invited the guards to step into the car and help us to find the all important button. Shortly, while one of the guards was still in the car, another guard came with a crowbar in his hands saying, "For American car this is the best." We held our breaths and just then the right button was located and the hood popped open.

Then we drove on a narrow highway lined with cherry trees laden with fruit. Many people were out picking cherries and putting them into huge bushel baskets. After a while I could not resist. Cherries have always been my favorite summer fruit. I stopped and offered to buy some cherries but I was happily given a big bag of cherries. It was a good welcome home.

Shortly afterwards we noticed a big accident involving a truck way ahead of us. In a few minutes two green ambulances passed by. They looked like props from *All Quiet on the Western Front.*. From that minute on we drove very slowly. After being away for several decades one easily forgets that long distances are not as long as they appear on the map. We were approaching Moravia, the territory of the homestead. We stopped for lunch at a small inn, after having investigated several inns before. We learned that in the Soviet territory most eating places are almost the same. The menu is the same but most appealing dishes are "no longer available," and you can bet that you will get stuck with goulash. Since it was a lovely day we took our lunch outside.

Late in the afternoon we were approaching Vir and I could see what used to be our beloved homestead. Gone was the tennis court, gone was the orchard, and there was a whole colony of brick houses. We stopped by the side of the road, and everything around appeared as a devastation. The formerly well kept forests looked like a jungle. Suddenly we heard the singing of children. The more carefully we listened the more we were shocked. They were singing the Battle Hymn of the Republic. Muriel smiled. Soon the children appeared on the road. They were the Young Pioneers, coming from their work in the fields to their camps. They sang with great gusto. I listened very carefully, yes, they loved to sing, "Glory, glory Hallelujah," but to my horror the text was different, describing the horrid slave task masters. The slaves were organized by a certain John Brown. He was the victim of the oppressors. He is dead but his spirit in all lands is marching on.

This was a shocking welcome, and as I was trying to investigate it, and find out the text of the hymn as taught by the Communists, everybody looked at me in amazement almost saying, "What's the fuss, it's a lie, and so what? The truth is only that which is in agreement with Marx-Leninism in its latest version."

Everyday I spent most of my hours with Nadia, and we had a wonderful visit. She lived in a small charming cottage in the woods above the homestead.

One of the last days, after I said goodbye to Nadia, I felt the need to be alone, and I walked through the woods which were formerly ours. I came to a beautiful clearing with a wonderful view of the entire village. I sat down, and as long as nobody was around the old magic was there, the old paradise, the old home. As I sat there, I reviewed our days at the homestead. Of course our visit became common knowledge over night, and the old friends baked cookies, and pastry, and came to say "welcome" but they all came to the back window, not to be seen. The kitchen now was in the former pantry with a big window. That is where the visiting took place. A few ministers and former classmates stopped by night. It was in the summer of 1988 and these friends did not show any hope for any liberty, the dearest hope for them and for their church people was to survive.

I looked at the beloved valley, and tears came to my eyes for I knew that I could never live there any more, it was now mostly the land of those who lied and for those who knew how to lie. No matter how much I tried to scold myself for being harsh I knew with my whole being that this no longer was my home.

IF NOT BY US, BY WHOM? IF NOT NOW, WHEN?

At last I was at peace with myself. I saw it with my own eyes, life under the Communist dictatorship. I saw the homestead, the drabness of Prague, the shop windows with merchandise which was not available. I thought of a few friends with whom I visited. From a distance it seemed to me that they did not want to talk, they had enough of debating. They were surviving the monotony of their days, the long hours of hard work in the presence of their enemies by a steady refusal to think. The only thing which kept their spirit alive was the thought of Friday. I was surprised by the number of people who bought some old, abandoned farm houses, and every Friday afternoon, rain or shine, there was a huge exodus from Prague, everybody was escaping to their old farm house in the country. There they cultivated their little gardens and enjoyed a bit of privacy. There they held reunions with families and friends, secured some food which was not available in the city, laughed at the latest political jokes told by friends and neighbors, hoping to tell the same jokes to others in Prague.

Although I was at the homestead only for a few days, I was amazed by the time spent listening to jokes. The old Postmaster, Vlada Stastny was in his element, always introducing a joke by saying "Did you hear this one?" There was one told by Vlada so masterfully that I shall always remember it. "Well," he said, "In spite of all that we say, this is a wonderful world. Just think that under the leadership of the Soviets we are exploring outer space. Who could ever predict that? You know all about Kagarin, don't you? You don't? I can't believe it! Well, when Kagarin returned from his first exploration of outer space, Kruschev invited him to the Kremlin and at last when they were alone, Kruschev asked Kagarin "Comrade, when you were way out there in space, did you, by chance, hear any music sounding like Mozart, and did you see any silver or gold naked boys with wings, playing flutes, harps or trumpets?" "Thousands of them," said Kagarin.

"I have always thought that such would be the case," said Kruschev, "but in the name of Lenin swear that you will not tell a soul!"

Some months later Kagarin was invited to travel to Rome and to visit the Pope. When the two were alone, the Pope asked, "My friend, when you were way up there in space, did you by chance hear any music like Mozart or Vivaldi, and did you see any silver or gold naked boys with little wings playing harps, flutes or trumpets."

"Nothing of that sort" answered Kagarin.

"It does not surprise me," said the Pope, "I have always though that such is the case but in the name of God, and for the sake of humanity, brother Kagarin don't tell a soul!"

Yes the old humor was still there, the people were able to laugh at the folly of dogmatism, but otherwise they were willing to accept things as they were and to live just for themselves, their families, their farm houses. Even the ministers who came to visit me from their nearby parishes spoke about their churches, their families and the hope for survival, but any hope for a change was not verbalized.

I returned home to my own realistic conclusion. No, I could never accept the thought that the Soviet system was permanent. I learned from Spinka to believe that every evil ultimately would destroy itself, but I came home believing that for the time being the communists largely succeeded in scaring people into passive obedience, they succeeded in teaching materialism, in eliminating a sense of history, the best of the past. It was perfectly normal to come to one of the farm houses so dearly loved by my friends. Somewhere on the bookshelf was a statue of Masaryk or Commenius, but when one asked about the writings of Masaryk they were totally blank and that was exactly what the communists wanted. Never mind the statutes, in a few more years they will be like the old Russian grandmothers, who insist on wearing large icon pins and have no idea who the saints on the icons are. We do not mind the statues as long as the ideas of Masaryk are dead.

After our return many people asked us if we sensed any brewing opposition to the Communist dictatorship and we sadly shook our heads. Of course, the people of faith have never been automatically endowed with unusual perception of reality or understanding of God's timing. In the nineteenth chapter of 1 Kings, Elisha, is escaping from Jezebel, and at last finds a cave where he can rest. He is rather shocked when God says to him, "Elisha, what on earth are you doing here?" Elisha takes it upon himself to inform God Almighty about the state of affairs, about the horrid persecution of God's people by Jezebel and he concludes his report to God by saying, "I alone am left, the last decent man!" and he is terribly shocked when God says to him, "And how do you know that you are the only decent man left? Behold I have left seven thousand men and women whose knees are not bowed to Baal." In prose, God was really saying to Elisha, "You have no business to be here hiding, and staging this melodrama about wanting to die, your job is in Israel!"

Undoubtedly here our egoism comes in conflict with our faith. After all, I was there, I saw the bloody persecution by Jezebel. How could this God question my courage? How could I know that he had seven thousand faithful people in Israel? Then comes the question of timing. To this day there are many who keep saying that Christianity is lovely but this is no time for it. Christ came too soon. We are not ready for him. Maybe in hundreds of years after we spill so much human blood that we shall be ill, we shall be ready, but now time is not yet. Others keep saying that since this Christianity did not work in the past in the days of our grandmothers and grandfathers, it's too late. Time is ripe for something new. Certainly one of the most magnificent narratives of the New Testament is the story of Joseph of Arimethea. He loved Jesus when nobody dared to love him. He asked Pilate for permission to bury the body of Jesus in a grave in his own garden. "And Joseph rolled a great stone to the door of the tomb and departed." (Matt. 27:60). Here is the prose; Joseph buried here not only his best friend, but a man whom he believed to be the Savior, here he buried his dearest hopes and dreams for Israel, and he departed. What is the use of hanging around grave yards?

Little did my wife and I know as we walked in semi-darkness down the Wenceslaus Square, the only neon light being on the top of the building housing the Secretariat of the Communist Party, that in less than a year this square would be filled with people singing of freedom and truth. We surely had no inkling that any underground movement was getting ready for any offensive nor that the Communist President Gustav Husak was shaking in his knees. We stand judged by the magnificent events which followed under the leadership of Václav Havel in December, 1989.

Here is the dreadful irony: The General Synod of my native church was in session discussing the great issues and priorities of the church printed on the agenda. This is one thing which is the same all over the world. If you ever attended a Synod of a church or an Ecumenical Council, or a convocation called to deal with a special issue, you saw it all. Some call it a celebration of diversity as so many people of different views line up in front of the microphone at different occasions and perceive this as a marathon of individual ego trips. I do not think there were as many rushing to the microphone at the General Synod in Prague as we see on this side of the Atlantic, but the fact is, that only a few city blocks away, on Narodni Trida, students courageously marched against the heavily armed anti-riot units shouting, "If Not By Us, By Whom? If Not Now, When?" If we compare those who affirm their right to be free, who affirm their idealism, their faith in the presence of their enemies with the churchy delegates at the General Synod we know where vitality and faith lie. Professor Lochman from Basel described the scene of the young people marching and shouting. "If Not By Us, By Whom? If Not Now, When?" as one of the most moving and most provocative scenes of the century. I do not know the details but I do know this: after the fact when the delegates of the Synod were notified of the unrest only a few blocks away, after they heard that some young people were hurt, the representatives of the church felt that some expression of solidarity with the protesters was needed. Indeed, later on, after the overthrow of the Communist government, thanks to the graciousness of Václav Havel, the head of the church of Czech Brethren, Dr. Hajek, was asked to serve as a member of the provisional government, but not all members of the Synod were happy with it.

Although history does not repeat itself it is interesting to note that the churches in critical periods of this century showed a total lack of political perception. In the critical era before the Octo-

ber Revolution the leadership of the Russian Orthodoxy was preoccupied with changes in liturgy and hymnology. In my life time as a
boy I saw in the movies an armada of tanks being blessed by the
Holy Church, the tanks which Mussolini was sending to Abyssinia
to murder the innocent. As Hitler was coming to power and was
cleverly dragging the young people away from the church to party
camps and Hitler Youth meetings, the church did not show any
concern. The churches began to be alarmed when it was too late.
The Nazi's plan to eliminate the Jews was known, and we just
whispered, and as the new brand of Communism appeared on the
scene we were so afraid of becoming the allies of the reactionaries
that as Hromadka's case points out, many were actually helping
the communists to achieve their victory. We had better look at our
selves and our agenda. Well, in most churches we have survived
the fight in selecting a new hymnal, and we have discussed whether God was he or she or it, the liturgical renewal has required quite
a bit of time and money in high places, some Christians still have a
hard times deciding whether or not the gays and lesbians are really
equal human beings. I really have no idea how the national "priorities" of our churches suddenly become such priorities that we cannot get away from them. The late Methodist Bishop Gerald Kennedy had a gift for poking fun at his own denomination. He was
masterful in comparing the choice of priorities in our churches to a
peasant woman coming to a Post Office asking for some stamps.
The postmaster got out a sheet of stamps, and the woman paused
for a moment and then pointed at a stamp in the middle of the sheet
and said, "I think I shall have that one." Here we are touching on
something which is familiar to us but which we are not obligated to
perpetuate.

　　　Private piety, detached from social and political problems
has become extremely popular, and ever since the seventies the
churches have been criticized for being too politicized. Indeed we
do not go to church to listen to his or her interpretation of what we
read in the papers, yet we do live in the realm of Caesar and it is
not as simple as it seems to obey the admonition of Jesus to "ren-
der unto Caesar the things that are Caesar's and to God the things
that are God's" (Matthew 22: 21) when Caesar finds the portion allotted to him totally unsatisfactory, or when that which is given to

Caesar is not used for the good of all. Christians always had difficulty in loving their neighbors as themselves, when loving one's
neighbor demanded an opposition to Caesar, yet *Christians cannot
afford neutrality as if this or that social evil were outside the range
of religion.* Many have found the solution to the problems of Christian social ethics by maintaining a double standard: one for personal life and another for the society at large. This double standard
ethics is becoming more and more difficult as the world is shrinking and we can see each suffering, and in our churches we dare to
speak about "the global village." It is interesting to observe how
quickly "private religion" which is to practice "traditional values"
and which refuses to mix politics and religion becomes self right-
eous and blind to the needs of others. How kind and loving we can
be to each other in the fellowship of the church, and the minute we
meet at the town meeting, we forget all about Jesus loving little
children, we protect our own interests even if it means sacrificing
the education of our children. The former Surgeon General Everett
Koop, a life long Republican who cannot be accused of liberal rad-
icalism spoke at our colleges and universities about his great disappointment in the general rejection of the national health insurance
as presented by Hillary Clinton. Dr. Koop is convinced that it is
the best health plan for America. Interestingly enough while the
fight about the national health insurance raged, in our churches it
was all quiet. The catholic bishops at least expressed themselves
because of the issue of abortion, in the Protestant churches it was
put aside as if the issue of the old who are being punished for being
old, of the ill being punished for being ill, as if the children are being punished for being children, was outside the scope of the
present priority. Will it be a priority two years later? Sorry, the
polls are closed!

At the same time Jesus is more and more venerated, and I
often think of the haunting narrative in John's Gospel. Jesus is
teaching in the temple. His teaching is extremely upsetting, and the
crowds get ready to stone Jesus to death and "Jesus went out of the
temple and hid himself" concludes the evangelist (John 9:59). In
another narrative in the Gospel of John, Jesus feeds the hungry.
They are so excited that they want to proclaim him the King, but
Jesus runs away, to be alone in the mountains. Obviously God has

this habit of hiding himself, "Surely, the Lord is in this place . . . and I did not know it." (Genesis 28:16) is the testimony of Jacob. As I am nearing the conclusion of these pages, I must admit, that every so often when I was looking for this God who was hiding, I was looking for Him in the wrong places! Who would have ever thought that liberty was marching on Narodni Trida, the youngsters proclaiming, "If Not By Us, By whom? If Not Now, When?" Suppose once in a while God is hiding from our churches, and Jesus is running when we desire to make out of him an object of worship rather than follow him. When God is hiding, when Jesus has gone to the mountains, where do you think they would most likely be found?

TOWARD THE NEW WORLD ORDER

For a long time after my visit of my native country and the opportunity to see the socialist society behind the Iron Curtain, I was deeply depressed. The glorious Metro built by the Soviets in Prague, the magnificent stolen villas effectively used as recreation centers for the members of the working class, and even such social advantages as free education and medical care could never outweigh the general shabbiness of the cities, the devastation of fields and forests, the old factories with outmoded machinery, the dirty table cloths in the communal restaurant in the formerly elegant French cafe "Repre," everything in sight in need of repair, the total neglect of ecology. Above all, the sad people whose hope for the success of their Prague Spring was crushed by the Soviet, Polish and Hungarian tanks, and who absolutely refused to think or to talk about politics. I could not be blind to the policy of "Bread and Circuses." The new upper class of the Communist system could eat extremely well, while the intelligentsia was systematically being punished. One marveled at the number of theaters, opera houses and symphony halls offering good performances of standard works approved by the communists, at very reasonable prices. Over and over again I could see myself sitting in the deep grass at the edge of our former woodland, looking at the ruined homestead saying to myself "l could never live here again!" Recalling that moment I felt guilty for seemingly overlooking so many wonderful people, simply saying that my native land was then a country "of the liars, by the liars and for the liars." I would not change a word in describing the Czechoslovak government of that era, but then I thought of the millions of men and women, blindly, even without a thought, going through the motions dictated by the political system, their minds and hearts being in some other kingdom of an often forgotten dream. As anybody else in the sphere outside of the former Soviet countries, I am not in any position to be judgmental. I do not

doubt that if I had stayed I would not be any different than anybody else, I would blend. It belongs to the genius of the totalitarian
regimes to convince people that they are caught, that it makes no
sense to walk into blazing fire. Countless people of this century realize how true this is. How many believed in the progressive coming of political freedom in the framework of Prague Spring, they
remember their gallant stand and then ending in a merciless prison.
They agree that it is not common sense to walk into fire. Of course,
Joan of Arc, during her trial heard those voices encouraging her to
be reasonable, to use her common sense, to understand that she
was all alone; and at least in the great portrayal by G. B. Shaw, she
cried, "I am not alone, God is alone, and what is my loneliness
against the loneliness of God?" Perhaps in our society in which
there is so much at stake we need to repeat for ourselves this para-
phrase of Shaw's thought, "God is alone!"

In every country in which some human rights are ignored,
and especially in totalitarian empires, God is ignored, God is alone,
and one is easily aware of it. In South Africa, just when freedom of
the oppressed seemed unreachable Athol Fugrad, a South African,
wrote a significant play entitled, "A Place With the Pigs." I saw
that play at Yale with Fugrad playing the leading role. The playwright describes something of the situation of the oppressed in the
world. Every day he says that he has enough of living in the land
of pigs. He starts plotting, soon he starts packing planning to leave,
and at last, he is leaving for good. This happens over and over
again, and every time he comes back, cursing his being alone, post-
poning the best and highest, at last he gives up. Perhaps here is the
tragedy of this century, of the pigsty of the Soviet Union, of Franco's Spain, of Mussolini in Italy, the pigsty of Hitler's Germany
and of Peron's Argentina, the pigsty of the former colonial nations
in which so many millions of tired, oppressed people are giving up
and leaving things as they are. After World War II many politicians announced a new world order forgetting that a new world order is a matter of a change of hearts and not of political pronouncements alone. We are constantly observing the enormous struggle to
get out of the pigsty of selfishness, the pigsty in which so many cry
for the return of their historic lands while they totally ignore those
who live in those territories. Some of the holy places in this world

are not so holy. A former confirmand, and a deeply thinking Christian wrote to me that he does not feel exactly safe in the town of Bethlehem in which Christians are oppressed. He wrote about his driving to Jerusalem, the Holy city in a rented car. Since he did not have an Israeli licence he had to leave the car outside the city and walk. Quite obviously the privilege of driving in Jerusalem is reserved only for those who claim to own it. Jerusalem, a Holy city? God is terribly lonely! We do not need to tolerate such a pigsty, but we do, and God is alone and we are alone, terribly alone, as we think of taking some risk not for selfish interests, but because we feel accountable to God, and strangely enough, as we take courage and go against what our common sense forbids, we meet brothers and sisters who are kin in spirit, we join hands, and God smiles. It surely seems easier to write about it now than in 1988 when the Soviet Union was respected as a permanent superpower. I was appalled by my own cowardice, and depressed by the millions and millions of people capitulating.

Later on, it was Václav Havel who helped me immensely by persistent treatment of the idea of "living in truth" and "living the lie" in his volume on human identity, *O Lidskou Identitu*. In his description of the realm of falsehood he underlines that there is always an enormous distrust of anything which seems even a bit out of the ordinary. Uniformity is a requirement, anyone stepping out of the required uniformity is suspected as dangerous. Masterfully, Havel portrays an ordinary merchant with vegetables. Every morning he arranges the vegetables in his store window, and as always he places a sign in the very same place in between the cabbages and carrots and a small Soviet flag. He has gone through this motion for years, he does not even remember what the sign says. It says "Proletarians of the world unite!" He could care less, but he knows that if he changed the political decorum he would be suspected by the landlords and by some of his customers.

From John Hus on, the great leaders of the Czechoslovak nation echoed him in saying that the truth prevails if we speak the truth, love the truth and defend the truth. Havel adds to the crescendo that we have to decide between living in falsehood and living in the truth. He points out that the shopkeeper selling vegetables may have limited opportunities in "living in truth," but this shopkeeper simply will stop doing certain things, he will not be putting a political sign in his window because somebody may report him, he will not participate in the elections which as everybody knows are not elections. He will not hide his views from his superiors. His effort may be in the refusal to do what the system requires, which is not a little. He may grow in spirit and desire to do more, this shopkeeper may do something concrete, something which goes beyond the protection of self interest. He may help other people to think, to organize his fellow workers to say something in behalf of others who are unjustly suffering, he will be constantly pointing out this or that unrighteousness and injustice . . . Life in truth is not a revólt against a system, it is the affirmation of the truth and the rest is the outcome of that affirmation. Millions of shopkeepers in this world will ask: Why bother when it is difficult and it may bring me into deep trouble? Presently I put the sign in my window, keep my opinions to myself and have peace. Why bother?

Here Havel answers with a deep sense of calling. He speaks and writes as a man who has lived out a sense of calling, and his words have a deep theological meaning. Havel was profoundly influenced by Heidegger and his concept of Being. Already in his *Letters to Olga* he wonders about the existence of God, acknowledging that the finite could never define the infinite, but he goes on to say "I only know this; that Being . . . as the principle, direction and meaning of everything that is . . .within the sphere of our inner experience . . . One thing seems certain to me: that our "I" has a sense of responsibility purely and simply because it relates intricately to Being as that in which it feels the only coherence, meaning and the somehow inevitable "clarification" of everything that exists!![18]

He cannot imagine any new world order without a spiritual foundation. There cannot be any life in truth without a sense of responsibility to Being. He wants us to understand that the so called "dissidents" were *not striving to defeat communism and take over the power of the communist leaders*, they were "dissidents" because they were yearning *to affirm the truth*. "Those who still claim that politics is chiefly the manipulation of power and public opinion, and that morality has no place in it are wrong. Political intrigue is not really politics, and although you can get away with the superficial politics for a time, it does not bring much hope of lasting success. Through intrigue one may easily become prime minister but that will be the extent of one's success, one can hardly improve the world that way. I am happy to leave the political intrigue to others. I will not compete with them, certainly not by using their weapons. Genuine politics, worthy of the name—and the only politics I am willing to devote myself to—is simply a matter of serving the community, and serving those who will come after us. Its deepest roots are moral because it is a responsibility expressed through action, to and for the whole, responsibility that is what it is—a 'higher' responsibility—and only because it has a metaphysical grounding: that is it grows out of a conscious or subconscious certainty that our death ends nothing, because everything is forever being 'above us,' in what I have called 'the memory of Being'—an integral aspect of the secret order of the cosmos, of nature, and of life which believers call God and to whose judgment everything is subject. Genuine conscience and genuine responsibility are always, in the end, explicable only as an expression of the silent assumption that we are observed 'from above,' that everything is visible, nothing is forgotten and so earthly time has no power to wipe away the sharp disappointments of earthly failures: our spirit knows that it is not the only entity aware of these failures."[19]

I shall return to some thoughts of Havel, and I am grateful to him for his underlining that living in lie means ignoring the responsibility to Being, or as the Christians would put it, outside God and responsibility to him there is no hope, there is death.

In the long winter months, seeing the enormous power of the Soviet Union, the millions subjected to living in falsehood, and the countless men and women in the free world totally enslaved by self interest, and yet saying with president Gerald Ford "America is morally and spiritually number one."[20] Our intentions to do justly, to love mercy, and to walk humbly with God easily turn into idolatrous nationalism which does not understand the social dimension of living in truth.

It is time for praying and hoping that the churches everywhere will be renewed in spirit so that they will be able to lead to a new future.

Although in our family we are not exactly disciplined people yet in Christmas preparations there is a definite unwritten agenda, a schedule in our household. Perhaps the agenda is a result of the many years when our hospitality was dictated by the church calendar; first Sunday of Advent: Concert, second Sunday of advent: the Christmas pageant, third Sunday: supper for the confirmands and the fourth week: a party for the staff.

The day after Thanksgiving the Christmas greetings are written. The goal is that all greetings are mailed by the first week of Advent, the packages have to be mailed at the beginning of the second week. By the second Sunday in Advent, the house has to be decorated outside, and the candles placed in the windows. The schedule is detailed, yes, we may say that we have a definite plan so that on Christmas we may have a bit of peace, time for reflection, time to enjoy loved ones and friends. We have never joined some of our friends in their fervent effort to put Jesus Christ back into Christmas because he has always been there, and he is hard to put anywhere. If anyone needs to be put in the framework of the Christmas Gospel it is us. It took us years to develop our plan, the trouble is that Christmas never seems to come according to our schedule. It never fails, there is always a funeral or two. I always think it is terribly inconsiderate on the part of our friends and relatives to die in December. There are unexpected guests, and uninvited illnesses, and world events, and wonderful plans are in shreds.

Our Thanksgiving in 1989 was reasonably quiet, and our Christmas preparations began according to schedule. The table in our breakfast room was covered with envelopes to be addressed, and cards to be written. We turned on our T.V. and instead of a repeat performance, there was a new drama from Prague. We could not believe our eyes as we watched the enormous crowds on Wenceslaus Square, and, to us unknown, Václav Havel standing on the balcony of some hotel telling the crowds that the prophecy of John Amos Commenius was fulfilled, and liberty once again returned to the Czech and Slovak lands. We forgot all about writing Christmas cards, holding hands, remembering the short lived joy followed by the massacre of 1968 when the Soviet tanks went against innocent people. This time we saw on the T.V. screen the familiar streets filled with joyful people, but no soldier in sight. For the first time in our lives we witnessed a bloodless revolution, which became contagious. President Bush appeared on television and confirmed the news from Prague of the collapse of Communism. He underlined that this event marked the beginning of the new world order.

Havel, who on earth is Havel? We were not alone that evening in asking this question, and I think Václav Havel, a playwright and a man dedicated to the principle of living in truth was shocked himself when the Communist power was giving in to the dissident's pressure, and Havel was swept by the sudden events into the leadership role. Our distinguished politicians, diplomats and foreign affairs analysts were shocked that a playwright, unknown to them could accomplish a revolution without a bit of bloodshed, a revolution which within days would spread.

Late, late at night I read for myself that remarkable 45th chapter of Isaiah in which God calls the pagan king Cyrus to deliver Israel from the oppression of Babylon. Quite obviously when God cannot count on his own people, he is not stuck, he does not mind calling a pagan to achieve his purposes. The chapter begins with the word "Thus says the Lord to his anointed Cyrus whose right hand I have grasped . . ." later on, this God introduces himself, "For the sake of my servant Jacob, and Israel my chosen, I call you by your name, I surname you, though you do not know me, I am the Lord and there is no other, besides me there is no God. I guide you though you do not know me, that men may know, from the rising of the sun and from the west, that there is none besides me. I am the Lord and there is no other."

I have preached on different verses of that chapter many times, and through the years it has been a great comfort to me that God does not depend on us alone. That night as I was thinking about Václav Havel and his companions, that chapter spoke to me with a new power.

Havel who never wanted to be a president writes about that eventful day and his presidency that followed; "I was simply 'pulled forward by Being.' With no embarrassment, no stage fright, no hesitation, I did everything I had to do . I was capable of speaking extempore (I who had never before spoken in public) to several packed public squares a day and of negotiating confidently with the heads of great powers . . . In short, I was able to behave as masterfully or as if I had been prepared and schooled for presidency all my life. This was not because historical opportunity suddenly uncovered in me some special aptitude for the office but because I became an 'instrument of time.'"[21] Havel never fails to acknowledge that he was "grasped" and that a very special strength was given to him during the exhausting struggle for Czechoslovak liberty.

That night I could not sleep, the excitement was too much, and then there was the dream to visit my sisters, my brother, to be in Prague and at the homestead and see it all with my own eyes.

My dream came true early in May just as the lilacs and chestnut trees were beginning to bloom. At the Ruzyne airport the old Communist bureaucracy still ruled, suitcases were carefully examined, a sphinx like officer behind a reinforced window carefully studied my passport, but the minute I stepped out of the airport I could sense a glorious change. While in the past one had to order a taxi a week ahead, now there was an armada of taxis ready to take the arriving travelers down town. According to my luggage the taxi man knew right away that I was a gold plated American, and he started to explain to me that there was terrible traffic, and that for a few more dollars he was willing to take me the round about way to my sister's apartment, and that the round about way would actually be cheaper than going in the bumper to bumper traffic. I could not imagine that kind of traffic at eleven in the morning. The driver was absolutely disgusted when I answered him in Czech suggesting the short way which was familiar to me. The driver was anxious to talk, he asked about the cost of cars in the USA, and about life in America in general. At the same time, I was hungry to study every street on which we drove and every house which we passed by. One thing which I noticed right away was the number of stone pedestals, differing in height and width. The driver enlightened me, that these were the pedestals of the statues of the communist saints. "In the middle of this square was a huge statue of Lenin," the taxi driver went on "and wait until you see the pedestal of the former statue of Stalin on the top of Letna hill! You could see it from all parts of Prague, it was the biggest statue of Stalin in the world! Some idiot saw a picture of the statue of Christ in Rio de Janeiro, and was determined to build something much bigger but also on the top of a hill in honor of Stalin. It took years to build." Then with typical Czech humor and some vulgarity he described the enormous effort in taking the statue down without damaging the houses in a whole section of Prague. He punctuated every sentence with "Jesus, Maria" (Jesus and Mary). We were passing through the suburbs. I was ecstatic in seeing the mighty old chestnuts in bloom lining the streets. I studied the broken torn lace of the wrought iron fences of the formerly elegant villas and town houses. I was horrified to see almost every house in need of repair. The formerly clipped gardens looked like overgrown jungles. The lawn around the former statue of Lenin was not mowed and was covered with dandelions. As we were coming closer to the city, construction was everywhere in sight. When I inquired about it, the driver proudly told me about all the building projects accomplished in less than six months. "Everybody wants to restore and rebuild houses that have been falling apart for years, all we need is money. What worries me is that Americans and Germans and other foreigners are coming here and are buying like crazy, and then building this and that. Jesus, Maria! I keep saying to myself if the Americans and Germans are buying everything, this will no longer be my home, and what will be the difference between them and the Communists, except the freedom of speech, and the vote, and other things, but it worries me."

We passed by a big food store, and quite a few people who were holding suitcases stood outside.

"What's that?"

"Jesus! You will never believe it, but it's true. These are Germans. For their Marks they can buy a lot for practically nothing. They are ashamed to go into a food market with a suitcase, therefore one or two stay outside with the suitcase, and others go shopping, many times twice and three times. Be sure to watch this. They come in the morning by cars or by buses, they eat in the best restaurant, they spend the day shopping and congratulate themselves on their bargains. It turns my stomach, my brother died in a concentration camp. My wife and I have been helping his kids . . . and now as it goes, by the time we have some money and time to go to a store, much has already been sold to our German visitors. Something must be done! Jesus. Maria! If they do not have any shame to stay away from the land they plundered, something must be done."

We were in a familiar territory not too far from where I used to live. Indeed, on one side of the street was a football stadium but on the other side where there used to be a row of big houses, there was an enormous field. Obviously there was some huge gathering there. The field had rows of chairs and benches, and a resplendent podium in front.

"What is that?" I asked.

"Jesus, you do not know? The Pope was here! Everyone, I mean everyone went to see him, Havel was the only one who got a good seat. We all stood there for hours, and when the Pope finally arrived we were all falling on our knees having no idea why but I guess we wanted to be blessed. Later on, yet before the mass, he stood by the altar and said 'Pax Vobiscum' or something like that, and we all yelled 'Hurrah!!' while the priest and nuns and the religious people were hitting us with umbrellas, telling us to shut up because the Pope was praying. Jesus, Maria! How would anybody know, when he prays in Latin! After all, when we clapped, and yelled, well, instead of a Communist leader, we voluntarily cheered the Pope. To tell you the truth, we have been doing the cheering for so many years, that at times we do not know what is what." I chuckled, and registered that after forty years, the Communists did not succeed in eliminating from the Czech vernacular the horrid habit of taking the Lord's name in vain. In my childhood the expression "Jesus, Mary!" was a mark of a certain religious orientation and class. Through the decades of living in a Communist society the expression lost any religious meaning. It does not mean that the people are religious, they may not even know who Mary and Jesus were, and the expression is as meaningless as our local expressions, "Holy Toledo!" or "Holy Mackerel!" but any professor Higgins interested in language may find it interesting that all kinds of religious expression survived decades of scientific atheistic indoctrination.

The family reunion was marked with much love and laughter. Although I was very tired after the flight, we talked until late at night, not minimizing the difficulty of rebuilding democracy but nevertheless celebrating the great miracle of liberty. Next morning

I was up much earlier than expected and as a curious kid I rushed to take a long walk through Prague. I had thought that during the years of my exile I had glamorized the image of Prague, but as soon as I reached the marvelous lookout in Letna park, and could see the exquisite panorama of the city: the river with its numerous bridges, the marvelous mixtures of baroque and Gothic, the buildings, the statues with their language of history and although I could not ignore the blemishes, the horribly neglected parks and gardens, the old houses in desperate need of repair, Prague spoke to me with the same old magic. I rushed down town. The Communists spent a great deal of money on the so called Royal Way, and the restoration of the Old Town Square with its Town Hall, the astronomic clock, and the Tyn Church in which the reformers preached. The huge statue of John Hus dominates the square. I was surprised by the number of outdoor cafés, I could not resist. I felt hungry. I had to go to one of the cafés for lunch. I did not know where to go next. I decided to go to the remnants of Charles University, founded in 1348. I was delighted to notice that all the buildings of Charles University were buzzing with activity, and with crowds of students, eager to learn. When I spoke with them I noticed their generous usage of the word "Sensational." They were happy to be free to choose their courses of study, and everything was simply "sensational." Alma Mater Pragensis appeared to be ready to return to its 1348 charter ". . . that this kingdom of Bohemia should abound in learned men and women as much as in worldly riches; that the faithful subjects of this kingdom who ever hunger for the fruits of beautiful arts should not in foreign lands beg for alms, but that they themselves should always have a table set for all; that they should not be forced to seek enlightenment in foreign parts of the world, but themselves enjoy the honor of inviting others to participate in happiness."

The theological studies were moved from the ancient Klementinum to new and bright headquarters. Father would be envious! The lecture rooms were nicely furnished, the professors enjoyed their rooms, and students were everywhere. I realized the great promise in these men and women, saying to myself "In three years, at least these young people will be able to take over the churches served by aged ministers, many of them in their late seventies." I stayed quite a while, visited some of the old professors. Finally I got acquainted with some of the students. To my surprise the name "Bednář" did not mean anything to them. One of them had a slight recollection of my father's books in history. Indeed, Father's books were not available, and I witnessed the genius of the Communist movement, the ability to erase the name of a prominent person as if he or she never existed. At the same time these students were quite well acquainted with the work of Hromadka. The students invited me to go with them to a nearby pub, and I learned a great deal from them,

On the way home, I realized the great difference between the collapse of Nazism and the consequences of the Velvet revolution. In 1945 the Nazis were gone and as foreigners they were brought to justice. The Velvet Revolution was considered an internal affair of the Czechoslovak State. The Soviets were gone trying to save their necks, but the Czechoslovak Communists in general were let free. Some of them made a complete turn about and posed as passionate defenders of democracy, others changed their jobs and in talking with them one could easily sense a passive resistance. This solution was in harmony with the philosophy of "living in truth" of President Havel. It will be interesting to watch. Indeed, it is in the interest of all, including the former Communists, that the Republic should succeed, but only the future will show whether it is possible to apply the law of loving kindness and truth to people grown accustomed to force and falsehood. Quite rightly, President Havel constantly calls for a spiritual and moral revolution, and strenuous development of the spiritual foundations of the Czech Republic.

The very next day we drove to the homestead. Considering that we were discussing every subject under the sun, it was a special grace that we arrived home safely. Of course, seeing the workers homes standing in our former orchard still turns my stomach, and I am not ready to accept it—the land was stolen from us. The homestead of course still holds an incredible charm. My brother with his wife developed a beautiful rose garden and it almost looked as in the days of my mother. The lilac hedges were nicely trimmed and instead of a gate there was a charming entrance to the garden through an artful opening in the lilac hedge. The homestead itself was in a sorry state, everything calling for repairs. It seemed incredibly ironic. The homestead was again ours but no one had the money to repair it. The woodland was returned to us but for years it was a public domain, everybody was delighted that these forests provided enough wood for their stoves. Of course we remembered our father taking long walks with the old forester, discussing which trees ought to be replaced. As many, many Czechs, we faced the same situation of receiving back the ruins of ancestral lands and homes, and not having the funds to make the necessary repairs.

We walked through the woods to the graveyard and I was very saddened by the many new graves of family members along the picturesque wall of the cemetery. On the way home we met a dear old woman. She covered me with kisses as she welcomed me. To my surprise she was still working in the factory "How do you like it?" I asked.

"It's horrible, it's a hell!" She burst into tears. "For thirty years I was making cotton pants for the Russian soldiers, ordinary fatigues. Oh God, now the Austrians bought it, and we are making fine night gowns. Rows and rows of lace around the neck. You have no idea how hard it is to make, and the worst of it all is, that the foreman stands by me or not too far from me, saying 'How do you expect anybody to buy such sloppy work! The lace must be absolutely straight.' At times, I have to make it over and over. I don't know if I can stand it much longer." After she wiped her tears, she remarked that thank goodness there was more food available in the local store, and she promised to make for us some *buchtas*, a promise which she kept and already in the morning there was a tray of these pastries for our breakfast.

Later on one of the neighbors invited me and served Slivovitz, a very strong plum brandy. We toasted each other, and the room was full of affection and good will. I noticed that the fine glasses were exactly like the glasses my mother had. I admired them.

"Of course you like them," the hostess exclaimed, "I use them only for very, very special occasions. Your dear mother gave them to me. I can just see her. Like a prophet she saw what was coming and she gave me those glasses saying, "Take them, dear- take them, before somebody steals them."

This testimony which did not make any sense, left me sad, puzzled and mad. My mother as I pointed, out, died during the Nazi occupation of the country. She already saw the freedom approaching and certainly she was not giving things away foreseeing the future of the house. It was quite obvious to me that these people really convinced themselves that they never took anything from the homestead, that the dear Mrs. Bednář gave it to them.

My visit was very short, because by then my wife was too ill to travel and a dear friend was taking care of her and the household. The visit left many impressions in my mind. I was tremendously impressed by president Havel, and, although he was already criticized, because of him I was extremely hopeful. The new World Order announced by president Bush certainly was not yet in sight, and considering the situation in the former Soviet Union, the announcement of the New World Order was more wishful thinking than reality. It was obvious to me that the Czechoslovak Republic-simply could not make any recovery without foreign aid. The whole Republic was in the same situation as we were, in facing the depleted homestead.

After forty years of complete Marx-Lenin indoctrination enhanced by the enormous Soviet hate for the West, here and there I felt the stench of Communism, realizing that it would take many years just to change the Communist mentality. This came particularly to my mind as I went with my sister to worship at St. Kliment, the dear church in which all of us were confirmed, and I had such special memories for the custodian, the late Mr. Vancura and the splendid organist, professor Urbanec. The church building is now recognized as one of the oldest sanctuaries in Prague, dating to the twelfth century. Behind Dad's pulpit are fascinating, recently discovered frescoes. The church has a magnificent organ and a remarkable organist. Because the church has good acoustics it is also used for concerts, and recordings of chamber music.

Since the church which I previously served donated a considerable amount of money through the World Council of Churches for the restoration of the organ, right after the service I climbed the stairs to the balcony to get acquainted with the organist and to thank him for his fine artistry. He looked at me as if he wanted to say "and so what? . . . what do you want?" I explained myself and our interest in reporting to the church at home about this particular organ, and he said "We know all about America, I was there for a few months before I went to Cuba. Americans never do anything without wanting something."

I tried to change the subject, I asked what was going on in his department and told him about the direction in which hymnology was moving in the United States. "Of course" he replied, "in American churches they play nothing but shmaltz." I could not believe it, but I smelled the stench of Communism on the balcony of my native church. The church was almost empty, the poor old minister tried his best to overcome his limitations in preaching the Gospel. I was glad to notice a few young couples, and then I discovered that they were foreigners! I may say, therefore, that no young people were in sight. I realized that it was unreasonable to expect some immediate change after forty years of oppression. The Roman Catholics had a tremendous advantage in the financial support of Rome. Before the evening news, and on Saturday several times during the evening, there was a very attractive T.V. commercial portraying our need of God and of Christian community. The Protestants do not have that kind of money, and also have to wait for the new generation of clergy to attract the young and to develop some significant Christian Education. A former nominal member of the Communist party was telling me that Communism for him meant a definite call to do something significant for the party and, therefore, for the future of the world. "When Communism collapsed, I had no illusion of its evil, but there has been an enormous void in my heart. Nobody seems to call me to perform some service, nobody assures me that I matter to society."

I returned to our home in New Hampshire full of impressions, hopes and fears. A new world order surely was only an illusion, but there was no doubt that genuine liberty was once again at home in Prague.

It has been almost ten years since my first visit to Prague. The new world order seems far away, the lands of the former Soviet Union are in chaos, and represent danger. Czechoslovakia no longer exists, since the Slovaks under the great influence of a former Communist leader decided to establish a separate, independent state. This is not an era in which common denominators unite, this is an era of grouping. The Czech Republic has made tremendous progress. The United States generously supported its development and, ironically, our son James was the Director of the Agency for International Development in Prague for five years. Prague has been beautifully restored, and has become a mecca for tourists, second to Paris. The AID office closed, and the Czechs walked the road of progress with all their energy, never shaking off the materialism placed in their souls by the Soviets. They have been possessed by the USA, unfortunately copying America even in enterprises which are not admirable. The material progress has never been matched by spiritual development. President Havel has not changed his philosophy and has become much admired throughout the world, yet among his own he is often criticized for moralizing and preaching, and yet the same critics admire him and three times elected him to the presidency. One of the remarkable things about Havel is that he can be perfectly candid in describing the follies of his fellow citizens. We remember the annual State of the Union addresses in which our presidents usually elaborate their achievements, and their goals. We are not used to the Churchillian promises of blood, sweat and tears. Our leaders can be bombastic and we applaud even when they make promises which we know will not be realized in a short time. Havel is just the opposite. Recently in his address to all members of the government and to the Czech parliament he elaborated the dissatisfaction of many people with the present economy and especially with the political process and said, "I will simply mention the causes or rather sets of causes of this situation. First is what I would call the 'historical' cause. It is, in fact, the Czech version of a phenomenon that has made itself felt in different forms and with different intensity, in all the countries that rid themselves of Communism. We may perhaps call it post-Communist morass. Something like that was bound to come. Every person of sound judgment must have known that. Hardly anybody, however, foresaw how deep, serious and protracted it would be. *The collapse of communism also brought down, virtually overnight, a whole structure of values that had been kept in existence for several decades, and with it the way of life based on that construction. The "time of certainties"—that were limited and dull, even suicidal to society, but still represented a certainty of a kind—*

was suddenly replaced by a time of freedom. Given the previous experience, it was inevitable that many took this new freedom to be boundless. The new life which held dozens of temptations, also made entirely new demands on individual responsibility. I have compared this strange state of mind to a post-prison psychosis, experienced by those who after having been constrained for years to a narrow corridor of strict and detailed rules, suddenly find themselves in an expanse of freedom that is strange to them. *The new conditions make them believe that everything is permitted; at the same time, however it thrusts upon them the tremendous burden of having to make their own decisions, and to accept responsibility for those decisions.* It is my firm belief that the young generation, those who grew up after the fall of Communism will not be affected by this terrible post-Communist syndrome, and I am looking forward to the time when these people take over the administration of public affairs. That time has not yet come, we are still living in a situation which makes us wonder how long it will take society to adapt to the new, more natural conditions of life, and how deeply the totalitarian era affected our souls. However, it would not be honest to ascribe all blame in the way that was so well known to the Marxists—to some blind laws of history . . . . First of all it is necessary to identify our faults.

"It appears to me that *our main fault was pride*, because of the fact that the transformation process progressed in our country practically continuously since November 1989 without being impeded by any major political changes. We really grew, in some respects, farther than others, or at least it seemed so. Apparently, this went to our heads. *We behaved like a spoiled child in a family or like those at the the top of the class who believe they can give themselves an air of superiority and be everyone's teacher.* Oddly enough, this pride was combined with a kind of provincialism and parochialism."[22]

Havel went on and on identifying the faults of the nation and speaking about the preparation for becoming a part of NATO. He declared "a relentless war on Czech provincialism, isolationism and egoism, on all illusions about a clever neutrality, on our traditional shortsightedness, on all kinds of Czech chauvinism. Those who now refuse to take upon themselves their share of responsibility for the fate of their continent, and of the world as a whole, are signing a death sentence, not only for their continent and the world but primarily for themselves."[23]

There is so much in what President Havel says which is important for us all. He does understand the post-Communism ethos, the hopes and dangers that are real. In his call for the new renaissance of culture by which he means not just the books we read, and the plays and films we see, and the symphonies we hear, but the way we speak, the way be behave toward fellow human beings especially toward those who differ from us, or who are of different color of skin or national heritage. Havel speaks to us all.

President Havel likes to speak about his appreciation of the Czech perception of the world, about the Czech historical experience, the Czech modes of courage and of cowardice, the Czech humor but then he goes on to affirm "My home is not only in my Czechness, of course, it is also my citizenship and beyond that, my home is Europe and my Europeanness and ultimately, it is this world and its present civilization and for that matter, the universe. But that is not all, my home is also my education, my upbringing, my habits, my social mileu . . ."[24]

Indeed in President Havel is a Czech gift to humankind. He understands our deepest hopes and our most dreadful follies. He does not mind elaborating them, and he understands what must take place before a new world order can be established.

WHERE IS MY HOME?

The meaning of the word home has certainly diminished in this century. At the back of my memory is a contest for children to give the best definition of the word home. I cannot remember the winning definition but I do remember a child who defined home as a place where we stay when we have no other place to go. That definition seems to fit the majority. Since both men and women are working, and our children spend long hours in schools, and then in their jobs or extra curricular activities, our homes in comparison with the homes of our childhood are like hotels, we are hardly ever there, and yet the place we live, our address is important. The answer to the question "Where do you live?" labels us, and many people seem to judge whether or not we are important and trustworthy according to our address. When we meet strangers at some gathering our first questions is "Where do you come from?" What luck it is when the people who want to know our whereabouts light up, they know our town, they know other people who live on the same street!

When I took my early retirement, hoping to spend our golden years in New Hampshire we moved not from a "mean address," after all, Wilton, Connecticut is the bastion of Fairfield County, definitely a prestigious address. It was delightful to move to our New Hampshire farmhouse late in the fall, but we were there only four days when my wife was taken very ill, and although I was totally unprepared for the task, I have been a care giver ever since. Naturally when my wife was taken to the hospital, we were far from being unpacked, and to the horror of our children the garage was still full of boxes of books and other unnecessary items. Our daughter finally got the courage, and told me "Dad, winter is at hand, we will have snow now any day. You simply have to get somebody to help you get the stuff out of the garage to make space for your car. You cannot leave your car outside anymore." It is very strange, but our grown up children all of a sudden have the ability to scare us to death. Right away I tried to get some help and called a number of people. I was amazed that the first questions of everyone I called, and to whom I explained my dire need, was "and where do you live?"

The minute I proudly said "Philbrick Hill" I knew that I made a fatal mistake. One after another, the people said "Philbrick Hill? Forget it! We know those rich people. Their checks always bounce . . .!" Yes, I did recall one of our neighbors living in a palatial setting and not paying his bills. Immediately I kept saying "I know what you mean, but we live almost at the bottom with all ordinary people and we try to pay cash!"

It worked. Knowing my home, these people at least would look me over. In the pages of the New Testament Jesus Christ is often referred to as Jesus of Nazareth. That address did not help him. When Jesus spoke with power and crowds followed him, many were shocked, saying "What good can come from the hick town of Nazareth? Well, the people may be saying that he is the promised Messiah but we know that he is from Nazareth, a son of a carpenter. We know his family!"

Later on we read about two young men who were captivated by Jesus and asked him "Master where do you live?"

"Come and see," he answered, and the two men followed him and stayed with him as his disciples. Quite obviously Jesus did not have a permanent address but we know that there were people like Mary and Martha and their brother Lazarus in Bethany, and that Jesus felt at home among them. Similarly, there was a tremendous difference between his disciples but Jesus loved them, and felt at home among them.

The zealots yearned for nothing but liberty. They believed that Jesus alone was strong enough to overthrow the Roman Empire. How can we ever maintain our homes when we are second class citizens, yes, the property of Rome? They were upset with him when he unflinchingly proclaimed that where the Spirit of the Lord rules, we are free to be brothers and sisters, in the very presence of the Lord is the foundation of that wonderful feeling of being at home.

* * * * *

At the beginning of the nineteenth century, a Westphalian lawyer was deeply troubled by his Jewish ancestry. For generations many of his male ancestors on both sides had been rabbis. In 1818 when his son was born, to the great sorrow and disappointment of his mother, the child's grandmother, he refused to give his son his name of Hirschel. What on earth can you do in anti-Semitic Germany with a name like Hirschel? No, the boy was given the pleasant sounding name of Karl Marx. The grandmother was heartbroken. Hirschel waited until his mother's death and then purely for practical reasons he submitted to baptism and changed his name to Heinrich.

Changing of names in order to have a better chance in the largely anti-Semitic society was quite common, and one hundred years later when Hitler was rising to power, determined to eliminate the Jews, all of a sudden many men and women having names of Christian saints were horrified when they found out that they were of Jewish origin, that their great grandparents had changed their names, and that in spite of their bearing Christian names they had to face the road leading to gas chambers. Several of my classmates faced this fate. Even more tragic seemed to me the case of the Czech Jews, that is of the Jews born in Bohemia, who felt that only the German speaking people belonged to the upper crust, and therefore they spoke German, they sent their children to German schools, and then early in the thirties, panic stricken, these Jews desperately tried to learn to speak Czech and to support the national cause but it was too late.

The Czechs and Slovaks certainly did not escape the temptation to survive, to blend with the ruling class by changing their names. After more than three hundred years of German oppression and systematic germanization it is really a miracle that the Czech and Slovak language has survived. Unfortunately the corruption of the Czech language has continued. One marvels at the number of Russian words which have become a part of the Czech vocabulary, and most shocking is the impact of English on contemporary Czech. The English speaking world certainly has no nationalistic interests in Central Europe, but especially the USA represents power, prestige and, as disgusting as it is, the Czechs use many Anglo Saxon words even though they have Czech words. At the same time we must admit that in the world of computers, outer space technology and our culturally shrinking world, languages in general have changed and have been embellished by such untranslatable terms as "Big Mac."

Early in the nineteenth century, exactly at the time when the father of Karl Marx decided to change his name to Heinrich, a great many Czechs, after centuries of oppression did not see any hope for freedom or opportunity. The question for many was not how to succeed in business without trying, the question was how to succeed in business trying hard but having a Czech name. Thus as a last resort some popular names were germanized. Jan, Honza became Hans. Anthony in Czech Antonin became Anton. The name of the river Vltava sounded more cosmopolitan as Moldau but many found a wonderful compromise in adjusting their names or the names of their establishment to the French chic. Whoever thought of a barbershop? How vulgar! Of course it is Frizeur! The variation of giving Czech words a German-French sound is just amazing. Of course, there are slavic names which are totally unpronounceable to German or English speaking people. I came to America with the perfectly good Czech name of Zdeněk, and before I knew it I became Denny!

The Czech national anthem "Where Is My Home?" is the first stanza of an aria from a musical named *Fidlovacka*, a musical which to a point is poking fun at people who were changing their names, who were germanizing the Czech language in order to be more successful in the given society. The main role is given to a blind grandfather who likes to remember the beauty of the Czech country side, and who likes to sing. It is this blind grandfather who sings the beautiful and gentle poetry by J. K. Tyl, "Where Is My Home?"

The first stanza is really a celebration of a sense of place and space, of the rushing brooks through meadows, of the beautiful blooming orchards. The blind grandfather sings of the beauty of his homeland, he claims it as his own. "And this land of wondrous beauty is the Czech land, home of mine!" This hymn has three stanzas. The second and third stanzas reach nationalistic heights and the refrain is "where the Czechs live is my home, where the Czechs live is my home." The producers of *Fidlovacka* staged the first performance with fear and trembling, but to their amazement the aria "Where is my home?" was an immediate hit. It has a very singable gentle melody. On the second verse the deeply moved audience joined the leading man in singing. Over night "Where Is My Home?" became a national folk song, and in 1918 when Czechoslovakia became an independent state the first stanza of "Where Is My Home?" became the national anthem. I do not doubt that the choice of the first verse was intentional, because it affirms a sense of belonging, this beautiful country is mine. The second and the third stanzas on the other hand have nationalistic crescendo; "where the Czechs live is my home, where the Czechs live is my home."

It does not take too long to understand that just being with the people who speak the same language does not make us comfortable. Why is it that every so often family reunions are painful? Why is it that the days after Thanksgiving and Christmas, the days of family togetherness, are the busiest days for counselors and psychiatrists? In the long run it is not the same language but what we communicate in the spirit of love and freedom which make us feel at home. Our yearning for home is then primarily a yearning for spiritual brothers and sisters with whom we share the vision of life and the world as it is meant to be.

*   *   *   *   *

Some of these pages were written when both my wife and I were hospitalized, and at one time we shared the same hospital room. After ten years of being a care giver any uncertainty has another dimension: Who is going to take care of my wife? My first encounter with a serious illness took me by surprise. I was in Connecticut at Darien's fabulous country club attending a wedding reception dinner. Since the bride was my former confirmand the huge room was full of old friends. It was good to see them. I surely hoped to visit with them but before we sat down for the first course, I felt wobbly, and disappeared to rest in one of the spacious reception rooms. I was not hiding very long. Soon I was surrounded by several friends who seems concerned about me. As it happened there were six doctors in the wedding party, and they took

over. In a few minutes an ambulance was taking me to a hospital.
As a young man was taking my blood pressure and another atten-
dant was giving me oxygen, I heard one whispering to the other
"Good Lord, he is going!" and I knew that I was not on the way to
the Ritz! While I was still being examined in the emergency room
of the Norwalk Hospital, only a few miles away from Wilton,
where I was a minister for a number of years, several members of
the wedding party and a few friends arrived. I felt badly but they
convinced me that this was what they wanted to do. I think they
were afraid that I would die without knowing that they loved me. I
was very much touched as they took turns standing by me and wiping my forehead. At one moment I remarked that it reminded me
of our rehearsals for the Easter Pageant and they cracked up laughing. Of course I was worried, but soon I was assured that my wife
was notified and that our daughter would take care of her.

I was taken to my room, and I do not remember anything
about that night except that I was very ill, hardly aware of where I
was. Next morning another of my former young people, Jeff came.
He is a scientist and an actor in one body. He knew exactly what to
say, it was good to have him near. While he was there a minister
came and brought me a nice flower arrangement. I admit that I was
frightened, worried. Yes, I was in need of prayer, in need of reaffirming what I have always believed, but the minister joked and
talked to me as if we were buddies from some fraternity organization. He left rather quickly wishing me well, and reminding me to
let him know if I needed anything. When he left, overcome by immense spiritual homesickness, I could not control my tears. Jeff
understood, gently he touched my shoulder, he did not say anything except "That idiot."

Later that day two, young, black, vivacious ladies came to
visit me, and told me that they were friends of Jeff. They told me
about their jobs, and their studying for masters degrees at night,
and about their church. Shortly Jeff came in, but instead of chatting
the ladies affirmed the purpose of their visit. They knew that Jeff
was worried about me, that I was very ill, and they came to offer
their prayers. We all joined hands. One of the women was obviously a leader, a definite soprano, her friend was an alto, the tonal difference was distinct. At first the soprano told the Lord that I was

real sick "Yes" repeated the alto "real, real sick!" The Lord was asked to look upon me a miserable sinner and have mercy on me. "We read in the Gospel," said the leading woman, "that we must preach the Gospel in season and out of season. The Gospel must be preached."

"Yes, O Lord, the Gospel must be preached!" echoed the other one. "We thank you Lord, that you gave this man the ability to preach your Word so we pray make him well again."

And then came a wonderful twist. "We sincerely ask you Lord, to heal this man that the Gospel may be preached . . ."

I fully registered that I was to be healed not to loaf in New Hampshire but that the Gospel would be preached.

We, the strangers, embraced and my visitors left.

"Actually," said Jeff, "it was not bad . . . The Gospel must be preached!"

"Yes," I replied, "it felt like a touch of home."

*   *   *   *   *

A dear old friend of mine, Ben, is a good doctor and a Roman Catholic. It is a strange combination, and we have been wonderful friends because Ben is first of all a Christian. We discussed many good books, we argued. Ben learned something about the Reformation from me, the word, "something" in this case is an understatement. We talked about St. Francis, and we both loved Henri Nouwen. Ben was very active in his church, maybe it was because his mother never forgave him for his decision to be a doctor and not a priest. We often laughed. His mother did not want another woman in Ben's life, and now, when he is a doctor, she has to tolerate his beautiful and intelligent wife. As busy as Ben is, every Sunday he goes with his wife to the early mass and then they go to visit some of the lonely parishioners. "There are so few priests left," complained Ben, "that we are getting worse than the protestants! We have to do the work of the priests . . . I could tell Luther something about his priesthood of all believers!"

It was natural that Ben, came to visit. Typically, he checked on my physical record first physical record first. "Well, your body is not too wonderful," he said, "what about your spirit?"

We talked about many important things. Ben told me that on Sundays after the mass he goes to bring holy communion to his fellow parishioners. He paused, gave me a long look and said "Would you like me to bring you Holy Communion?" I nodded, big tears were rolling down my cheeks. He gave me a hug. I felt as if I were at home. As Ben left I was humming "A Mighty Fortress is Our God." Who could ever, ever believe it! A catholic bringing holy communion to me, that insolent protestant cub! A Catholic doctor bringing me Holy Communion when all the professionals were rather busy. Realizing that Ben made this offer in the same spring of 1998, when an African priest was severely reprimanded by Rome for offering the Holy Communion to the President of the USA and his wife during their Aftrican journey not only pointed out for me the special spiritual freedom of Ben but also increased my joyful hope for a New Reformation, dictated by men and women who take the Gospel of Jesus Christ seriously.

*   *   *   *   *

One of my dear friends came to visit and brought me a book to read. It was a best seller paperback called *The Color of Water* by James McBride. It is a marvelous saga. As a boy James McBride knew his mother was different. But when he asked about it she would simply say "I am lightly skinned." Of course, he knew that he was lighter too and asked his mother whether he was black or white. "You are a human being," she answered. One day when James asked his mother what color God was, she said, "God is the color of water . . ." and when he grew up, at last, he knew the story of his mother. She was a rabbi's daughter born in Poland. She fled to America and later on as a widow she married a black man. She founded a Baptist church and put twelve of her children through college, all remarkable human beings.

The reading of this book was a true benediction for me, and since I was in the hospital I read it slowly, leisurely, thoughtfully, and I even read the acknowledgement at the back of the book, which I never do. I read the acknowledgement of this best seller and I could not believe my eyes as I read the first sentence: "My mother and I would like to thank the Lord Jesus Christ for his love and faithfulness to all generations."[25]

I was at home.

Theologians and the publishing departments of our denominations are trying so hard to be "with it" and not to offend anybody in our diversity that they probably do not even think of saying something as strong as the words which come to James McBride naturally.

I do not want to make any simplicity out of pain, suffering and sorrows, yet I would not want to skip even a moment of my life so richly permeated with tremendous gifts of love and friendship, certainty and hope.

As a lover of life, I have never been inspired by the admonitions of positive thinking to believe in the future, having justified doubts about seeing that future. "This too shall pass! It is not as bad as you think!" These have not been the slogans for me but I do want to underline here: all right suffering is suffering, pain is pain, injustice is injustice, and the cross is not any metaphor, but God is there, in the midst of it all, not only as a sustainer but as a Creator. I constantly marvel at God's respect for our freedom of will. When we want to make him our errand boy or a king whose job is to approve and bless the conclusions of our wisdom, he runs away from us to hide. Then we are truly homeless, on our own, but what a thrill it is to feel the prompting of his spirit in the pseudonyms of his choice, in the most ordinary people and events, in those who come to laugh with us or to cry with us, in those who perhaps do not know how to say anything but who do know how to stand by a person who is suffering, in a doctor who is not consulting any dogma as he offers to bring the Holy Communion!

There is a sculptor's chisel in our experiences, in a paperback which is waiting to be read, in some beauty which is yet to be seen, in some flaming bush in which God is hiding, ready to speak to us afresh as a present reality. In the rawness of life there were many who exclaimed, "Well, if this is God's world, forget it!" and who joined Job's wife in saying "Curse God and die!" From the perspective of years, however, I am ready to bow down in awe and wonder, and join Browning in whispering, "Hush, I pray you, what if these hands, the hands of loved ones and friends were the hands of God upholding us, and shaping us?"

As a teenager I admired human wisdom. I was awed by the brains of the University, how I yearned to be just a bit smart! Of course, as any adolescent I thought that real faith begins when our reasoning is defunct. After all, Freud in one of his weaker moments tried very hard to convince us that whatever science cannot discover, just is not there!

In my teenage years I certainly kept my church going as a very private affair, in order to escape the laughter of the wise protagonists of the age of unbelief, "Oh, you poor thing, going to church! Who needs the church except the feeble-minded!" Once in a while we still hear the echo of this arrogance from the lips of the enlightened. "The church is good for those who need it. Personally, we don't."

It has been a tremendous liberation for me to see the bloody collapse of "Scientific certainty" proclaimed both by Nazism, and especially by Communism, the collapse of the world of our own making, and the realizations that precisely the opposite of the adolescent thinking is true, that only as believers attune with God's will for human life and for the world, can we be sound reasoners. The Nazis and the Communists were fanatical believers. They wanted to destroy the Christian faith and replace it with faith in their own doctrines. Interestingly enough, as Christianity in the western world was becoming more and more secularized, the Communists in the last phases of their movement, were borrowing more and more from Christian usages to make Communism more attractive. They even developed a form of Confirmation! We are emerging from a century of pseudo-religious and demonic movements. We analyze our experiences and say with Edison, "at least we know that these nine hundred ninety nine things positively will not work!" At the same time one is appalled not only by the enormous cost in human blood for this experimental conclusion but also by the multitudes who insist on perpetuating the old follies in a new dress. Nevertheless, what we have seen, what we have experienced, what we have endured seems to support the integrity of believing in Jesus Christ and his proposals for human life, and for the world. In this faith we have dreams, visions and hopes, searching for brothers and sisters, the kin in spirit, who would constitute one's family and home.

Recently I had another legitimate reason to go to Prague: the eighty-fifth birthday of my oldest sister, Vera. Some were shaking their heads at the thought of my traveling to Europe. Everybody would understand the reasons for my staying at home. After this winter of our illnesses, our physical and financial strength have been largely exhausted, but I could not imagine my sister being alone on her big day. At times I was anxious about the trip primarily because the carcass of my body often refuses to obey the commands of my mind. All of a sudden, two of my young friends were eager to go with me: Kristian Whipple, a photographer who designed the cover of this book, and Jeff, who watched over me when I was hospitalized in Connecticut, an actor, balladeer and scientist in one. Laughingly we agreed that they would be my body guards in exchange for my giving them a good tour of Prague.

We were a good trio, spending memorable days together, walking through the ancient city, visiting galleries and art shows, attending theater performances, and then stopping at cafes and discussing our experiences. After seven days we even had "our table" in one restaurant. The evenings were spent with Vera in whose presence one cannot help but feel at home.

I had forgotten the terrain of Prague, the steep hills and steps one has to manage to see its lovely face. One day after going through the Prague castle, as we walked down the castle steps, which really are a narrow street in the shape of stairs, I felt weary, and just then I noticed the gentleness of my friends. Without a word, one walked in front of me, and one behind me, in case of a fall, they were ready to catch me. They never told me that this or that was too much for me or that I ought to sit down, they were just there. Their presence gave me a wonderful sense of liberty and security, I walked more than I had walked in months, and on the way home I did not even notice that I left my cane at the airport in Frankfurt. A home is not a home without this feeling that we are there one for another, ready to uphold, and catch one another.

One bright day we made it to the observation tower on the top of the hill named Petrin, which offers a spectacular view of the city. The aging cashier was obviously alarmed by the number of tourists. As we came forward to the admission booth, she looked us over and asked "Are you Czech or foreigners?" When I answered in Czech that we were foreigners she invoked Jesus, Mary and the Holy Ghost saying, "How can you be a foreigner when you speak Czech?"

Fortunately, thanks to the crowd, I did not have a chance to answer the question, but she let me in free.

How can you be lonely, how can you be a stranger, when you speak the same language? Of course, one could also reverse the question and ask: How can you, a foreigner, expect to feel at home at the dinner table of the natives? Was this on the mind of Jesus as he was narrating his parable of an uninvited guest appearing at a wedding feast? "But when the king came in to look at the guests, he saw there a man who had no wedding garment, and he said to him, 'Friend how did you get in here without a wedding garment?'" And the man was speechless.[26]

Of course, the purpose of my short visit in Prague was the celebration of my sisters eighty-fifth birthday. We gathered in a restaurant, ironically because the most precious commodity is time, and because no one has a place big enough to accommodate "the crowd" of twelve. Among the twelve around the table were also the great nieces and great nephews. It was my duty and honor to propose a toast. I gave it a great deal of thought, wondering: Why is this old, cultured, highly educated woman of strong convictions so dearly loved especially by the young? The remarkable assertion of Paul that perfect love casts out fear was constantly coming to me as an answer, reminding me that we felt at home in my sister's presence, because we are free not to pretend, not to hide behind evasive phrases, we are free to be as we are, knowing that she will understand us, that her love is big enough to forgive us.

Recalling the days of our years and the years of our days, I was thinking of the paradoxes expressed by the Irish poet George Matheson. He was a tragic, blind man who gave us one of the much loved hymns at the beginning of this century, "O Love That Wilt Not Let Me Go." The hymn has a rather unfortunate sentimental melody, and since we seem to adhere to L. P. Hartley's motto, "The past is a foreign county," the hymn is missing in most contemporary hymnals, but as Matheson in this hymn speaks about the joy that seekest us through pain, and tracing the rainbow through rain, of the cross that liftest up my head, and the ground of blossoms red, he speaks about that which every Christian knows.

We are told that shortly before his death, Matheson asked his dearest friend to take him to the sea shore. For a long, long time Matheson stood there on the rocky coast of Ireland, his blind eyes turned to the sea, deeply inhaling the salty air, then he smiled and cried, "How beautiful this is!"

His friend was puzzled, and whispered, "Do you know?"

"Yes I know!" answered Matheson in a voice of certainty, and after a pause, filled with emotions, he added "and most of it is only because of you!"

I used this thought in my toast, and I rejoiced that this framework gave me a chance to say it in full: because of you, we have known truth even when we lived in falsehood, because of you we have known beauty even when life was shabby, you have shown us kindness when rudeness was the rule of the day, certainty for our fears, the wonder and excitement of living even when living appeared only as something to be endured.

Undoubtedly all of us can recall someone because of whom we have seen beauty and known some truth. To them we owe a toast of gratitude, but it would be a dreadful homelessness just to have a passing glimpse of that for which we yearn, and then to be left only with a memory and a desire. It belongs to one of the great miracles of living, that by God's grace, those who in their blindness have seen beauty, love and truth, are bound to find their spiritual kin. The given vision is the common denominator of men and women with whom we feel at home.

NOTES

1. Frederick Buechner, *A Room Called Remember* (New York: Harper & Row Publishers, 1984).

2. Exodus 3:14.

3. Exodus, 3:7.

4. Luke 10:42, Goodspeed Translation.

5. Albert Speer, *Inside the Third Reich,* 133, (New York, The Macmillan Co. 1970).

6. William Blake, *Complete Poetry* (New York: Random House, 1941) 614.

7. Prokop Drtina, *Ceskoslovensko Muj Osud,* Vol. 11, (Praha:Melantrich, 1991) 41.

8. Ibid.

9. Stephen L. Carter, *Civility, Manners, Morals, and the Etiquette of Democracy.* This chapter was published in "Christian Century," April 8, 1998, 367.

10. Taylor Branch, *Pillar of Fire* America in the King Years, 1963-65 (New York: Simon and Schuster) quoted in the New York Times Book Review, 18 January 1998, 13.

11. T. S. Elliot, *The Cocktail Party* (New York: Harcourt, Brace and Co., 1959) 133-34.

12. T. S. Elliot, *The Confidential Clerk* (New York: Harcourt, Brace and Co., 1959) 48.

13. Matthew Spinka, "Church in Communist Society A Study in J. L. Hromadka's Theological Politics." *Hartford Theological Seminary Bulletin,* 17 June 1954, 52.

14. Ibid., 53.

15. Ibid.

16. Ibid., 55.

17. *Evangelicky Kalendar* 1998. Praha-Kalich, 22.

18. Václav Havel, *Letters to Olga,* trans. Paul Wilson (London: Faber and Faber, 1990) 346.

19. Václav Havel, *Summer Meditations*, trans. Paul Wilson, (New York: Vintage Books, a Division of Random House Inc., 1993) 6.

20. John C. Bennett and Howard Seifer, *US Foreign Policy and Christian Ethics* (Philadephia: Westminster Press, 1977) 20.

21. Havel, *Summer Meditations*, 8.

22. "Speech of President Václav Havel At Czech Parliament, 1998," reproduced by the Office of the President of the Czech Republic.

23. Ibid.

24. Havel, *Summer Meditations*, 31.

25. James McBride, *The Color of Water*, (New York: Riverhead Books 1996) 287.

26. Matthew 22:12.